JURISPRUDENCE

JURISPRUDENCE

Fifth Edition

Raymond Wacks

BA, LLB, LLM, LLD, MLitt, PhD

Professor of Law and Legal Theory,
The University of Hong Kong

Series Editor: C.J. Carr, MA, BCL

BLACKSTONE
PRESS LIMITED

This edition published in Great Britain 1999 by Blackstone Press Limited,
Aldine Place, London W12 8AA. Telephone: (020) 8740 2277
www.blackstonepress.com

© Raymond Wacks, 1987

First edition, 1987
Second edition, 1990
Third edition, 1993
Fourth edition, 1995
Fifth edition, 1999

ISBN: 1 85431 994 9

British Library Cataloguing in Publication Data
A CIP catalogue record for this book is available from the British Library

Typeset by Montage Studios Limited, Horsmonden, Kent
Printed by Bell and Bain Limited, Glasgow

CONTENTS

PREFACE

It is hard to believe that thirteen years have passed since the first edition of this book rocked the foundations of legal theory. It remains deeply gratifying to learn that students (even my own) continue to find it helpful. For this edition I have corrected some errors, expanded the discussion in one or two places, and mentioned a little of the more accessible recent literature to which serious students may wish to turn. I am again grateful to the remarkable team at Blackstone Press — who still dominate the Premiership of law publishers — for cheerfully steering this new edition from my screen to your desk.

Raymond Wacks
1 October 1999

PREFACE TO THE FIRST EDITION

Legal theory is a formidable discipline. Several dangers lie in wait for anyone unwise enough to attempt to condense or elucidate some of its principal concerns, especially in a book such as this one. In embarking upon so foolhardy a course, I have been mindful of these perils. Two things have, however, fortified me.

First, my students, past and present. As a teacher of jurisprudence in three jurisdictions over the past decade, I have no illusions about the place of the subject in students' hearts. In the absence of compulsion, few would choose to study it at all. Yet, having been obliged to do so, many find it a challenging and even a rewarding exercise; it is often the only opportunity in a crowded curriculum for reflection upon, and critical analysis of, law and the legal system. Given proper guidance and encouragement, even the least compliant student may develop a genuine interest in, and even an affection for, jurisprudence. And here lurks a significant difficulty. Much of the literature is an impenetrable thicket to all but the professional jurisprude, or wholly dedicated and gifted student. It is the chief object of this book, without avoiding the subtleties and complexities of legal theory, to provide (in what I hope is not an unduly idiosyncratic manner) such guidance and encouragement. The perplexed and occasionally bewildered faces of hundreds of my long-suffering students over the years have been in my mind's eye throughout the writing of the pages that follow.

Secondly, I am myself extremely fortunate to have received certain guidance and encouragement in writing this book. A number of friends and colleagues have been kind enough not to howl in horror and alarm at my attempts to identify and unravel some of the mysteries I have selected for discussion. This has sustained me during periods when I feared that the task I had undertaken was a hopelessly intractable one. I am very grateful to Ronald Dworkin, Joseph Raz, Alice Tay, and especially to Roger Cotterrell, John Finnis, Eugene Kamenka, and Katherine O'Donovan for reading and commenting on earlier drafts of various parts of the text. I have, needless to say, been swift to take into account their suggestions and, in some cases, to amend certain chapters as a result. Of course, I alone, must bear full responsibility for any errors, misinterpretations, and misconceptions that remain. Heather Saward of Financial Training has been a most friendly and helpful editorial director.

This is a book for students. It is not, however, a textbook. I have selected its subject-matter on the simple ground that it reflects what tends to be taught in most jurisprudence courses. Inevitably, a number of subjects have had to be omitted; it is therefore neither comprehensive nor exhaustive. Nor is it intended to replace the books and essays to which reference is made throughout, and to which all serious students will want to turn. My objective is to point students of jurisprudence in the right direction. If my book is as helpful to students as I know the other books in the SWOT series to be, I shall be more than gratified. If it awakens in students an interest in this absorbing and important subject, or, better still, enables them to enjoy it, I shall be delighted.

For tolerating my long absences and short temper while I grappled with the manuscript, my wife, Penelope, deserves special praise and gratitude. She was, moreover, estopped from complaining: as a recent convert to the charms of the law, and devotee of the SWOT books, it was her idea that I should write this one. She now knows the true meaning of *volenti non fit injuria*.

Raymond Wacks
January 1987

TABLE OF CASES

1 JURISPRUDENCE WITHOUT TEARS?

Impossible! A contradiction in terms! Fraudulent misrepresentation! For most law students jurisprudence is pain. Given the choice, they would not take the subject at all. And it is little consolation for them to be told that one day they will look back and recognise the value of their exposure to legal theory.

How then can this book live up to its promise? You are probably a student in your second or third year of study (the stage at which jurisprudence is taught at most universities). Having got this far, you have become hardened to the lecture/seminar/essay/examination ritual that remains the predominant mode of legal education in most countries. You have sussed out the system and learned to adapt to its demands. You know which lectures are worth attending, how to appear intelligent in seminars, and how to pass examinations with minimum effort. But jurisprudence comes as something of a shock. Unlike the 'black letter' courses you have taken (and miraculously passed) you are now expected to think, to read a great deal of often turgid — and even incomprehensible — literature which has little connection with 'the law' and frequently presumes an understanding of philosophy, sociology, economics and even anthropology. There is little security here: you long for the friendly reassurance of a statute or the simple pleasures of a Denning judgment. Suddenly you are plunged into the perilous depths of grand theory, a world inhabited by epistemology, teleology and metaphysics. And your apprehension is compounded by the fact that some of your peers actually seem to understand it all!

The first and most obvious point is that this book is not intended to be a substitute for your reading of the materials prescribed by your lecturer. No single text could ever achieve that objective. Nor should it. Jurisprudence is a rich and diverse subject which is in a constant state of growth; most textbooks (and, indeed, courses) cannot aspire to much more than an eclectic skimming of its vast depths. And the book in your hands is *not* a textbook. Secondly, and almost equally obviously, no two courses in jurisprudence are the same. There are a number of theorists and theories that are common to most university syllabuses (and it is this 'core' that is the subject-matter of this book), but beyond that, every teacher has his or her own preferences (conditioned by a wide range of factors) and you will inevitably be required to consult *several* books, essays and articles which pertain to these topics. This book is intended to develop your skills in getting to the heart of the matter and, though it deals only with the major strands of legal theory, it aims to equip you to apply similar techniques in respect of the more exotic issues covered in your particular course.

Thirdly, the affliction most commonly associated with the study of jurisprudence is lack of confidence. Overwhelmed by the enormity of the subject and its attendant reading materials, many students experience a combination of frustration and despair. Having ploughed through the often rarefied works of leading legal philosophers, they throw up their hands in resignation at their complexity, density or their sheer impenetrability. It is hoped that the chapters which follow may, while avoiding oversimplification, facilitate a better understanding of the ideas so as to increase your confidence both in reading and writing about them.

Fourthly, many students fall at the last fence: the examination. There are a number of dos and don'ts (discussed in chapter 2) which, if followed, will considerably improve your performance in the examination (as well as in essays you may be required to write). Some of the best and brightest students in seminar discussions turn out to be indifferent examinees as a result of their poor mode of expression, weak presentation of argument, superfluous discussion and other avoidable (or, at least, curable) defects.

In short, then, this book will help you to think more clearly about jurisprudence. It should encourage you to approach the literature with greater insight and understanding. And it may even enable you to *enjoy* the subject. To this extent, much of the pain will be relieved and any tears you shed will be crocodile ones.

TEXTBOOKS

Jurisprudence has a prodigious literature. You will have been prescribed or recommended one or more textbooks, in all probability, *Lloyd's Introduction to Jurisprudence*.

There are a number of other texts which, though they are no longer particularly fashionable, may be consulted with profit (Friedmann's *Legal*

Theory, Dias's *Jurisprudence*, and Paton's *A Textbook of Jurisprudence*). Each has its strengths — Dias, for example, devotes the major part of his book to what he calls 'aspects of justice' (which includes discussion of, amongst other things, statutory interpretation, custom and values). Few teachers of jurisprudence have the time to deal, in any depth, with these questions (which is a pity), and spend an overwhelming proportion of their course grappling with legal theory, i.e., the views of leading jurists on the central problems of law and the legal system. If your course does consider in greater detail the application of theory to practice you will find Dias's book a useful friend. Another helpful collection is *Jurisprudence: Texts and Commentary* by Davies and Holdcroft, see, too, McCoubney and White's *Textbook on Jurisprudence*.

My own preference is for *Lloyd's Introduction to Jurisprudence*. It contains not only a very large number of extracts from the most important writings (sensibly organised and well edited), but provides reliable accounts of the various theories themselves (richly footnoted) expressed in an admirably lucid and lively manner. Acquiring a copy could save you many frustrating hours searching for texts that some law libraries may not hold at all. Make sure you obtain the latest edition (currently the sixth, by M. D. A. Freeman). An important new series of readers on a wide range of theoretical subjects has been published by Dartmouth. Called the *International Library of Essays in Law and Legal Theory*, it is divided into three sections: schools, areas, and legal cultures. Each volume contains about 20 essays. They are fairly expensive, but it is very likely that your law library will have copies. New titles are constantly being added to the 80 already published.

There are, of course, a number of more specialist works (to which reference is made in the chapters below), and if you are a keen student (or simply an affluent one) it would be very useful to own copies of them. Full details of books are given in the 'Futher reading' sections at the end of chapters. You will certainly be expected to read parts or all of them. Much depends, of course, on what your course attempts to cover. No course in legal theory is, in my experience, ever large enough. There is never enough time to devote to this vast and ever-expanding subject.

The Top Ten

Times change. But the golden oldies seem to be holding their ground. The latest charts certainly indicate that issues and tastes are not static; it would be odd if they were. New artists come on the scene, old standards occasionally have to give way. On the basis of theorists that are read 'in depth' in 64 British universities in 1994, as compared with 1984, the Top Ten is as follows. (The information is drawn from H. Barnet, 'The province of jurisprudence determined — again!' (1995) 15 LS 88, 111–12.) Note that the criterion 'read in depth' is by no means a rigid one, and the percentages below exclude the extent to which the work of each of the theorists is read 'in outline' or 'in brief'. Thus, to take one example Kelsen is read 'in depth' in 47 per cent of courses, but he is read 'in outline' in 29 per cent, and 'in brief' in 18 per cent. He is therefore not read at all in only 6 per cent of jurisprudence courses. The ⬆ means the theorist has improved his (there are no women represented in the Top Ten) performance over the past decade. The ⬇ indicates a slide in popularity. In only one case did the theorist's position remain the same.

Position	Theorist	*Percentage of courses where read in depth*	
1	Hart	87%	—
2	Dworkin	83%	⬆
3	Rawls	71%	⬆
4	Finnis	70%	⬆
5	Marx	67%	⬇
6	Austin	59%	⬇
7	Fuller	57%	⬇
8	Mill	52%	⬆
9	Bentham	48%	⬇
10	Kelsen	47%	⬇
10	Llewellyn	47%	

Bubbling under: Aquinas (44%), Devlin (40%), Unger (38%), Raz (37%)

The performance of some writers over the last 10 years has been meteoric. John Finnis, for example, was, in 1984, read 'in depth' in only 29.8 per cent of courses surveyed. In 1994 this had risen to 70 per cent. Almost 20 per cent of legal theory teachers did not bother with him in 1984. In 1994 those who shunned the work of the leading natural lawyer had shrunk to 7 per cent.

Articles in journals and essays in collections are, of course, every bit as important as books. I shall resist the temptation to formulate a further 'Top Ten' of the most important or useful articles or essays (you might challenge your lecturer to do so!) but it is obviously important to read the works referred to by him or her, many of which you are likely to find extracted in *Lloyd's Introduction to Jurisprudence*. Apart from the leading law journals with which you are already familiar, there are a number of specialist journals to which you may be referred. These include the *American Journal of Jurisprudence*, the *Juridical Review, Philosophy and Public Affairs*, the *Philosophical Quarterly*, the *Journal of Law and Society*, the *Law and Society Review, Political Studies* and the *Proceedings of the Aristotelian Society*. A new journal called *Legal Theory* was launched in 1995. It may be necessary to forage in the depths of the main library for these (and other) periodicals which are not, strictly speaking, legal.

LECTURES

Why bother? So many lectures are so indifferent that it is hard to blame students for preferring another cup of coffee (or even something stronger) to an hour's misery at the hands of a wretched lecturer who succeeds only in alienating you from his or her subject for ever! Things are changing and there is a growing awareness of the self-evident proposition that unless students actually *gain* something from lectures, they might as well be dropped altogether. Certainly many students feel that their time would be more profitably spent (rather than in the refectory or common room) in the library reading the material 'covered' in the lecture.

The teaching of jurisprudence calls, if anything, for more inspired, imaginative and stimulating teaching methods than other subjects. A dreary lecturer can easily murder the subject and inflict grievous intellectual harm on his students. If you are among the minority who are in this unfortunate position (your complaints to the lecturer him/herself, the head of department, dean etc. having proved fruitless) you should nevertheless seriously consider *attending* these laborious sessions. This is because lectures should, in any event, *never* be regarded as note-taking exercises. However dynamic or dull your teacher may be, it is essential that you come to the lecture having done some preliminary preparation. Only by equipping yourself in advance to follow the general drift of the lecture can you really expect to achieve very much by attending. And in this respect, therefore, it is not so important (though none the less disappointing) if your lecturer is below average (unless he or she is downright incompetent).

In other words, you ought to regard *all* lectures as an opportunity to listen to (and where appropriate to take notes of) your lecturer's discussion or explanation of the subject-matter under consideration. This may sound like a counsel of perfection, but unless you are willing to relegate yourself to the role of automaton (which too many students are) you are wasting valuable energy which could be far better spent in gaining a proper *understanding* of the subject. You may find the chapters in this book useful in this respect. So, for example, if the lectures are devoted to legal positivism, it might be a good idea to read chapters 3 and 4 to give you a general picture of the landscape that is likely to be traversed. You might follow this up with a closer reading of the specific topics being discussed. Thus if (as is fairly likely) your lecturer's first 'positivist' is Jeremy Bentham, you could read the section on Bentham in chapter 3 and then look at the essay by Hart referred to (or the readings recommended by your lecturer), jotting down a few essentials to be used as the basis of your preparatory 'lecture notes'. In simple terms, therefore, the normal procedure is reversed: lecture notes are actually written *before* the lecture! Naturally, you will supplement your outline by specific observations, references or criticism made in the course of the lecture. Your preparatory notes for the first lecture on Bentham might look something like this:

Bentham

Discovery of *Of Laws* in 1832. B more sophisticated positivist than Austin?

Def. of law: S. V. Scem. (See SWOT Ch. 3.)

Commands: Imperative & permissive laws. Penal & civil parts of law. (NB *Of Laws* 176–83.)

Sovereignty: May be limited and divided (advance on Austin). Refusal to obey = limitation on sov. (But see Hart *Essays* 228–39.) Judicial review? See const. law cases.

Sanctions: No necessity.

These very brief notes (which are likely to make sense only after you have read chapter 3) will serve as an extremely useful outline in the lecture. So, instead of furiously attempting to scrawl down the lecturer's words (as most of your fellow students are doing), you may relax and reflect upon these points, adding the occasional enlightening comment that happens to fall from his or her lips (e.g., 'Higginbottom finds Hart's analysis of B on sov. unconvincing. Check Hart and B.).

You will find also that you have a far better grasp of the subject which will, in turn, provide an efficient means of preparing for seminar discussions, to say nothing of the examination later. A further important benefit of this system is that you will be reading *to some purpose*. Instead of losing your way in the labyrinth of Bentham's sonorous prose, you will be evaluating his arguments against the backdrop of a broad understanding obtained from your own reading combined with the guidance of your lecturer and tutor. The notes that you make of the primary and secondary texts will, as a result, be more concise, lucid and pertinent to the course you are taking. Your final set of notes (from which you will eventually revise for the examination) will be considerably more reliable and accessible, and you will find them easier to remember when it comes to those crucial three hours.

SEMINARS AND TUTORIALS

Much turns on the method adopted by your tutor. The most common form of seminar or tutorial is the informal 'discussion' of material covered in the lectures. You are normally given a question or series of questions in advance, the 'answers' to which you are expected to prepare for the seminar. Some tutors favour the (generally less satisfactory) method of asking one or perhaps two students to prepare a 'paper' which is then read to the group and subsequently 'discussed' (frequently only by the presenter of the paper and the tutor, with the rest of the class as innocent bystanders). Whatever method is used the general objective is to encourage you to participate in the discussion.

You may be a retiring or diffident soul, reluctant to spellbind your tutor and fellow students with a profound exegesis on the mysteries of the *Grundnorm*. Or you may feel that the exercise is largely futile for you have understood (or, more likely, read) so little on the subject under discussion that you would prefer to give the whole thing a miss, preferring to leave such arcane matters for consideration until a few weeks before the examination. You would be misguided. *Discussion groups are the best means by which to test your own comprehension of a subject.* And if you have followed the advice above about 'lecture notes', you will seize the opportunity afforded by seminars to ask questions, raise difficulties, make points, disagree with your tutor and your peers, and so on. This is also an ideal time to determine where the significant areas of controversy and debate lie (and these, needless to say, often surface in examination questions). Moreover, informal discussion groups provide an ideal method of gauging the performance of your fellow students ('How does she know *that*?') and the expectations of your tutor. Use the group to test your own ideas, to clarify difficult points you have encountered in the literature or lectures, and to further expand your 'lecture notes'.

I would go even further. I would suggest you form your own small discussion group in which (in an even more relaxed, less competitive atmosphere) you can really develop your understanding of the subject-matter being dealt with in the lectures. Books, photocopies of articles, and even notes can be swopped, compared and talked about. You do not need me to tell you how valuable such 'extramural' education can be. And it is especially helpful in legal theory where, unlike the 'hard law' subjects, knowledge is constructed on a variety of foundations. You may be adept at logic, while another member of the group may have a sociological turn of mind. A third may have studied economics. Pooling these different backgrounds and abilities will not only assist all of you in reaching a better understanding of the literature, but it is more than likely to enhance your appreciation of jurisprudence and of law itself.

FURTHER READING

Ackerman, Bruce A., *Reconstructing American Law* (Cambridge, Mass; London: Harvard University Press, 1984).
Attwooll, Elspeth (ed.), *Perspectives in Jurisprudence* (Glasgow: University of Glasgow Press, 1977).

Bryce, James (Viscount Bryce), *Studies in History and Jurisprudence* (Oxford: Clarendon Press, 1901).

Cotterrell, Roger, *The Politics of Jurisprudence: A Critical Introduction to Legal Philosophy*, 2nd ed. (London: Butterworths, 1992).

Davies, Howard and Holdcroft, David, *Jurisprudence: Texts and Commentary* (London: Butterworths, 1991).

Dias, R. W. M., *Bibliography of Jurisprudence*, 3rd ed. (London: Butterworths, 1979).

Dias, R. W. M., *Jurisprudence*, 5th ed. (London: Butterworths, 1985).

Finch, John, *Introduction to Legal Theory*, 3rd ed. (London: Sweet & Maxwell, 1979).

Friedmann, W., *Legal Theory* (London: Stevens & Sons, 1967).

Harris, J. W., *Legal Philosophies* (London: Butterworths, 1980).

Hart, H. L. A., *The Concept of Law* (Oxford: Clarendon Press, 1961).

Hart, H. L. A., *The Concept of Law*, 2nd ed. by P. A. Bulloch and J. Raz (Oxford: Clarendon Press, 1994).

Hart, H. L. A., *Essay in Jurisprudence and Philosophy* (Oxford: Clarendon Press, 1983).

Honoré, A. M., *Making Law Bind: Essays Legal and Philosophical* (Oxford: Clarendon Press, 1987).

Lloyd, Dennis (Baron Lloyd of Hampstead), *Lloyd's Introduction to   Jurisprudence*, 6th ed. by M. D. A. Freeman (London: Sweet & Maxwell,   1994).

MacCormick, Neil, *Legal Rights and Social Democracy: Essays in Legal and Political Philosophy* (Oxford: Clarendon Press, 1982).

Mace, E., *British Philosophy in Mid-Century* (London: George Allen & Unwin Ltd, 1957).

Marmor, Andrei, *Interpretation and Legal Theory* (Oxford: Clarendon Press, 1992).

McCoubrey, H., and White, N. D., *Textbook on Jurisprudence* (London: Blackstone Press, 1999).

Morrison, Wayne, *Jurisprudence: From the Greeks to Post-modernism* (London: Cavendish, 1997).

Paton, G. W., *A Textbook of Jurisprudence*, 4th ed. by G. W. Paton and D. P. Derham (Oxford: Clarendon Press, 1972).

Patterson, Edwin White, *Jurisprudence: Men and Ideas of the Law* (Brooklyn, NY: Foundation Press, 1953).

Posner, Richard A., *The Problems of Jurisprudence* (Cambridge, Mass.: Harvard University Press, 1990).

Pound, Roscoe, *Jurisprudence* (St Paul, Minn: West Publishing Co., 1959).

Raz, Joseph, *The Concept of a Legal System: An Introduction to the Theory of Legal System*, 2nd ed. (Oxford: Clarendon Press, 1980).

Raz, Joseph, *Ethics in the Public Domain: Essays in the Morality of Law and Politics* (Oxford: Clarendon Press, 1994).

Riddall, J. G., *Jurisprudence* (London: Butterworths, 1991).

Schauer, Frederick, *Playing by the Rules: A Philosophical Examination of Rule-Based Decision-Making in Law and Life* (Oxford: Clarendon Press, 1991).

Simonds, N. E., *Central Issues in Jurisprudence: Justice, Law and Rights* (London: Sweet & Maxwell, 1986).

Simpson, A. W. B. (ed.), *Oxford Essays in Jurisprudence*, 2nd ser. (Oxford: Clarendon Press, 1973).

Smith, Patricia (ed.), *The Nature and Process of Law: An Introduction to Legal Philosophy* (New York: Oxford University Press, 1993).

Stone, Julius, *Human Law and Human Justice* (London: Stevens & Sons, 1965).

Summers, Robert S. (ed.), *American Legal Theory* (Aldershot: Dartmouth, 1992).

Twining, William (ed.), *Legal Theory and Common Law* (Oxford: Basil Blackwell, 1986).

2 READING, WRITING AND REVISING

You've heard it all before. The three Rs discussed in this chapter are not only common sense, but they are the stuff of a cornucopia of 'study guides', 'aids to effective learning', and the sagacious advice of teachers, elders and betters. Nor will you be short of exhortations to sleep well the night before the examination (as if that were possible!) to participate in gentle physical exercise before the examination (as if you had the desire!) and to keep calm, relaxed and clear-headed during the examination (as if you had the time!). These are, as you know by now, all sensible ideas; the problem is that the proverbial road to hell is paved with good intentions. You promised yourself *last year* that come *next year* you would not leave all your revision to the last minute, that you would keep up to date with the prescribed reading, that you would isolate yourself in the far corner of the law library (away from talkative friends) and devote yourself scrupulously to serious reading, and so on. And now — a week before the examination — as you gasp under a pyramid of unread books, illegible notes, and incomprehensible past examination papers, you are tempted to give it all up, wander down to the union bar, and make resolutions about *next year*!

Jurisprudence imposes its own special problems. Quite apart from the formidable demands it makes upon your time, you are expected, normally in the space of no more than (and often less than) 30 weeks, to become reasonably proficient in aspects of several, often diverse, disciplines. Moreover, much of what you are expected to read, absorb, remember and write about is technical, complex and often profoundly intimidating. How are you expected to stay afloat? The object of this chapter is to offer you a lifeboat. It obviously helps if you are able to swim, but even the strongest of swimmers may require help when the waters are rough. A quick disclaimer is, however, in order (I am not a lawyer for nothing!): I profess no special expertise nor even any scientific foundation for what follows. As a teacher of jurisprudence in three jurisdictions over the past decade, I claim only that I have watched (often with surprise and even horror) while students have sought to keep their heads above water. Most have managed to do so. Some, sadly, have sunk without trace — and I think I know why. It is, in the hope that, by following my advice, you will not suffer a similar fate, that I have attempted to identify the most important lessons that they have not learned.

Few students fail jurisprudence examinations, but many fail jurisprudence. They regard the subject with such disdain and displeasure that they are inevitably disappointed and even disenchanted. This is to fail jurisprudence. It is the complaint of many teachers of the subject that, in order to maintain student interest (or even attention!), they try to 'spice up' their courses. There is nothing wrong with this if it means they attempt to relate 'dry theory' to 'relevant' practice. But sometimes it assumes a more disturbing form: 'difficult' areas of legal theory being oversimplified or avoided altogether. You may, as a student, applaud this phenomenon. It certainly makes life easier! But jurisprudence is not an easy subject. Indeed, I am always suspicious of any student who describes it as such. That student must have missed something! The subject calls for a determined and sustained attack on a massive body of literature which, as a student said to me only today, is 'too heavy'. But this does not mean that you should not make the effort. And I will suggest how you might approach this task. Secondly, since most courses in jurisprudence require students to write essays or produce written assignments of some kind, I shall consider not only how you might improve your writing of examination answers, but also how to develop your essay-writing skills. Thirdly, I shall suggest various methods of revising jurisprudence for the all-important examination.

READING

A new trend arrived about 10 years ago, and it still seems to be in evidence. I call it the 'Technicolor treatment'. Vast tracts of text are liberally and luminously highlighted in almost every colour of the rainbow. I have noticed in recent years that students come to seminars or tutorials with their notes and materials copiously decorated in this way. Yet, as far as I can tell, while they have obviously applied their multicolour pens to paper, they have not necessarily understood what they have 'read'. Like the photocopier (which has usually been employed to produce personal copies of these texts) an otherwise valuable technical advance has been used as a substitute for genuine 'reading'. You will, I think, know what I mean. If not, let me make myself clearer. Highlighting pens are undoubtedly useful for doing just that.

But two problems seem to arise: first, many students appear to highlight almost *everything* — and often with more attention to the aesthetics of their colourful creation than to its meaning. Secondly, and more importantly, by using this method, students frequently imagine that because they have so adorned a text, they have actually *read* it! In the same way, there is a modern syndrome (as yet unrecognised by psychologists) that consists in the patient believing that what he has photocopied he has also read. And this is an affliction suffered not only by students. I have known several law teachers who store (completely unread) huge quantities of photocopied articles, reports of cases, and extracts from books, which they are unlikely ever to read. Sufferers seem to labour under the delightful delusion that in the process of photocopying, the material is instantaneously transferred to their brains. Would that it were true!

There is, I am afraid, no simple substitute for reading in order to understand. But there are certainly a number of ways in which you may improve your capacity to read *effectively* — to read *to some purpose*. Obviously, the faster you read, the more efficiently will you use the time you spend engaged in the process. And, by reading more rapidly, you are likely to improve your grasp of the argument being developed. John F. Kennedy, it is often claimed, was able to read complex government documents at the rate of 1,200 words per minute. That is roughly equivalent to two-and-a-half pages of this book — in one minute! This is probably apocryphal. Most of us read about 200–300 words per minute (unless it is Austin or Kelsen, you may be tempted to add). But there is no reason why, with practice, you should not be able to increase your speed well above 500 per minute. If you are genuinely handicapped by your slow reading, there are a number of courses available which claim to be able to teach you to read dramatically more quickly. I have no idea whether their claims are justified, though I do not doubt that they cannot do much harm. A useful, short book is *Read Better, Read Faster* by M. and E. De Leeuw. The trick seems to be to learn to read intelligible groups of words rather than reading every word. You probably do this unconsciously anyway. Consider how you read a long judgment in the House of Lords. Your eye picks out key concepts or groups of words, and this facilitates a better comprehension of the general drift of what is being said. You will, of course, examine certain passages (or even the entire judgment) more closely later. But your first reading is likely to be of the kind I am describing. And this unconscious process ought to become commonplace. It is neither necessary nor sensible to read every word — unless, of course, you are closely analysing the subject-matter at hand.

Suppose you settle down to read Professor Dworkin's important essay 'Hard cases', which is ch. 4 of his *Taking Rights Seriously*. It is a fairly substantial piece (of some 50 pages) which may seem a little intimidating at first. Before you begin to attack it, page through the whole essay. It is divided into six sections. And Dworkin helpfully provides headings and even subheadings. Write these down as follows:

1. Introduction
2. The rights thesis
    A. Principles and policies
    B. Principles and democracy
    C. Jurisprudence
    D. Three problems
3. Rights and goals
    A. Types of rights
    B. Principles and utility
    C. Economics and principle
4. Institutional rights
5. Legal rights
    A. Legislation
        1. The constitution
        2. Statutes
    B. The common law
        1. Precedent
        2. The seamless web
        3. Mistakes
6. Political objections

You have now, in a matter of minutes, reduced a large body of forbidding text to a workable skeleton which provides a useful anatomical plan of the whole essay. Now read the introduction. You will see that Dworkin provides (as all good writers — including students — should) a lucid and concise statement of what is to follow in the next 50 pages. So (at p. 81) he states plainly, 'I shall argue that even where no settled rule disposes of the case, one party may nevertheless have a right to win'. And he expands on this a little in the next few sentences. We now know what to expect: Dworkin is seeking to show that in 'hard cases', contrary to the theory adopted by legal positivism, judges have no 'discretion'. Now proceed to the first section on the 'rights thesis'. Before you begin to read it glance at the four subheadings in this section; this will provide a clue to how the argument will develop. Then start reading. Always have a pencil in your hand; this will enable you to draw the inevitable question mark or to jot down any points in the margins. Try to read quickly: this does not mean that you should skim the pages, but that if (or, more likely, when) you encounter something you do not fully understand, scribble a question mark in the margin and proceed. You will return to these problems later. Underlining is extremely helpful — but within reason (see above discussion of the Technicolor treatment). So, looking at my own copy of the book, I see that on p. 82, I have underlined only two words: in the last paragraph the words 'policy' and 'principle' are underlined. This instantly directs my eye to this passage which contains Dworkin's important distinction between arguments based on these two conceptions. Sometimes a whole sentence warrants underlining (or, if you insist, highlighting). So, turning the page, I notice that on p. 84 I have underlined the first sentence of the third paragraph: 'I propose, nevertheless, the thesis that judicial decisions in civil cases, even in hard cases like *Spartan Steel*, characteristically are and should be generated by principle not policy'. This seems to be the only *really* important sentence on this page. It instantly jumps out at me when I look at this page.

Occasionally an 'NB' is merited. But they are to be used sparingly. I have sometimes bought second-hand books in which the previous owner has scrawled 'NB' alongside almost every line. Nothing is *that* important! And, of course, this lack of discrimination is self-defeating. You will have your own system of asterisks, squiggles and symbols which will have their own special meaning to you. One symbol that I have used for years is 'e'. This signifies that, despite its apparent complexity, the sentence or passage in question is actually 'easy'. This reminds me that I have (at least once) understood the argument in the text. It is a source of considerable security and comfort.

Apply the above treatment to the remainder of this section of Dworkin's book (which takes you to p. 90). Now flip back through the 10 pages you have read, looking only at the headings and your underlinings and markings. Think for a few moments about what you have read. If any questions or general difficulties come to mind, write them down at once. Then proceed to the next section, 'Rights and goals'. And so on until you have completed the chapter. Then go back to the beginning and commence a leisurely page-through, taking in the underlined or marked sentences or passages, and halting at any question marks. Do they *still* signify your inability to grasp a particular point of Dworkin's or, having read the whole essay, do you now understand what is being said: can you now replace any of the question marks with an 'e'?

Before leaving the chapter read *slowly* any section which you have identified as important. Add any further notes to your list (which you will incorporate into your notes or raise with your tutor) and then, for good measure, have one last look at your list of headings. This is no money-back guarantee. But I believe that by following this systematic approach to reading, much of your pain and tears will be obviated. It goes without saying that when (or perhaps, if) you attack a whole book, you would apply similar principles: listing chapter titles, headings, subheadings etc. In an ideal world, you should follow up any reading with the sort of group discussion suggested in chapter 1. As I said there, reading or discussion groups are the best way of consolidating what you have read, and dealing with any problems you may have encountered.

WRITING

We all have a voice. Whether we are speaking or writing, each of us has a unique manner of communicating what we want to say. And no one should be allowed to stifle your distinct mode of expression. Yet there are certain guidelines that should be followed, if only to make yourself clear and intelligible. In the words of Confucius, 'If language is not correct, then what is said is not what is meant: if what is said is not what is meant, then what ought to be done remains undone'. And, without putting too fine a point on it, what ought to be done in your case is to succeed at jurisprudence — or, at any rate, to pass the examination.

It has become commonplace to lament the decline in standards of written English. Nowadays elegant language which heeds the canons of grammar is unquestionably a rarity. Dreadfully constructed sentences, ill-chosen words, appalling punctuation, and atrocious spelling are by no means confined to students' examination scripts! Open this morning's newspaper. I suspect, though, that every generation decries the erosion of accepted standards. But it is especially painful to find law students, who ought to have developed a slightly deeper respect for language, mercilessly slaughtering it. And you will doubtless agree that your poor usage is likely to be more conspicuous in jurisprudence essays or examinations than in 'black letter' subjects. What is to be done? For a start, the more you read good writing, the greater the prospect of your absorbing and developing similar habits. Jurisprudence, like any discipline, has its own identifiable voice or voices. Try to listen to it. By reading the works of writers who express themselves with admirable clarity and intelligibility (Hart, Dworkin, MacCormick are examples of jurists whose writing rarely justifies the charge of obscurity) your own style ought to improve. I am not, of course, suggesting that you *copy* their mode of expression, merely that you learn to recognise a well-constructed sentence, a well-chosen word and a concise, uncluttered argument. A useful guide to the rules of grammar and to clear expression is Gowers's classic, *The Complete Plain Words* (revised by Sidney Greenbaum and Janet Whitcut). Though primarily intended for civil servants, it contains a wealth of invaluable advice and many an answer to the interminable debates about proper usage. Keep it close at hand at all times, next to your dictionary.

I shall not attempt to provide what books like *The Complete Plain Words* do with great skill. My concern is principally with writing in *jurisprudence*. Though I discuss how you should approach writing in the examination as well as in essays, there is one principle (I hesitate to call it a 'rule') which is common to both. It may strike you as somewhat idiosyncratic or even daft, but I urge you to follow it. Or at least to give it a try. *Use the present tense.* Students, when describing particular theories, tend to employ the past tense. They say, for example, 'Raz said that there is no prima facie moral duty to obey the law' or 'Finnis's account was based on Aquinas's theory of natural law'. This is hopeless. You must — unless the context requires otherwise — express the views of writers in the present tense — even if they are dead! This is, I think, a generally acknowledged, unwritten (and perhaps even unconscious) canon which good students adopt automatically. You will rarely find professional jurists lapsing into the past tense, unless, of course, the context requires it. Thus, in his essay 'Diamonds and string: Holmes on the common law', in *Essays in Jurisprudence and Philosophy*, Professor Hart employs the past tense when introducing the subject of his review (*The Common Law* by the long-deceased Oliver Wendell Holmes): 'In his preface of 1881 Holmes told his readers that his object in writing the book ... was to construct a theory' (p. 279). But once he begins to analyse the book, he switches to the present tense, for instance: 'He asserts that society frequently treats men as means' (p. 283). And you should adopt the same grammar. This sounds like a counsel of unmitigated triviality; it will, however, raise the standard of your writing — at a stroke.

There is another (almost indefinable) weakness that, in my experience as jurisprudence examiner, afflicts a very large number of students, especially (but by no means exclusively) in examinations. It consists, I suppose, in what might best be called, 'crude reductionism'. It demonstrates an almost total insensitivity to complexity. Ideas are expressed in a breezy, often journalistic manner, with almost no attempt at substantiation. Sophisticated or subtle nuances are entirely ignored. No one expects you (particularly in an examination) to express profound or original thoughts, but you should *never* state any proposition without supporting it. Nor should you employ phrases like 'Kelsen's pure theory is rubbish', 'Dworkin is great' or 'the American realists were stupid' — however true they may be. I am not, by the way, inventing these examples. Consider the following opening passages from two (genuine) answers to the same examination question on the Marxist view of the rule of law.

> Marxism is a good theory of law because it recognises class conflict which is present in our capitalist societies. The Marxists are opposed to the rule of laws [sic] because they argue that it is a con trick. There is an economic base which determines the system of law which is unnecessary in a socialist society where law and state withers [sic] away and there is no oppression.

> It would be misleading to talk in terms of a single Marxist *theory* of law and state, for Marxists are themselves divided about the extent to which the rule of law should be endorsed. It is true that certain Marxists reject the very idea of the rule of law as being incompatible with a class-based explanation of society. Legality is a mask that conceals the real inequalities of the capitalist mode of production.

Without even considering which passage is 'right', you will immediately observe how the first inspires little confidence. Imagine yourself as an examiner at midnight surrounded by a pile of scripts (which seems to grow every time you look at it). You are weary. You have already marked 50 scripts. Only 100 to go! You open the next script and begin reading the first passage above. The opening words inform you that you are in the hands of an oversimplifying reductionist. He (or she: there is only a number on the script) has not said anything profoundly 'wrong', but the way it has been said is so sloppy that you will be unlikely to read what follows with any great interest or enthusiasm. You probably know what the writer is trying to say in the last sentence, but it is said with so little precision or care that you will be inclined to doubt whether the student understands the point at all. Now compare the second extract. It starts with such confidence that you are willing to be swept along with what is likely to be a good answer. Two important morals arise for the student. First, your opening sentences create an initial impression which will probably stay with the examiner throughout the answer, if not the whole script. A sharp, arresting first sentence is (within obvious limits) a desirable goal. Secondly, avoid being silly (a theory can rarely be described as 'good' in this sense), avoid colloquialisms ('con trick'), avoid long, meandering sentences which confuse several ideas. Strive for clarity, short sentences (each containing a single idea), and, above all, treat the subject-matter in a less cavalier way. At least *appear* to recognise the subtleties of legal theory.

EXAMINATIONS

According to a recent survey, only 14 of the 52 responding law schools rely *exclusively* on formal examinations. But the majority have *some* form of examination, though the extent to which it counts toward the final mark obviously differs widely (H. Barnett, 'The province of jurisprudence determined — again' (1995) 15 LS 88, 124).

All examinations are artificial tests of your knowledge, but jurisprudence examinations are more so. Many expect you to answer five questions in three hours. This means that, after, say ten minutes to read through the paper to decide which questions to attempt, you have 34 minutes to answer each question. And even if, as is often the case, you are required to answer only four questions, you have under 43 minutes per question. To answer satisfactorily almost any question asked in a conventional three-hour examination in this period of time, requires a range of skills which are not necessarily a fair reflection of your understanding. Thus, you will need to be able to compress a considerable amount of information into a fairly short space; you have to recall it and write it down pretty swiftly; and you must do all this under the pressure that inevitably accompanies all examinations. Nor is there much consolation in Isaiah Berlin's observation that 'Everything in life, including marriage, is done under pressure'. The premium on time in the examination hall means that there is little time to gaze into space and reflect on the verities of life or law. In fact, as I often tell my students (half seriously), if you have time to think in the examination, you must be doing something wrong. Far from inviting you to engage in the sort of philosophical cogitation that legal theory ought to encourage, the three-hour examination frequently seems to assess only your ability to succeed in examinations.

I shall resist the temptation to identify and analyse the numerous limitations of examinations as a means of testing — in three hours — your knowledge and understanding of a year's work — this will hardly assist you. There is, I am pleased to report, an increasing acceptance by law teachers of the weaknesses of the examination — especially as an *exclusive* test of skill (as it once was). Hence, it is highly likely that you will be asked to write an essay or paper which will constitute 25 per cent or more of your final mark. And I discuss these below. Nevertheless the examination still constitutes the *principal* mode of assessment in most law schools. So you will have to learn to live with it for a while yet. My misgivings about examinations should not, however, be taken to imply that I think they are devoid of merit. A well-set examination paper can certainly test a variety of skills which unquestionably provide useful evidence of the candidate's level of understanding and knowledge. In particular, the manner in which you *interpret* the question posed is a good index of your grasp of the material being sought. It goes without saying, therefore, that the question which asks you to 'write notes on' Savigny's *Volksgeist* does not exactly offer a satisfactory means of testing much more than your memory. Such questions are (happily) becoming rare, and examiners are, if anything, displaying considerable ingenuity and creativity in setting questions in jurisprudence. Yes, I know you'd prefer the former kind!

The first step to success in any examination obviously lies in careful and thorough preparation and revision (see below), but so many well-prepared students destroy their hopes of success in the three hours during which they are actually taking the examination, that I want to consider this subject first. You do not, at this stage of your career, need to be told about the importance of reading the whole question paper closely, before selecting the questions you wish to answer (or, in the case of many students, which questions you want to *avoid*). However, there are eight points that warrant emphasis.

(a)   *Scribble as you read.* It is a curious phenomenon, but as you read the examination paper, ideas, thoughts or information may (assuming you have them) flood into your mind. Yet, when — a few moments later — you attempt to recall them, they are gone — for ever (or at least until a few seconds after the examination is over). My advice is simple. As you read each question, jot down anything that comes to mind. Many students have told me they have found this helpful.

(b)   *Read questions with suspicion*. Suspend your trust. The examiner does not deliberately set out to trick you, but the manner in which you interpret the question is crucial — for at least two important reasons. First, if you misinterpret the question you may decide *not* to answer it or, worse still, you may decide *to* answer it. Secondly, if you follow the latter course, your answer may win few marks. You know the feeling. In the course of the post-mortem, several friends reveal that question 8 required X, while you (vainly and weakly) insist that it called for Y. Had you read the quetion more carefully, you might have avoided it altogether and answered question 3 instead (to which you would have given a brilliant answer). Alternatively, you may have given a *good* answer to question 8 for (as you now confess with horror) you actually 'knew' *that* aspect of Nozick's theory far better. These problems cannot be entirely obviated, but you can at least reduce the possibility of their arising by spending a little longer analysing the questions *before* you make the (almost irrevocable) selection from the menu. Table 2.1 (which I have adapted from H. Maddox, *How to Study*, pp. 119–20) should alert you to the range of directive words employed by examiners, and their meaning. Note that they apply equally to essay topics which are often formulated in the same way as examination questions.

Table 2.1   Directive words in examination questions

Analyse	Show the essence of something, by breaking it down into its component parts and examining each part in detail.
Argue	Present the case for and/or against a particular proposition or theory.
Compare	Look for similarities and differences between propositions or theories.
Criticise	Give your judgment about the merit of theories or opinions about the truth of facts, and support your judgment by a discussion of the evidence.
Define	Set down the precise meaning of a term or phrase. Show that the distinctions implied in the definition are necessary.
Describe	Give a detailed account.
Discuss	Investigate or examine by argument, sift and debate, giving reasons for and against.
Enumerate	List or specify and describe.
Evaluate	Make an appraisal of the worth of something, in the light of its apparent truth or utility; include your personal opinion.
Examine	Present in depth and investigate the implications.
Explain	Make plain, interpret and account for in detail.

Illustrate	Explain and make clear by the use of concrete examples, or by the use of a figure or diagram.
Interpret	Bring out the meaning of, and make clear and explicit; usually giving also your own judgment.
Justify	Show adequate grounds for decisions or conclusions.
Outline	Give the main features or general principles of a subject, omitting minor details, and emphasising structure and relationship.
Prove	Demonstrate truth or falsity by presenting evidence.
Relate	Narrate/show how things are connected to each other, and to what extent they are alike or affect each other.
Review	Make a survey of, examining the subject critically.
State	Specify fully and clearly.
Summarise	Give a concise account of the chief points or substance of a matter, omitting details and examples.
Trace	Identify and describe the development or history of a topic from some point or origin.

I cannot, of course, warrant that your examiner will use these terms with the precision indicated in this table. It might be a good idea to show it to him or her — just to make sure! But it will give you a sensible starting-point from which to launch your attack on the questions set.

(c)   *Err on the side of a narrow construction.* It is a common fault of students to seize upon a question as a vehicle to 'show off' their wide knowledge of a subject. This could be fatal. There is a natural tendency to want to *use* the information which you have so diligently stored in your memory bank. But, more often than not, this is counter-productive: it may lead your examiner to think (with some justification) that because you cannot see the target you are spraying arrows in a wide arc in the hope that some of them might hit. When trying to discern what it is the question is actually seeking, unless you are convinced to the contrary (and the actual directive words used will be a useful guide — see Table 2.1), assume that the examiner is asking for *less* rather than more. And this has important consequences for the *manner* in which you answer the question (a point that I stress throughout this book). Questions are obviously 'pitched' at different levels, from the broadest to the narrowest. Thus, consider the following development in descending degrees of generality:

Realism
Scandinavian realism
Alf Ross
'Valid law'
'Feeling bound'

From a broad question on realism in general (which would call for a fairly rapid sketch of a map of the vast territory of the 'realist movement', including its American and Scandinavian varieties) we move down through a less ambitious question confined to the latter 'school', to the theory of a single member of that group, and a particular aspect of his theory, and eventually down to a very specific element of that aspect. It does not require me to tell you that Ross's identification of 'valid law' by reference to 'feeling bound' would be unlikely to merit more than a mention in a question on realism in general. Your brief account of Ross in such an answer would obviously assume a very different form. Yet I find a disturbing tendency among students to blur this distinction: many answer a general question with an attention to detail that is hopelessly inappropriate. Needless to say, they inevitably run out of time and their answer is a truncated jumble of detail which inspires little confidence in the author's ability to see the wood for the trees.

(d) *Tell the examiner what you take the question to mean.* Once you have arrived at the conclusion above, it is essential that you make this *explicit*. I cannot emphasise too strongly the importance of *telling* the examiner how (and even why) you propose to answer the question in the way you intend to. I do not mean that you should devote pages to a detailed exegesis upon the semantics of the question, its ambiguities and possible interpretations. A short paragraph will suffice. So, for example, the following question appeared in a fairly recent examination paper of an English university which provides a well-subscribed external LLB degree:

> Evaluate critically the following statement concerning Roscoe Pound: 'For him, jurisprudence is not so much a social science but a technology' (Charles Conway).

At first blush this question could involve a wide-ranging discussion of Pound's jurisprudence. But a closer reading reveals two important factors. First, the directive word is 'evaluate' (see Table 2.1) — with the somewhat redundant adverb 'critically' — but (consequently and thankfully) there is no possible tension or contradiction between the quotation and the actual question posed (see below), and, secondly, the quotation itself supplies an important clue to the limits of your answer. In other words, the reference to 'technology' may legitimately be regarded as an invitation to traverse not the entire field of Pound's sociological jurisprudence which includes a detailed evaluation of his analysis of 'law in action', his 'jural postulates', and his account of 'social interests' (see chapter 8) but, while *referring* to these aspects, to concentrate on the technological 'social engineering' advanced by Pound, and the limitations of his arguments. You might therefore conclude that your answer should give a brief introduction to Pound's assault on analytical jurisprudence and his concern to harmonise 'law in books' with 'law in action', and a general sketch of his attempt to classify social interests under various heads. But the focus of your answer would be upon his argument that by identifying and protecting these interests, the law ensures social cohesion: his analysis of the various legal means by which they are secured, how they are to be weighed or balanced against each other, and how the recognition of new interests is to be tested by reference to certain 'jural postulates of civilisation'. A large part of your answer would, of course, be devoted to the many criticisms that have been made of his (and other) attempts at 'social engineering'. But, however you construe the question, make sure you *inform* the examiner. Thus, you might begin by saying something along these lines:

> Since the quotation in the question refers to Pound's conception of jurisprudence as 'technology', I shall evaluate his analysis of 'social engineering' and the extent to which his theory of social interests provides a satisfactory account of 'law in action'.

Even if your interpretation is misguided, your examiner will be so impressed by your confidence and assertiveness that he may even mistake them for brilliance!

(e) *Give primacy to the directive words.* It often happens (but should not) that a question contains a quotation the import of which is at variance with the directive words of the question. This will not arise where, as in the question just considered, the directive is simply to 'evaluate' or, more frequently, simply to 'discuss'. But where the actual question posed is more detailed, problems can arise. There are many forms this sort of difficulty may take. Usually, the quotation is considerably wider than the question posed, as in the following example:

> 'American realism provided the bridge between sociological jurisprudence and the sociology of law' (A. Hunt).
> What are the principal contributions to legal theory of the American realist movement?

The problem is that Hunt's observation is a large one whose substantiation would require a fairly detailed analysis of both the main elements of the American realist movement as well as a discussion of *the other two movements.* A tall order! But the directive (fortunately) restricts the scope of the question fairly considerably. The best you can (and should) do is, while considering the leading American realists (see chapter 7), to emphasise their contribution to the sociology of law and how far they succeeded in developing sociological jurisprudence in this direction. In other words, though you ought always to obey the command in the question, you must take into account the quotation on which it is (apparently) based. You should assume that the quotation has been included *for some purpose* — even if (as I am sometimes inclined to suspect since I am sure I have myself committed this sin) it seems that the only reason was that it was such a juicy quote that the examiner found its inclusion in the examination paper irresistible!

A slightly more serious problem arises where you actually *recognise* the quotation — and realise that (accidentally or by design) — it does not 'jell' with the question posed. This could be because the quotation has been taken out of context or because it does not represent the view of the author who uttered it. An example will explain what I mean.

'The law is, perhaps more clearly than any other cultural or institutional artefact, by definition a part of a 'superstructure' adapting itself to the necessities of an infrastructure of productive forces and productive relations. As such, it is clearly an instrument of the *de facto* ruling class: it both defines and defends these rulers' claims upon resources and labour-power — it says what shall be property and what shall be crime — and it mediates class relations with a set of appropriate rules and sanctions, all of which, ultimately, confirm and consolidate existing class power. Hence the rule of law is only another mask for the rule of a class.' (E. P. Thompson.)
Examine this account of law and the rule of law.

You will, I hope, have recognised that Thompson's elegant denunciation of the rule of law (from *Whigs and Hunters*) is the precise *opposite* of his own view of the ideal as an 'unqualified human good' (see chapter 9). If you did *not* know this you might imagine that the attack on the rule of law represents Thompson's actual view, when in fact he is here describing the account which he subsequently rejects. So what? At worst, it could expose, as it would in this case, a major lacuna in your knowledge. At best, where the quotation is not fundamental to the question posed, you could look a little silly. The best course of action is: if in doubt, do not rely on the quotation to advance your argument. Refer to it, analyse and examine it, by all means, but do not slip into the self-made trap of assuming that the words cited actually represent the view of the writer to whom it is attributed.

(f) *Draw comparisons.* Some questions, of course, explicitly ask you to compare two or more theories, concepts or ideas. But even where they do *not*, you should always attempt to do so *where this would illuminate your answer*. This is often inevitable anyway, and hardly requires stating. So, for instance, a question that calls for a general survey of a particular subject ('What is natural law?', 'Is justice synonymous with law?', 'Analyse Marxist theories

of law and State', 'Does legal positivism clarify thinking about law?')
obviously requires you to examine a number of theories, issues or ideas,
and, in doing so, you will often explain the differences (and similarities)
between them, rather than simply stating them. And often a question, though
it explicitly refers to only *one* theory etc. nevertheless requires a comprehensive comparison with one or more other theories etc. Take the following
question:

> Hart claims that the indeterminacy of legislative aim and the open texture
> of language guarantee that there will be 'hard cases' when 'the rules run
> out'. What does Hart mean? What implications does Hart draw regarding
> adjudication in such cases? Is his account correct?

You will at once realise that, notwithstanding the question's preoccupation
with Hart, your answer would obviously need to compare, in fair detail,
Dworkin's alternative account of 'hard cases' (see chapter 6), and, of course,
in so doing, to assess the validity of Hart's positivism in the light of Dworkin's
attack.

It is impossible (and undesirable) to offer cast-iron rules here. You will have
to use your judgment. But, in general, it is fair to say that your examiner will
regard pertinent comparisons as persuasive evidence of your wider grasp of
legal theory. So, even though a question is manifestly limited to a *single*
subject ('How pure is the pure theory?', 'Does Austin's sovereign really
exist?', 'How does Bentham analyse commands?', 'In what sense is Hart's
description of 'social rules' hermeneutic?', 'Is Hume's noncognitivism
destructive of all natural law thinking?'), your answer can only be improved
by *brief* and *relevant* comparative references. Hence, in the case of the question
about the pure theory, you might, in demonstrating some of the 'impurities'
that creep into Kelsen's system (e.g., how do we *measure* 'by and large
effectiveness' except by reference to *factual* circumstances? — see chapter 4),
mention the American realist or sociological method of determining whether
laws are actually being obeyed or effectively enforced. Or, in answering the
question on Austin's sovereign, you might, for example, compare his account
of sovereignty with Olivecrona's theory of law as fact or refer to Hart's attack
on (and refinement of) Austin's argument that sovereignty is based on
'habitual obedience', or compare Austin's illimitable, indivisible sovereign
with Bentham's model. And so on. I will suggest below that an essential part
of your revision is the drawing of comparisons of this kind.

(g) *Refer to examples from the substantive law.* Where it will clarify or
illuminate your argument, draw on cases or statutory principles from your
'black letter' law courses. I have tried to suggest some ideas in the chapters
that follow. There are obvious opportunities for doing this (Kelsen and cases
dealing with illegal regimes, Dworkin and examples of 'hard cases') but you

should find your *own* illustrations from contract, tort, criminal law, land law and so on. A good use of common law cases in an unexpected area is to be found in Hugh Collins's *Marxism and Law*. He uses (pp. 59–60, 71, 86, 99) the case of *Sagar* v *H. Ridehalgh & Son Ltd* [1931] 1 Ch 310 to demonstrate how the Court of Appeal when faced with a conflict between 'pre-capitalist' conceptions of the master-servant relationship, on the one hand, and the doctrine of 'freedom of contract', on the other, compromised by finding that the term (which permitted an employer to deduct money from an employee's pay for poor workmanship) had been incorporated into the contract by virtue of long-established custom. And there are equally felicitous applications of a criminal law decision on rape (*R* v *Miller* [1954] 2 QB 282) to show (pp. 64–6, 68–9, 72, 108, 113) how the 'dominant ideology' affects legal doctrine, and of the nuisance action in *Duke of Buccleuch* v *Alexander Cowan & Sons* (1866) 5 M 214 (CSess), (1876) 2 App Cas 344 (HL) to demonstrate (pp. 79–85, 90, 93) the limitations of the base-superstructure model (see chapter 9). Dig into your own mine of common law cases and materials for similar explanatory devices. The major textbooks on jurisprudence will provide you with some helpful clues; thus Lloyd's table of cases runs to some 500 decisions. Examine them to discover how they have been employed in a subject which, for many law students and lawyers, has almost no practical relevance. Few things will warm your examiner's heart more than your providing evidence that his or her subject is not merely dry, abstract theory.

(h) *Always give your own views.* It is never adequate merely to regale the examiner with the views of others. Every question (often explicitly, but otherwise implicitly) calls for some statement of your own position on the subject. This does not mean that you have a licence to discuss *only* your own views, as some students have discovered to their cost. The examiner is interested in your reflections upon natural law, but only once you have considered the classical doctrine of Aquinas, the development of the theory in political theory, Finnis's account of the matter and so on. The most sensible (and obvious) approach is to examine the various views of jurists etc. and then to submit (with the requisite humility expected from law students) that 'in my view' or 'it seems to me' that natural law provides a useful yardstick against which to measure positive law or whatever. There is no uniquely correct answer to any question; you may therefore proffer your own views with confidence — provided, of course, you support what you say.

ESSAYS

Much of what I have said above about your approach to writing examination answers applies to the writing of essays or assignments. But essays are, of course, designed to test a range of different skills: your ability to research a particular question and to produce a sustained argument of a reasonable length. They are also a relatively successful method of compelling students to read material they might otherwise be tempted to avoid. A well-set essay ought to encourage its victims to spend a few weeks poring over primary and secondary sources in search of a coherent, systematic analysis of a problematic subject. But, while they serve different purposes from examinations, there is no good reason why an examination question could not serve as the topic of an essay. Where this is the case, your essay will, of course, assume a different form from the answer to a question under examination conditions. In particular, your essay will draw on a variety of sources and examine the matter in far greater depth. This does not mean, however, that you are free to ramble at will; the attention to the purpose and scope of the question (discussed above) is no less crucial. And at least nine other principles (discussed below) should be observed. Much has been written on the subject of essay writing. Two useful guides are R. Lewis, *How To Write Essays*, and C. Turk and J. Kirkman, *Effective Writing*. You will also find helpful chapters in L. A. Marshall and F. Rowland, *A Guide to Learning Independently*, and R. Palmer and C. Pope, *Brain Train: Studying for Success*. You may feel that it is too late in your career to begin learning about writing essays. I shan't make the obvious comment, but I am afraid very few students that have come my way could legitimately claim that they are not in need of improvement. The following nine points may be of some assistance.

(a) *Plan carefully what you are going to say.* The heat is off. Unlike the circumstances under which you have to think and write in an examination, your essay is written under relatively calm conditions. Having interpreted the question posed (with the considerations above taken into account: it will be just as important, for instance, to err on the side of a narrow construction or to draw illuminating comparisons), set about planning how you might approach the subject. You will need to consider: your purpose, your principal arguments or theses, the most appropriate approach to adopt, the most likely sources to consult, how you will introduce and conclude the essay.

(b) *Plan carefully which sources you will consult.* This is not normally a major problem (the reverse is usually the case — how to *reduce* the material to be consulted). Your first port of call is obviously the standard textbooks on jurisprudence. You will scour their texts, footnotes and bibliographies for appropriate references which will, in turn, lead you to further references. The *Index to Legal Periodicals* and, for British journals, the *Legal Journal Index* is likely to be useful. Many libraries have them on CD-ROM.

(c) *Start in the middle.* We all know that any introduction is best written *last*, and the conclusion can only be written *after* you have written the main body of the essay. It is therefore quite logical and sensible to begin sketching the middle *first*. Once you have drafted the main body of your essay, you may then go on to think about what conclusions may legitimately be drawn from your arguments. Having done this, you may write the introduction.

(d) *If stuck, write.* You may have what is loosely known as a 'mental block'. You sit for hours staring at the endless pages of notes you have photocopied or scrawled down — and nothing happens! You cannot decide what to *say*. The so-called method of 'free writing' is suggested by educationists as a means of coping with this malady. The idea is that, like the process of brainstorming, you simply allow your mind (and pen) to run freely. Keep scribbling down whatever comes into your mind about the subject, then edit what you have written. It may be that you will have to discard much of what you have written, but it ought to assist you to clarify your mind.

(e) *Argue.* This is the single most important piece of advice I can give. The overwhelming majority of essays consist in the regurgitation of large tracts of texts that have barely been paraphrased. Think of an essay as an *argument:* you are engaged in developing, step by step, an argument towards a conclusion. It is essential and perfectly proper, in marshalling your argument, to draw on the work of relevant jurists, but you are doing so only in order to strengthen the case you are presenting. Some essays, you may object, do not lend themselves to the presentation of a case. You should nevertheless attempt to interpret the topic in such a way that it enables you to progress through the stages of a reasoned argument.

(f) *Do not plagiarise.* In referring to the thoughts of others, do not present them *as your own.* This is plagiarism. And the reader of your essay is unlikely to be fooled. Yet many students — despite a hundred warnings — persist in this foolhardy practice. I have even had students passing off *my own* published writing as theirs. It is a pointless exercise. There is no objection to *quoting* from the works of a writer (provided, of course, you acknowledge the source in the accepted way; see below), but a good practice is to limit the quantity of quoted material. A distinguished Oxford law professor who was once my supervisor advised me never to quote more than six lines from any source. And, I have noticed that he himself, in his prodigious writings, always follows his own counsel. But I have, needless to say, breached this admirable rule (both in this book and elsewhere) on many occasions. Some quotations capture so effectively the essence of the author's views that to truncate them is easily resisted! Be brutal. If you really must quote, then edit the quotation by the liberal use of dots, or, while attributing the ownership of the idea, simply paraphrase it. But do not extract huge chunks from book to essay. If you suffer from this weakness, an effective treatment is to read the section concerned, set the book aside, and express the idea in your own words.

(g) *Evaluate your rough draft.* Having produced a complete first draft, subject it to close scrutiny, asking the questions (adapted from L. A. Marshall and F. Rowland, *A Guide to Learning Independently*, pp. 152–4) in Table 2.2.

Table 2.2 *Assessing your first draft*

The purposes

Does the draft reflect your purposes in:

    (a)   Undertaking the essay or assignment in the first place?
    (b)   Writing this particular essay or assignment?
    (c)   Selecting this particular topic?
    (d)   Selecting your theme and focus within the topic?

The content

    (a)   Is your topic clearly defined?
    (b)   Does your definition fit in with the topic?
    (c)   Is your material relevant to your definition?
    (d)   Do you have adequate (or inadequate) material for the length of the assignment? Do you repeat yourself often?
    (e)   Does the material you have selected reflect your approach to the topic?
    (f)   Have you selected your material too subjectively or partially?
    (g)   Have you incorporated your own ideas and supported them?
    (h)   What are the main points or arguments of your essay?
    (i)   Have you included reasons or evidence or examples to support your main points?
    (j)   Are quotations and examples which you have used integral to your assignment?
    (k)   Have you plagiarised?
    (l)   Have you clearly defined any central concepts or terms?

The structure

    (a)   What is the structure of your essay or assignment?
    (b)   Does your structure logically and effectively develop your arguments about and definition of the subject-matter?
    (c)   Have you clearly indicated to the reader the stages by which you develop your thesis/argument/theme?
    (d)   Does your introduction accurately outline your definition of the subject-matter and is it sufficiently inviting?
    (e)   Are your main arguments presented as clearly and fully as necessary?
    (f)   Is there a balance between your main arguments?
    (g)   Have you linked your main arguments clearly?
    (h)   Does each paragraph contain only one main idea?
    (i)   Have you clearly connected your paragraphs?

(j) Does your conclusion:

(i) reflect the material presented in the essay?
(ii) relate to your introduction?
(iii) finish smoothly, and
(iv) suggest any further areas or questions to be followed up without introducing any major new ideas?

(k) If you are expected to conform to a certain format, have you done so?

Your style

(a) Have you expressed yourself clearly and simply?
(b) Is your writing style your own?
(c) Have you incorporated any formal style requirements into your writing (proper references to cases etc.)?

(h) *Ensure all citations are correct.* This means both that you have cited the work properly (according to convention) and correctly (the details of the work cited, the page numbers etc.). You will, by now (I hope), know the accepted mode of citing cases, books and articles. Just in case, I shall state the main principles below. One mistake that seems fairly common is to confuse the citation of a book (the title of which is always underlined, italicised, or put in capital letters) with that of an article (the title of which is always placed within quotation marks). Skim the rest of this book for examples of both.

(i) *Provide a bibliography.* Your reader wants to know what works you have consulted (or, at any rate, *claim* to have consulted). It may also save you repeating the full title of the works to which you have made reference or from which you are quoting. This is because there is no reason (unless you are instructed otherwise) why you should not follow the sensible practice, long used in social science literature, of merely stating in the text 'Bohannan (1967)'. In your bibliography, of course, you will have a fuller reference: 'Bohannan, P. (ed.), *Law and Warfare* (1967)'.

Strictly speaking, you should, in your bibliography include more information than this. It is normal to give also the place of publication and the name of the publisher. Thus, a proper citation would be:

Bohannan, P. (ed.), *Law and Warfare: Studies in the Anthropology of Conflict* (Garden City, NY: Natural History Press, 1967).

For student essays this is, I think, an unnecessary affectation; it is highly unlikely that you will refer to a work that is unknown to your reader. But it is not a bad habit to get into, in which case you should follow the correct sequence which is:

Book

Author's surname, followed by forename or initials.
Title (underlined, italicised or perhaps in capitals).
Place, publisher, date.

Note, too, the correct punctuation.

Essay, article or chapter in book or journal
Author's surname, followed by forename or initials.
Title of essay or chapter, enclosed by quotation marks.
Author or editor of book in which the item is found.
Title (underlined, italicised or in capitals) of the book, journal etc. from which the item was taken.
Publication details of book.
Page numbers of article, chapter or essay.

So: Nagel, Thomas, 'Rawls on justice', in Daniels, Norman (ed.), *Reading Rawls: Critical Studies on Rawls' A Theory of Justice* (Oxford: Basil Blackwell, 1975), pp. 1–16.
Or: Kantorowicz, H. U., 'Savigny and the historical school of law' (1937) 53 LQR 326.

There are a variety of 'modern' forms of punctuation (for example, full stops are now unfashionable). It does not matter which practice you adopt — *provided you are consistent.* Note, too, that if you choose to provide a reasonably full reference in the text (as opposed to the brief 'social science' method suggested above) certain differences in usage are necessary. In particular, reference notes in the text normally give the author's surname *after* his or her name or initials; they normally omit full publication details; and there are certain differences in the punctuation used. You should ask your teacher what the preferred style in your law school is. Ideally, you should be provided with a full guide of the 'house style'.

This may be an appropriate place to mention the use of other conventions. I shall confine myself to the 'famous five' abbreviations most likely to be encountered in texts on legal theory (and much loved by students):

et seq.	'and following' (as in 'pp. 94 et seq.').
ff.	'and the following' (pages).
ibid.	'in the same work' (as previously cited).

loc. cit.   'in the same place [already] cited' (this means in the same
                   passage referred to in a recent reference note).
op. cit.   'in a work [recently] cited'.

Use them sparingly. I am not sure that I always do!

REVISION

If you follow the advice offered in the previous chapter about adopting a
systematic approach to lectures and classes, you will need to expend
considerably less time and feverish energy in the run-up to the examination
itself. If, on the other hand, you do not, you will end up furiously attempting
to cram a year's work into a few frenzied weeks. I shan't preach, but you *know*
which approach makes sense. In either event, you will still need to process
your data into a form that may be easily recalled for examination purposes.
There are as many techniques as there are students. But I shall suggest a few
tips that may lighten the burden a little.

REMEMBERING

Why do we remember certain things and forget others? Is it possible to
improve our capacity to remember? Are some of us born with superior
memories? Though our brain works in mysterious ways, a fair amount of
research has shed light on the processes of memory. An important distinction
is between short-term memory (STM) and long-term memory (LTM). The
former enables us to perform our daily tasks (it tells you, for instance, that
today is Thursday or that you have a lecture at 10 o'clock). LTM, on the other
hand, stores data for a very long time (it tells you, for instance, that 10
years ago you broke your arm). In Palmer and Pope's *Brain Train*, Richard
Palmer has compared STM to a handbag which contains all the material we
need to remember for a short time for 'immediate, imminent, or temporary
use' (p. 29). LTM, however, is like a deep-freeze: it is filled with materials
that can be stored indefinitely: 'You can ignore its contents for months on end
if you want to, and then raid it for something which can be cooked at once'
(p. 31). The importance of this dichotomy lies in the fact that your LTM
contains the data you really *know*. In addition it seems that, like a freezer, the
more you store in it, the better it operates.
  The process of learning really consists in transferring material from your
STM to your LTM. But these fascinating questions are not your principal
concern. (A readable introduction is P. Russell's *The Brain Book*.) You would
like a simple method of securing this transfer or, in other words, of
remembering more effectively. There is, as far as I am aware, no such thing.
But there are, as you will yourself know by now, a variety of devices that may

assist you. Repetition, mnemonics, visual aids, songs, symbols, cartoons and a score of other *aide-mémoire* have won the hearts and minds of generations of students. I shall not attempt to discuss these here. As a student, I always relied on mnemonics (especially to assist in memorising case names) and you will meet S. V. Scem in chapter 3 (where I offer a possible (highly utilitarian) mnemonic). Do not scorn these devices; even the great American realist (and amateur poet), Karl Llewellyn (see chapter 7) used verse, as a means of remembering the limits of federal jurisdiction:

> Dangerous weapon, intent to kill,
>   Killing in either shape,
> Robbery, burglary, larceny, will
>   Go to the Feds, like rape
> And burning down a barn or house
>   Or screwing family, like a louse.
> Embezzlement, fraud and fornication
>   Are safe, within the reservation.

(Quoted in W. Twining, *Karl Llewellyn and the Realist Movement*, p. 474.)

It is up to you to devise the method that best suits your personality. Many students report that they remember better the things that they *say*: they therefore read their notes aloud, sometimes strutting around the room (simulating perhaps an impassioned lecturer). Others use tape recorders to record the material, though I never believed the student who claimed he listened to recordings of my lectures on his Walkman! I can only suggest that you experiment with all these methods. They certainly cannot do any harm.

SWOTTING

Read this book! Well, that's a start. The single most important thing is to ensure that, by the time the actual swotting begins, you have a comprehensive, clear and reliable set of notes from which to study. To rely on a host of sources — textbooks, notes, photocopied articles — is likely only to precipitate panic and alarm. It is, I believe, essential to have a *single* source to use as the basis of your intensive, final preparation for the examination. And this is true of all subjects. I strongly urge you to begin, as early as possible in the year, to *summarise* your lecture notes, embellishing, expanding and improving on them by drawing on published material to which you are referred or which you regard as important. Having a concise, consolidated set of notes will save you considerable pain and suffering, and will, almost certainly, improve your performance in the examination substantially.

In preparing this summary you will, as I suggest throughout this book, draw comparative tables between different, or even similar, concepts, theories or theorists. And you will find a number of examples of these tables in the following chapters. They will not only assist your comprehension of the subject-matter concerned, but they are an excellent means of equipping yourself to answer comparative, or even other, questions that require or permit comparisons to be drawn. Make a habit of doing this throughout the year.

Finally, an obvious point. Obtain past examination question papers. These, of course, provide considerable insight into what your examiner expects of you, and even if they were set by someone else, they are nevertheless an invaluable guide to what the examination will be like. You may be sure that your examiner will consult these, or, at the very least, he or she will look at last year's paper when setting this year's. The style of questions and the rubric of the paper are very unlikely to change radically from one year to the next. But past papers are not merely for purposes of detection, you should attempt to *answer* them and, if possible, ask your teacher to *mark* your efforts. If this seems like a recipe for making yourself instantly unpopular with your teacher, fear not. So few students avail themselves of this 'service' that it will not be regarded as a burden. On the other hand, if too many readers follow my advice, I risk making *myself* instantly unpopular with harassed jurisprudence teachers everywhere.

FURTHER READING

De Leeuw, Manya, and De Leeuw, Eric, *Read Better, Read Faster: A New Approach to Efficient Reading* (Harmondsworth: Penguin, 1965)

Gower, Sir Ernest, *The Complete Plain Words*, rev. ed. by Sidney Greenbaum and Janet Whitcut (London: HMSO, 1986).

Lewis, Roger, *How to Write Essays*, rev. ed. (London: Heinemann Educational, 1979).

Maddox, Harry, *How to Study* (London: Pan Books, 1963).

Marshall, Lorraine A., and Rowland, Frances, *A Guide to Learning Independently* (Milton Keynes: Open University Press, 1983).

Palmer, Richard, and Pope, Chris, *Brain Train: Studying for Success* (London: Spon, 1984).

Russell, Peter, *The Brain Book* (London: Routledge & Kegan Paul, 1979).

Turk, Christopher, and Kirkman, John, *Effective Writing: Improving Scientific, Technical and Business Communication* (London: Spon, 1982).

3 LEGAL POSITIVISM: BENTHAM AND AUSTIN

Of all the labels you will encounter in your jurisprudence course, few have generated the confusion and the controversy that are associated with the apparently innocuous phrase 'legal positivism'. Use it with caution. To call someone a 'positivist' may excite an unexpected reaction: in some quarters it is regarded as a fairly serious term of abuse!

We are, of course, concerned here less about such sensitivity than arriving at a reasonably clear understanding of this frequently abused term and the theories of law espoused by those jurists who might legitimately be described as 'positivists'. It is therefore important that the confusion attending the use of the term be clarified at once — particularly because not only is a proper grasp of these theories an essential prerequisite to an understanding of a good deal of jurisprudence in general, but because your examination paper will contain several questions which require a fairly detailed knowledge of legal positivism and its principal exponents.

WHAT IS LEGAL POSITIVISM?

The confusion is so acute that, in the view of at least one distinguished writer, the term 'legal positivism' ought to be abandoned altogether (R. S. Summers, 'The *new* analytical jurists' (1966) 41 NYU LRev 861, 889–90). And he was driven to this conclusion by identifying no less than 10 different positions which are described as 'positivist'. It is, however, unlikely that, whatever the extent of the ambiguity surrounding the phrase, it will cease being a central term of art in jurisprudence — at least before you take your examination! It is essential therefore that you have a clear idea of what it is the positivists say about law and (as will emerge later) how this differs from other views (especially the natural law approach: see chapter 5).

A very useful starting-point is Professor Hart's important essay, 'Positivism and the separation of law and morals' (1958) 71 Harv LRev 593, 601 n. 25, and *The Concept of Law*, p. 253, where he suggests five principal views that are generally associated with legal positivism, as follows:

(a)   That laws are commands of human beings.

(b)   That there is no necessary connection between law and morals.

(c)   That the analysis of legal concepts is (i) worth pursuing, (ii) distinct from (though not hostile to) sociological and historical enquiries and critical evaluation.

(d)   That a legal system is a 'closed logical system' in which correct decisions may be deduced from predetermined legal rules by logical means alone.

(e)   That moral judgments cannot be established, as statements of fact can, by rational argument, evidence or proof (this is known as 'non-cognitivism in ethics', and is discussed in chapter 5).

While, in general terms, it is fair to describe certain jurists as 'positivists' (Bentham, Austin, Kelsen, and Hart himself, are the most important), students are sometimes too quick to treat them as if they belonged to a largely undifferentiated 'school' which adheres to certain general views about the law. At a fairly high level of abstraction, this is not entirely inaccurate (particularly when an examination question requires you to compare the positivist with, say, the natural law approach). But it is important to recognise that not only do each of these writers pose different questions, but their method of enquiry and general objectives are often as different as the features they share. This ought to become evident below.

If one were to express the highest common factor among these writers it would probably be point (b) above: that the law as laid down (*positum*) should be kept separate — for the purpose of study and analysis — from the law as it ought morally to be. In other words, that a clear distinction must be drawn between 'ought' (that which is morally desirable) and 'is' (that which actually exists).

WHAT POSITIVISM IS NOT

It does not follow from this (and this is a point that Professor Hart is at pains to stress in the essay mentioned above) that a legal positivist is unconcerned with moral questions or even that he rejects the important influence of morality on law. Indeed, all of these jurists have been deeply concerned to criticise the law and to propose means of reforming it. This normally involves moral judgments. But positivists do share the view that the most effective method of *analysing* and *understanding* law and the legal system involves suspending moral judgment until it is established what it is we are seeking to explain. In explaining the operation of the internal combustion engine, a positivist might argue, it would not help if we were to suggest alternatives to the carburettor or point out the limitations of the air filter. We should *first* want to know how the engine works. Criticism is a legitimate, but *separate* enterprise.

Nor do positivists necessarily subscribe to the proposition (often ascribed to them) that unjust or iniquitous laws must be obeyed — merely because they are law. Indeed even Austin (to say nothing of Bentham as utilitarian and Hart as moralist) acknowledges that disobedience to evil laws is legitimate if it would promote change for the good. As Hart puts it (*The Concept of Law*, p. 206):

> ... the certification of something as legally valid is not conclusive of the question of obedience, ... however great the aura of majesty or authority which the official system may have, its demands must in the end be submitted to a moral scrutiny.

And Kelsen insists that legal and moral discourse are so different that we cannot directly confront a legal 'ought' with a moral 'ought'. The important question of the relationship between legal positivism and natural law theory is considered further in chapter 5, where it will be seen that the general philosophy of positivism represented, in large part, a reaction against the allegedly unscientific metaphysics of natural law doctrine. Legal positivism has, in turn, been criticised for its preoccupation with the question 'What is *the* law?' and its failure to address the more fundamental question 'What is law?'. Some of these criticisms are considered in chapter 5. A good reader is M. Jori (ed.), *Legal Positivism*.

Law and Power

It would be folly to deny the persisting relationship between law and power. Little perception is required to discern that those who exercise political power normally do so through the enactment of law, whether or not they are themselves subject to it. This indisputable truth, while it may not take us very far, identifies an important distinction between law and other forms of social control. In particular, law's fundamentally coercive nature.

But this generalisation leaves unanswered many important, and often uncomfortable, questions about the nature of law. They cannot sensibly be considered, however, without an understanding of the claim itself. What does it mean to say that law is little more than the decisions of those in power? Is it to divest law of moral content? Does it entail a rejection of attempts to distinguish good law from bad, the just from the unjust? The next two chapters consider the theories most closely associated with a purely analytical view of law: so-called legal positivism. This chapter examines the two leading legal positivists of the 19th century: Jeremy Bentham and John Austin. Chapter 4 discusses the philosophies of some of the principal exponents of legal positivism, Hans Kelsen and J. L. A. Hart.

The 'debate' between legal positivists and natural lawyers is one of the central issues of legal theory. But the distinctions are not always simple and there are subtle gradations in the positions of those who adhere to either standpoint. Indeed one writer (Richard Tur in Tur and Twining (eds), *Essays on Kelsen*, pp. 165–6) has suggested a continuum along which may be placed, in various degrees of extremism, the main protagonists in the debate. His spectrum would look something like figure 3.1.

Figure 3.1

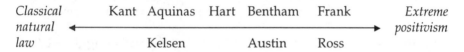

Of course, no scheme of this kind can do more than simplify the complex ideas adopted by the writers concerned. Nevertheless, it is a helpful representation, the import and utility of which should become clearer in the course of the following pages. It is, of course, premised on a set of defining characteristics of both legal positivism and natural law theory which will not be uncontroversial. I think, however, that the basis of Tur's paradigm is an acceptable one:

> ... classical natural law and, perhaps Kant himself might be placed at the natural law extreme and Frank, if interpreted as an extreme particularist, and the early Ross, adjacent to the positivist extreme. Bentham, for whom everything must pay up in the hard currency of fact, and Austin occupy a position fairly adjacent to the positivist extreme but, in comparison to Frank, the commitment to some degree of legal system would justify a slightly more central position. Hart's theory would be even more centrally located, not so much because of the minimum core of empirical good sense which he perceives in the terminology of natural law but because his positivism purports to be normative rather than fact-based. Given, however, the facticity of the rule of recognition, Hart might properly remain nearer the positivist end of the continuum. Aquinas, as interpreted by Finnis, clearly cannot go too far out from the centre towards the natural law end partly because, apparently, he allows that an unjust law is still a

law but primarily because he apparently rejects the rationalist stance that all decisions flow from logical deductions, allowing for 'determinations' in his system.

... given a stronger normativity than Hart's, [Kelsen] must be placed nearer to natural law than Hart's theory. (R. Tur, 'The Kelsenian enterprise', in Tur and Twining (eds.), *Essays on Kelsen*, at p. 166.)

JEREMY BENTHAM: THE LUTHER OF JURISPRUDENCE?

Bentham and Austin represent the classical school of English legal positivism, often disparaged by modern theorists as quaint or simply misguided. But they cannot sensibly be understood without an appreciation of the historical context in which they wrote and the objectives they sought to achieve. In particular, they were (in different ways) apprehensive about the manner in which the common law was explained and justified as the expression of community needs and interests. For them, law is an expression of political facts, as will become evident below. I shall briefly describe the main elements of their theories and then suggest where their strengths and weaknesses might lie.

Bentham's prodigious manuscripts lay unknown, gathering dust in the University of London for more than a century after his death in 1832. Especially since 1970, when Professor Hart published the first authoritative edition of Bentham's *Of Laws in General* (which Bentham completed in about 1782), it is clear that Bentham's work (including, in particular, *An Introduction to the Principles of Morals and Legislation*) constitutes a major contribution to positivist jurisprudence and the systematic analysis of law and the legal system. But it is a good deal more. With his 'extraordinary combination of a fly's eye for detail, with an eagle's eye for illuminating generalisations' (Hart, *Essays on Bentham*, p. 4), Bentham devoted himself to exposing what he saw as the shibboleths of his age and constructing a comprehensive theory of, *inter alia*, law, logic, politics and psychology, founded on the principle of utility.

Little escaped his meticulous and scrupulous attention. He dealt with the courts, prisons, procedure and reform of the law on almost every subject. And his sustained, often devastating, assault on the received wisdom of his day is magnificent in its destructive power, for, as Mill put it, Bentham found the battering-ram more useful than the builder's trowel (quoted in Postema, *Bentham and the Common Law Tradition*, p. 148). But it is his critique of the common law and its theoretical underpinnings that are especially important to the student of jurisprudence. Moved by the spirit of the Enlightenment, Bentham sought to subject (some would say reduce) the common law to the cold light of reason.

He attempted to demystify the common law, to expose what lay behind its mask. The use of fictions, the confusion and inconsistency of the Draconian criminal law with its disproportionate sanctions, including capital punishment, legal jargon, and the complex writ system were some of the features of the common law that he attacked in his characteristically stinging and incisive manner. The law was a perplexing network of technical rules created by lawyers, conveyancers, and judges ('Judge & Co.') which served their, usually corrupt, interests. Most people were too poor or ignorant to derive any benefit from a process which purported to be fair and rational:

> The techniques of manipulation of ignorance, complexity, and selective terror for sinister ends . . . could not be seen, according to Bentham, as mere aberrations of an essentially rational system of law. Rather, they comprised the latest expected chapter in a saga that had been written over the centuries. If society was to see any improvement, its law must be reformed; if its law was to be reformed it must be burned to the ground and rebuilt according to a new and rational pattern. (Postema, *Bentham and the Common Law Tradition*, p. 267.)

Bentham, says Hart, 'surely recognised in himself the Luther of jurisprudence' (*Essays on Bentham*, p. 29). He derided not only lawyers' language (which was designed to render the law incomprehensible to the layman and hence multiply lawyers' fees) but also their wigs, robes and anachronistic forms of address (which sought to lend legal proceedings 'lustre and splendour'), and the ambiguity, complexity and irrationality of the rules of evidence. His critique inspired the major legislative reforms of the law of evidence of 1843, 1851 and 1898.

There is, as has already been stressed, no substitute for the reading of primary sources (though the often turgid writings of Bentham and Austin demand a fair amount of patience and resilience). Indeed, Bentham himself described *Of Laws in General* as a 'dry cargo of speculative metaphysics' — not an entirely fair self-criticism, for there are certainly more laughs in Bentham than Austin. But you will find the principal features of Bentham's legal positivism (as well as other themes in his writings) analysed with characteristic clarity and elegance in Professor Hart's *Essays on Bentham* (1982). Make sure that you have, at the very least, read chapter 5.

In Search of Determinacy

Bentham devoted a significant portion of his onslaught against the common law tradition to the 'theory' of the common law and the extent to which this theory differed from its practice. The common law was, in the 18th century, considered to be the expression of immemorial custom and long-standing practice which embodied natural reason. The law was thus legitimated by its historical (and hence popular) antecedents as well as its inherent rationality.

Bentham regarded such ideas as dangerous fallacies: appeals to the Law of Nature were nothing more than 'private opinion in disguise' or 'the mere opinion of men self-constituted into legislatures'. The 'most prompt and perhaps the most usual translation of the phrase 'contrary to reason', is 'contrary to what I like' ' (quoted in Postema, *Bentham and the Common Law Tradition*, p. 269 and p. 270).

> The only determinate, concrete content that can be given to natural law or reason is entirely private and subjective because of the abstractness of these notions.... They offer no public shared standards for assessment of rules, laws, actions, or decisions. This has two disastrous consequences for law and adjudication. (a) Justification of judicial decisions is removed entirely from the public arena. Judicial decisions resting on appeals to natural law or reason rest entirely on private sentiment or whim. And (b) this opens the door wide for corruption and the manipulation by sinister interests of those who are subject to law. (Postema, op. cit., p. 270.)

Behind the mask of legal fictions (vaunted, especially by Blackstone, as the spirit of the common law) and the pretence of immemorial custom, lay an incomprehensible web of unjust laws perpetuated in the name of 'precedent' which Bentham ridiculed as 'dog law':

> Whenever your dog does anything you want to break him of, you wait till he does it, and then beat him for it. This is the way you make laws for your dog: and this is the way the judges make law for you and me. (Quoted in Postema, op. cit., p. 277.)

Such 'superstitious respect for antiquity' ensures that senseless decisions of the past are repeated in the future. But times obviously change:

> ... the more antique the precedent — that is to say, the more barbarous, inexperienced, and prejudice-led the race of men, by and among whom the precedent was set — the more unlike that the same *past* state of things ... is the *present* state of things. (Quoted in Postema, op. cit., p. 278.)

And, paradoxically, the doctrine of *stare decisis* produces greater rather than less arbitrariness. This is because despite the apparent rigidity of the doctrine, to avoid following a precedent judges resort to legal fictions, 'equity', 'natural law' and other devices which render the law even more uncertain. Moreover, a judge is at liberty either to observe a precedent or to depart from it. The doctrine thus defeats its own avowed purpose.

The indeterminacy of the common law is endemic. Unwritten law is, in Bentham's book, intrinsically vague and uncertain. It cannot provide a reliable, public standard which can reasonably be expected to guide behaviour. Bentham's positivist conception of law, in other words, is a profoundly purposive or functional one, informed of course by the principle of utility. The common law falls far short of this conception not only because it fails to express rules with clarity, but because (and as a consequence) its very validity is suspect. So law's indeterminacy infects its very legitimacy; to accept the authority of the rules themselves is often to accept the larger authority of the law itself. And this conflation results in a reluctance to question and criticise the law in general, to blind obedience.

The role of judges in this disorder is especially pernicious. As already mentioned 'Judge & Co.' conspire to preserve the common law's delay, expense and injustice. The judiciary was insufficiently accountable to the people and its method of resolving disputes unduly complex. The first deficiency could, he argued, be remedied by rendering the whole process of judging more open and public. Publicity, he wrote, is 'the very soul of justice'. It ensured that judges were legally and morally accountable. But it was not enough for the courts to be accessible, they had to use language which was comprehensible to the ordinary person (an ideal which still shows little sign of realisation!).

The second problem (which also continues to afflict modern courts) could, Bentham thought, be resolved by making judges more like fathers. He saw considerable merit in employing the method by which domestic disputes are resolved: a father quickly, justly and comprehensibly determines (without technical rules of evidence) whether a child (or perhaps a servant) has committed the act in question, and hands down the appropriate verdict and judgment or sentence. This cosy model of alternative dispute resolution assumes, of course, a number of social features from which it may seem dangerous to extrapolate a great deal, but it supplies a fairly graphic analogy in support of informal modes of adjudication.

Bentham's attack on the conventional common law model of the judicial function is entirely consistent with his argument for grounding the legitimacy of law in rationality, accessibility and utilitarianism, see below.

The chaos of the common law had to be dealt with comprehensively. For Bentham this lay, quite simply, in codification. Once the law is codified:

> ... a man need but open the book in order to inform himself what the aspect borne by the law bears to every imaginable act that can come within the possible sphere of human agency: what acts it is his duty to perform for the sake of himself, his neighbour or the public: what acts he has a right to do, what other acts he has a right to have others perform for his advantage. ...
> In this one repository the whole system of the obligations which either he or any one else is subject to are recorded and displayed to view. (Bentham, *Of Laws in General*, ch. 19, para. 10, quoted in Postema, op. cit., p. 423.)

Such a code would significantly diminish the power of judges; their task would consist less of interpreting than administering the law. It would also remove much of the need for lawyers: the code would be readily comprehensible without the help of legal advisers. Codification, in short, would wind up 'Judge & Co.'.

The principle of utility dictated that the code be structured in the most logical manner and formulated in the simplest language. It would lay down general principles in a coherent and fairly detailed way, as well as justifications for these principles (these are particularly important for the judge).

Though Bentham argued for codification with passionate conviction for most of his life, his views fell on deaf ears in both England and America.

JOHN AUSTIN: NAÏVE EMPIRICIST?

Austin was a disciple of Bentham as well as a friend and follower of both James Mill and his celebrated son John Stuart Mill. Austin's major work, *The Province of Jurisprudence Determined*, was published in 1832, the year of Bentham's death. A significant figure in legal theory and legal education throughout his life, Austin's influence on modern jurisprudence has declined considerably (indeed the bicentenary of his birth on 3 March 1990 passed virtually unnoticed in the common law world). For one of his most articulate admirers, however, Austin's contribution is not unlike Mozart's Clarinet Quintet, through which many people have been led to explore the world of chamber music:

> For all the unmusical qualities which many find in Austin's style and mode of presentation, it is through the gate of John Austin's work that thousands of people have been led to explore the world of jurisprudence in common law countries — and continue to do so. (Morison, *John Austin*, p. 192.)

Like Bentham, Austin's conception of law is also based on the idea of commands, though he provides a less complex account of what they are (see below). Both stress the subjection of persons by the sovereign to his power), Austin's definition is sometimes thought to extend not very much further than the *criminal* law, with its emphasis on control over behaviour; his identification of commands as the hallmark of law leads him, in the minds of most commentators, to a more restrictive definition of law than is adopted by Bentham. Bentham seeks to formulate a single, complete law which sufficiently expresses the legislative will. But both share a concern to limit the scope of jurisprudential enquiry. In the case of Austin, however, his map appears to be considerably narrower, as may be seen from figure 3.2.

For Austin, therefore, 'laws properly so called' fall into two categories: the laws of God and human laws. Human laws (i.e., laws set down by men for men) are further divided into positive laws or laws 'strictly so called' (i.e., laws laid down by men as political superiors or in pursuance of legal rights) and laws laid down by men not in pursuance of legal rights. Laws 'improperly so called' are divided into laws by analogy (e.g., laws of fashion and international law) and by metaphor (e.g., the law of gravity). Laws by analogy, together with laws set by men not as political superiors or in pursuance of legal right are merely 'positive morality'. It is only positive law that is the proper subject of jurisprudence.

And the central importance of definition and classification characterises the work of both jurists. For Austin, in jurisprudence, 'there abide three things: faith, hope and clarity. But the greatest of these is clarity and it is all that is needed in definition' (Morison, *John Austin*, p. 207). His concern with precision in the use of legal concepts does not, however, lead him to a linguistic analysis of the kind undertaken by Professor Hart (see chapter 4). He is, in Morison's words, a 'naïve empiricist' who regards the laws as an empirical reality rather than a 'concept'. But this does not mean that he neglects the subtleties of language:

> The naïve empiricist does not say that words or other things which have meaning may not function in other ways than by presenting the addressee with pictures of observable reality. What he does say is that representing the other functions as conveying meaning is highly confusing, even though in popular language we may speak in this way, and that it does lead to confusion. Nor does the naïve empiricist claim that there is any 'one to one' picture relationship between words that are commonly used and the observable reality which is pictured if the words have meaning.... For the naïve empiricist there is only one logic — covering the general propositional and implicational characteristics which everything we observe has — universally. (Morison, *John Austin*, p. 190.)

Unlike Hart, therefore, who attempts to define legal terms by reference to the *context* in which they are used, naïve empiricists such as Austin resist the temptation to develop particular forms of logic appropriate to specific legal statements or terms. Austin's empirical model of a legal system presupposes a single logical system.

Yet, for all his empiricism (and even reductionism) Austin exhibits a shrewd understanding of the nature of politics and the relationship between law and power. Not for him the liberal doctrine of demarcating the scope of individual freedom by rules, or the natural law idea of fundamental rights. For Cotterrell:

Austin ... sees law as a technical instrument of government or administration, which should, however, be efficient and aimed at the common good
as determined by utility.... All laws, rights and duties are created by
positioning rules, the laying down of rules as an act of government.
Consequently there can be nothing inherently sacred about civil or political
liberties. To the extent that they are valuable they are the by-product of
effective government in the common interest. (*The Politics of Jurisprudence*,
pp. 60–1.)

The Austinian view of law is, on this account, anything but naïve. (Note:
Morison's notion of naïvety is, of course, a different one and applied in a
different context. See Morison, *John Austin*, p. 189.) It represents an astute
acknowledgement of 'the phenomenon of centralised modern State power in
a way that classical common law thought seemed wholly ill-equipped to do'
(Cotterrell, *The Politics of Jurisprudence*, p. 82). (Professor Postema does not
share this view: 'Austin, it seems, is closer to the common law tradition than
would first appear. [Austin's] approach differs in motivation from the
traditionalist common law approach only in the substitution of the wisdom
of the utilitarian elite for the wisdom of the ages. Both define authorities
which no individual citizen is regarded as competent to challenge. This
departs radically from both the letter and the spirit of Bentham's utilitarian
positivism.') At the same time, however, it is essentially anti-democratic,
elitist, and not particularly concerned to postulate a system by which such
power might be controlled.

BENTHAM AND AUSTIN COMPARED

Their General Approaches

Bentham is, of course, best know as a utilitarian (see chapter 9) and law
reformer. But he insisted on the separation (already identified above as the
hallmark of legal positivism) between the 'is' and 'ought' of law, or what he
preferred to call 'expositorial' and 'censorial' jurisprudence respectively.
Austin was equally emphatic in maintaining this distinction, but his analysis
is now generally regarded as considerably narrower in scope and objective
than Bentham's. Even Professor Morison (who is Austin's most prominent
contemporary supporter) acknowledges this fact, conceding that 'Austin
wished himself to construct a science of law rather than involve himself in
Bentham's art of legislation' (*John Austin*, p. 47). Nevertheless Morison is
quick to defend Austin from the charge that Austin's concern with expository
jurisprudence (as contrasted with Bentham's inclusion of censorial jurispru-

dence) renders his work less valuable than Bentham's; such a conclusion is, in his view, 'unfair' (ibid.). The modern view is certainly that Austin was considerably more conservative politically than his mentor (see E. Rubin, 'John Austin's political pamphlets 1824–1859', in E. Attwooll (ed.), *Perspectives in Jurisprudence*). In fact, Austin eventually came to disown the principle of utility and to doubt the value of his own 'expository' jurisprudence: see Hamburger and Hamburger, *Troubled Lives*. Consider Rubin's argument (op. cit., p. 38) that Austin's jurisprudence 'was designed to defend the stability of a particular economic system and protect the interests of the middle class. A legal theory built on these premises can hardly be called value-free or impartial.' A tempting quotation for use in an examination question!

Your reading of both jurists will benefit from comparing not only their differences in respect of the specific issues referred to below, but also their respective starting-points and achievements.

Though they both adhere to a utilitarian philosophy (which Bentham, the Mills and others propounded with varying degrees of success; see chapter 9) and adopt broadly similar views on the nature and function of jurisprudence and the serious inadequacies of the common law tradition, there are a number of important differences in their general approach to the subject. In particular, Bentham pursues the notion of a single, complete law which adequately expresses the will of the legislature. He seeks to show how a single law creates a single offence defined by its being the narrowest species of that kind of offence recognised by the law (Bentham, *Of Laws in General*, pp. 170–6).

Austin, on the other hand, bases his idea of a legal system on the classification of rights; he is not concerned with the search for a 'complete' law (Morison, *John Austin*, p. 44). Secondly, in his attempt to provide a comprehensive plan of a complete body of laws and the elements of the 'art of legislation', Bentham develops a complex 'logic of the will' (see below). Austin, however, is more concerned to construct a science of law rather than involve himself in Bentham's art of legislation (Morison, *John Austin*, p. 47).

Similarly, while Bentham sought to formulate, in considerable detail, the means by which arbitrary power (exercised in particular by judges) might be checked, Austin did not really apply his mind to such questions.

Bentham regarded judicial law-making as a form of customary law with all its ambiguities and uncertainties (see below). Austin, however, was willing to accept that judicial legislation was capable of providing a basis for codification of the common law.

The Definition of Law

You should be able to give a clear (not necessarily verbatim) account of both definitions. For this purpose (and in the case of all important 'definitions' and 'concepts') I recommend the simple device of summarising the essential terms and then breaking them down into component items which may then be more easily remembered. Thus Bentham's definition of law might be divided into the following six elements:

(a) An assemblage of *signs*
(b) declaratory of a *volition*
(c) conceived or adopted by the *sovereign*
(d) concerning *conduct* to be observed by persons subject to his power;
(e) such volition relying on certain *events* which it is intended such declaration should be a means of causing, and
(f) the prospect of which it is intended should act as a *motive* upon those whose conduct is in question.

By underlining the essential idea (preferably a single word) in each term, both your comprehension and (hence) your ability to remember the definition are facilitated. Instead of attempting to memorise a large block of information, you ought to be able to recall it merely by remembering six words: signs, volition, sovereign, conduct, events, motive. By this stage of your career, this form of memorising material is probably old hat.

You should then give Austin's definition the same treatment: 'a signification of desire by a party with a power to inflict evil if the desire be disregarded, thereby imposing upon the party commanded a duty to obey': command and duty are therefore correlatives. You will see that while their definitions of law are very similar (particularly in respect of their emphasis on the subjection of persons by the sovereign to his power), Austin's definition does not extend very much further than the *criminal* law. His identification of commands as the hallmark of law leads Austin to a far more restrictive conception of law than is adopted by Bentham. Bentham is concerned to arrive at the conception of a single, complete law which sufficiently expresses the legislative will.

Both jurists share a concern to *limit* the scope of jurisprudential enquiry (and this is illustrated by the very titles of their works: Austin's *The Province of Jurisprudence Determined* and Bentham's *The Limits of Jurisprudence Defined* (published under the title, *Of Laws in General*). Austin is the more doctrinaire (and restrictive) in the map he draws, which may be represented as in figure 3.2.

Figure 3.2 Austin's province of jurisprudence

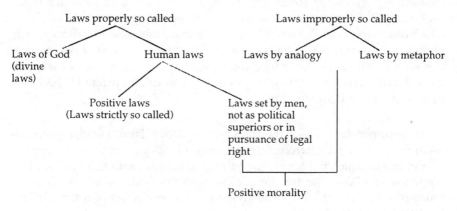

Commands

The central feature of Austin's map of the province of jurisprudence is, of course, the notion of law as a *command* of the sovereign. Anything that is not a command is not law. Only *general* commands count as law. And only commands emanating from the sovereign are *'positive laws'*. Thus Austin's analysis of commands may be represented as in figure 3.3.

Figure 3.3 Austin's commands

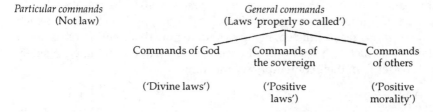

You should know the five elements of his definition of positive laws (which may be telegraphically expressed as wish, sanction, expression of wish, generality and a sovereign who initiates the command — or, even more simply, in the quasi-mathematical formula: $L = W S E G + S$). This insistence on law as commands has been a major focus of attack on Austin's theory. Not only does it require the exclusion of customary, constitutional and public international law from the field of jurispudence, but it drives Austin to the somewhat artificial conceptions of 'tacit commands', 'circuitous commands' (when a sovereign's 'desire' to require obedience to the commands of his predecessors is effected by his refraining from repealing them) and of nullity of, say, a contract, as constituting a sanction.

Bentham, on the other hand, argues that commands are merely one of four methods by which the sovereign enacts law. In developing his (far more sophisticated) theory of the structure of law, he distinguishes between laws which command or prohibit certain conduct (*imperative laws*) and those which permit certain conduct (*permissive laws*). In *Of Laws in General* Bentham is concerned with the distinction between penal and civil laws. Every law has a penal and a civil part; thus, even in the case of title to property there is a penal element: as Bentham puts it:

> Let the proprietary subject then be a certain piece of land, a field, the offence which consists in the wrongful occupation of this property will be any act in virtue of which the agent may be said to meddle with this field.... The offence then being the act of meddling with the field, the act which is the object of the law, the act commanded is the negative act of not meddling with the field. (*Of Laws in General*, p. 176.)

In other words, the owner's title is derived from a general (penal) prohibition against 'meddling' with the field. The owner is himself, of course, exempted from this prohibition. What Bentham seeks to show is that laws which impose no obligations or sanctions (what he calls 'civil laws') are not *'complete laws'* (in the sense in which Austin uses the term, see below), but merely parts of laws. And, since his principal objective was the creation of a code of law, he argued that the penal and civil branches should be formulated separately. You should be familiar with Bentham's strong views on codification (expressed, in particular, in *Of Laws in General*, pp. 183, 232 ff.). You should also read the important section in *Of Laws in General*, pp. 176–83, from which the above passage is extracted, being careful to note that Bentham's usage of certain terms such as 'penal' and 'offence' often conveys something considerably broader than their contemporary meaning.

Sovereignty

For both Austin and Bentham, sovereignty is a key concept. They both regard sovereignty as a matter of the social fact of the *habit of obedience*. Again, Bentham's views turn out to be more sophisticated and less doctrinaire than Austin's. First, Austin defines sovereignty as follows:

> If a *determinate* human superior, *not* in a habit of obedience to a like superior, receive *habitual* obedience from the *bulk* of a given society, that determinate superior is sovereign in that society, and the society (including the superior) is a society political and independent (*The Province of Jurisprudence Determined*, p. 194).

Bentham's definition is strikingly similar (and Austin's debt to him is clear):

> When a number of persons (whom we may style *subjects*) are supposed to be in the *habit* of paying *obedience* to a person, or an assemblage of persons, of a known and certain description (whom we may call *governor* or *governors*) such persons altogether (*subjects* and *governors*) are said to be in a state of *political* SOCIETY (*A Fragment on Government*, ch. 1, para. 10).

Notice how Austin refers to 'a society political and *independent*', while Bentham refers to 'a state of political society'. This explains why Austin's definition comprises two elements: one positive (the bulk of the population habitually obeys the sovereign) and the other negative (the sovereign is not in the habit of obeying anyone). Bentham, however, alludes only to the positive condition. This is only a minor difference and it is fairly likely that the issue of 'independence' (to which he refers elsewhere) is simply not germane to the point Bentham is here making.

The second difference is more significant. Whereas Austin insists on the illimitability and indivisibility of the sovereign, Bentham (alive to the institution of federalism) acknowledges that the supreme legislative power may be both limited and divided by what he calls 'an express convention'.

Both writers, by identifying 'commands' as an essential element of their theories of law, naturally require to explain *who* issues these commands and under what circumstances. For Austin, to the four features of a command (wish, sanction, expression of a wish, and generality) is to be added a fifth, namely an identifiable political superior, or sovereign, whose commands are obeyed by political inferiors and who owes obedience to no one. But, as several critics have been quick to point out, this is a *theoretical* guide to the nature of law. It led Austin to give a distorted picture of legal systems which impose constitutional restrictions on the legislative competence of the legislature or which divide such power between a central federal legislature and law-making bodies of constituent States or provinces (such as obtains in the United States or Canada).

Bentham, however, recognises not only that sovereignty may be limited or divided, but that limitation on the sovereign power is actually a correlative of limited obedience to the legislator's commands. What Bentham seems to be suggesting is that where the people decide not to obey a particular command this constitutes a limitation of sovereignty. This is not a wholly convincing argument (as Hart shows, *Essays on Bentham*, pp. 228–39), but it exhibits a willingness on Bentham's part to acknowledge political realities which often escape Austin. Indeed, Bentham goes so far as to accept (albeit reluctantly) the possibility of judicial review of legislative action. It has been suggested that Austin may have confused the *de facto* sovereign (or the body that receives habitual obedience) with the *de jure* sovereign, or the law-making body. Or that, because the Crown in Britain receives allegiance from its subjects, while the Crown in Parliament is the supreme law-making body, when he refers to the uncommanded commander who makes laws, Austin must mean the *de jure* sovereign. But these criticisms may miss the point of Austin's theory. His conception of sovereignty is not a legal one at all: it is pre-legal: 'the logical correlate of an assumed factual obedience' (Manning, 'Austin today: or 'The province of jurisprudence' re-examined' in W. I. Jennings (ed.), *Modern Theories of Law*, p. 192 at p. 202, quoted by Cotterrell, *The Politics of Jurisprudence*, p. 70). In other words, the sovereign (person or body) is a more abstract idea: it is the source of political authority and legitimacy.

Your reading on this subject should include those decisions of the court which you encountered in your constitutional law course (of which you obviously have the clearest recollection!) dealing with the question of the extent to which Parliament may bind its successor. This is further evidence of the practical relevance of jurisprudence, and your examiner will always be impressed by such reference (as well as being reassured that his subject is not merely dry theory.)

Sanctions

Austin, of course, regards the sanction as an essential element in the definition of law. And he does so largely on the basis that if the sovereign expresses a wish and has the power to inflict an evil (or sanction) then a person is under a duty (or is 'obliged') to act in accordance with that wish. Duty is therefore defined in terms of sanction. This is another aspect of Austin's system which has been widely attacked. (Make sure you have read the critique by Tapper, 'Austin on sanctions' [1965] CLJ 270.)

Though several major criticisms have been made, it is important to clarify exactly what Austin is saying. My own view is that (though he does occasionally suggest that the existence of a sanction supplies the motivation for obedience) his analysis of sanctions attempts to show that, in *a purely formal sense*, where there is a *duty* there is normally a *sanction*. In other words, he is not necessarily seeking to provide an explanation for *why* law is obeyed or whether it *ought* to be obeyed, but rather *when* a legal duty exists (cf. Tapper, op. cit., pp. 282–3). But this does not answer the more fundamental objection that *duty* is itself accorded undeserved importance by Austin: there are clearly many instances in the law where no legal duty arises at all (and hence there is no sanction) and yet we should not wish to exclude these examples from a sensible definition of law. The most obvious cases would be those laws which enable people to marry, to enter into contracts or to make wills: no one is under a *duty* to do these things, yet they are obviously part of the law. Hart calls these 'power-conferring rules' (see chapter 4).

Another objection is that, yet again, Austin's theory is too simple. The operation of law in society is a complex process which does not admit to Austin's somewhat ingenuous explanation based on compulsion and coercion. This, as will be seen below, is the linchpin of Professor Hart's criticism of Austin, and, despite the spirited defence of Austin's 'naïve empiricism' by Professor Morison (*John Austin*, especially ch. 6) it remains a pervasive weakness in Austin's command theory of law.

Bentham is willing to concede that a sovereign's commands would constitute law even in the absence of sanctions in the Austinian sense. For him law includes both punishments ('coercive motives') and rewards ('alluring motives'), but they are not the fundamental, defining characteristics of law that they are for Austin. Nor, therefore, is Bentham guilty of the limited social vision of law and the legal system that afflicts Austin in this respect.

THE EXAMINATION

In order to answer a question on the 'older' theories of legal positivism, it would obviously make sense for you to have read and summarised the primary works of Bentham and Austin as well as the leading commentaries on them. This is, for most students, an unrealistically ambitious objective. And, in view of the fact that you are normally expected to answer at least three questions covering different aspects of legal theory, it would be a misallocation of your time. Jurisprudence is, after all, not the only subject you are taking.

Having said that, however, I do not want to discourage you from attempting a measure of specialisation in your preparation for the examination. A thorough understanding of the theories of Bentham and Austin would stand you in very good stead, not only in answering questions on these jurists, but also in explaining or elaborating upon issues that arise in *other* questions. Consider for example, the following question from a recent LLB examination paper:

> 'While it is never wrong not to respect the law it is morally wrong to respect it in ... fundamentally iniquitous regions' (Joseph Raz).
> Examine this assertion and the general question of whether there is, in any event, a moral duty to obey the law.

On the face of it, this question appears to have little connection with the legal positivism of Austin or Bentham. You would be fully entitled to regard it as a question which requires a discussion of the problem of obedience to law and, in particular (as the question puts it), whether there is a 'moral duty' to obey the law. Professor Raz argues persuasively against such a duty (in *The Authority of Law*, pt. 4, from which this quotation is taken). You would obviously be expected to consider the various arguments about whether there is a prima facie duty to obey the law (e.g., social contractarianism, promise-keeping, utilitarianism, bad example, gratitude) and the more specific question of obedience to unjust laws (civil disobedience and conscientious objection). Nevertheless, you might illuminate your answer by referring to Bentham's aphorism, 'Obey punctually, censor freely', which makes plain his rejection of natural law and his view that law (if it accords with the standard of utility) must be obeyed (see chapter 9).

Or you might refer to Austin's similar sentiments concerning the claim that unjust laws need not be obeyed. This illustrates, of course, the difficulties of attempting to divide the subject-matter of jurisprudence into watertight compartments. To put it another way, *none* of the reading of the works of legal theorists is likely to be irrelevant in answering questions in the examinations. This is hardly surprising. Most of the writers you will be studying in your course are essentially pursuing the answers to similar questions. No reading is therefore wasted: Olivecrona, the Scandinavian realist (see chapter 7) propounded a theory of 'independent imperatives' which might be compared with Austin's notion of 'commands', Fuller is relevant to anthropological jurisprudence, Dworkin to the economic analysis of law, Kelsen to natural law, Rawls to utilitarianism, and so on.

But you must use your judgment. It ought to be apparent from your lecturer's advice or approach whether it would be worthwhile devoting a large proportion of your time to a detailed analysis of, say, Bentham. It is, however, a very good idea to concentrate on a particular jurist (and Bentham is not a bad choice) in order to follow the flow of his argument and the manner in which it develops and is, in turn, criticised (and not merely rely on second-hand accounts, such as this one).

While a growing number of examination questions call for a relatively straightforward *comparison* between the theories of Austin and Bentham (and this ought to be fairly simple) be on your guard for the examiner who, though he or she wishes to whet your appetite with a juicy quotation about the place of the two writers in the history of legal positivism (gems like 'If Austin is the father of English jurisprudence, then Bentham must be the grandfather' abound), specifies that you should analyse a *particular* element in their models (e.g., commands or sovereignty). You would be surprised how many students simply fail to see that what is being sought is not a general comparison of every feature of the two approaches, but a fairly detailed discussion of a *part* thereof. You can never read an examination question too carefully.

Despite the more limited scope of such questions, it is nevertheless important to show the examiner that you have an understanding of the theories and, in particular, where and how the specific features you are called upon to analyse *fit in* to the models proposed by the respective jurists.

Suppose, for example, the question, though it starts with a general statement of the kind suggested above, asks you to consider the importance of *sanctions* in the two theories. A sensible (brief) introduction to your answer would point to the *similarities* between the approaches of Bentham and Austin: that they both expounded an imperative theory of law, a theory which maintains that a law is the command of a determinate person or body of persons, an order to a person to do or refrain from doing something. You should show in what way their approaches may be described as 'positivist' by giving a very brief statement of the fundamental propositions of legal positivism: the separation of law and morals. You might then go on (concisely) to mention the significant features of their models of law, in particular their definitions of 'law' (showing that you understand that they were both reacting to the metaphysical speculations of natural law), their utilitarianism and the strong influence of Bentham's work on Austin (even if, as Morison puts it, Austin had a reputation as 'a retrograde or backsliding Benthamite' (*John Austin*, p. 42) (and see above). This sketch helps to give the impression that you have not merely learned the *details* of the theories, but have gained some insight into the theorists themselves.

The greater portion of your answer should, of course, be devoted to a discussion of the place of sanctions in each of the models of law. It is probably easier to treat each theorist separately and then to compare their differences. Thus, you would obviously be expected to demonstrate a clear understanding of the position of sanctions in each theory. Beginning with Bentham, you might point out that sanctions, though important, are less central to (though a more complex feature of) his analysis of law than is the case with Austin. It would be sensible to point out that you cannot (nor would you be expected to) provide a *detailed* account of Bentham's (fairly lengthy) discussion of this subject in your answer. (Always *tell* your examiner exactly what you propose to do and what you propose not to do in your answer. This inspires a certain confidence in you — even if it is misplaced!)

The concept of a command was important for Bentham. It captured, in Professor Postema's words, 'the *artificial* character of law':

> Law conceived as command could not be regarded as some mysterious, unalterable fact of nature, as common law theorists often tried to portray it. To conceive of law as command invites the questions *who* issued it? and *when*? and with what authority? Law is clearly portrayed as an artificial creation of human society. The paradigm captures the related important idea that law is not just descriptive of social order, but is its 'cause' — not an expression of some deeper reality, but the *instrument* by which the social relations necessary for human life are constituted and sustained. This has important implications for Bentham. For once this view is adopted, no existing system of law and legal relations can be protected as sacred. All

law, social relations, and institutions, are opened to critical assessment, challenge, and reform. (Postema, *Bentham and the Common Law Tradition*, p. 316.)

And Bentham did not, of course, shrink from vigorously pursuing all three.

It would be sensible to explain the relationship between 'commands' and sanctions in Bentham's theory (and perhaps even how this differs from Austin's approach); thus you would show how, for Bentham, 'command' is merely one of four manners in which the sovereign's will is manifested. There are two *imperative* aspects (command and prohibition), and two *permissive* aspects (non-prohibition and non-command). It would certainly help to give examples of each of these, such as those given by Hart (*Essays on Bentham*, ch. 5 (which you have, of course read and noted!), p. 113): command — 'shut the door'; non-command — 'you may refrain from shutting the door'; prohibition — 'do not shut the door'; non-prohibition — 'you may shut the door'. Bentham develops a complex system of what Hart (ibid.) suggests might be described by a logician as 'four imperative operators or deontic modalities'. Your examiner will not expect you to comprehend this sort of high-powered logic (even if he or she comprehends them); indeed, even Hart (p. 115) confesses that *he* lacks the 'technical logical competence' to explain Bentham's complete 'logic of the will', so you are in very distinguished company. You should nevertheless point to the relationship between the permissive aspects and the imperative (they release the subject from previously issued commands or prohibitions and are therefore dis-imperative) and refer to Bentham's view (discussed on pages 48–51 above) that all 'complete' laws are imperative in form.

For Bentham a law contains two parts: the *directive* part which announces the conduct to be done, not done etc., and the *incitative* part which predicts the sanction. The sanction is, at this stage, merely a prediction; it becomes a reality only when a subsidiary law is addressed to an official ordering him to impose a sanction in the event of a breach of the first law. This subsidiary law requires the support of another law and so on. Every law therefore has a sanction, but unlike Austin's fairly crude account of sanctions (see below) Bentham recognises that a sanction may be not merely coercive, but may also be in the form of a reward. If it is coercive it may assume one or more of several forms: political, moral or religious. And if it is a reward sanction (what he calls 'praemiary laws') it cannot be said to create an obligation; it is not therefore a 'complete' law (even though it is sufficiently similar to coercive sanctions to be called 'law'). This connection between sanction and obligation (the sanction creates or constitutes the legal obligation) is an important element in Bentham's theory and is, again, more sophisticated than Austin's account. You might here refer to his distinction between *contrectation* (the power to handle persons or property, e.g., the owner's power to walk on his land which is derived from a general prohibition against anyone else doing so) and *imperation* (the power to alter persons' legal position by making them subject to commands or prohibitions) to demonstrate the manner in which a particular sanction (e.g., damages for breach of contract) may be used to make laws 'complete'.

As far as Austin's theory is concerned, the relationship between commands and sanctions is equally important. In particular, the fact that Austin's very concept of a command includes the likelihood that a sanction will follow failure to obey the command. A sanction is defined by Austin as an evil which is conditional upon the failure of a person to comply with the wishes of the sovereign. Thus unless a sanction is likely to follow, the mere 'expression of a wish' is not a command. Obligations are therefore defined in terms of sanctions: this is a central tenet of Austin's imperative theory. The 'likelihood' of a sanction is always uncertain, but Austin is driven to the position that a sanction consists of 'the smallest chance of incurring the smallest evil'.

His analysis of sanctions is adduced as evidence of the 'muddled, inconsistent and ambiguous' theory of Austin in general in the sharp (and very useful) article by Colin Tapper [1965] CLJ 270 (referred to on page 50). The whole question of the efficacy of sanctions in motivating obedience is controversial (you could here refer briefly to Milgram's experiments and the general question of social and psychological factors explaining obedience, described by Lloyd, *Introduction to Jurisprudence*, p. 223). 'Austin seems to assume', says Tapper (p. 281) 'that if evil is certain to be inflicted upon some who disobey, all who disobey run some risk of having it inflicted upon them. This is plainly false.'

Moreover, if all laws are commands then how is one (or more especially Austin) to explain those rules which confer power on persons to alter their legal position (by contract, trust etc.)? Austin attempts to squeeze them into his scheme by suggesting that the sanction is nullity and the likelihood of this makes these rules duty-imposing in common with other commands. Hart, of course, demonstrates the artificiality of describing these 'secondary, power-conferring rules' as duty-imposing. It would be sensible to refer to this criticism of Austin's limited account of law as commands which is an important element of Hart's critique in *The Concept of Law*. Indeed, you might want to point out that, despite Hart's attack on Austin, he acknowledges *The Province of Jurisprudence Determined* as constituting an important statement of legal positivism.

You would conclude your answer with a general consideration of the superiority of Bentham's theory (if this is what you believe to be the case) referring perhaps to Morison's defence of Austin's 'naïve empiricism' as well as a brief discussion of some of the criticisms that have been levelled at both imperative theories. Thus, you might point to the fact that, in spite of the importance of sanctions in any account of a legal system, it is highly questionable whether they ought to be accorded so central a place in the *definition* of an individual law and its accompanying obligation. In other words, there are many obligations imposed *by the law*, the breach of which carries no sanction at all. There are even situations in which there is *no* likelihood of the sanction being enforced (e.g., the offender has died), yet we would not want to deny that the obligation exists.

For the rest, you should always include some of your *own* views on the subject (see chapter 2). No one expects you in 43 minutes to present a trail-blazing, original analysis of the subject, but you ought to have, at the ready, a few comments and observations of your own which you have arrived at after attending lectures and seminars and, especially, after reading the theories themselves. Those I leave to you.

Another kind of question (which is becoming increasingly popular with examiners in the light of Bentham's new-found prominence as legal positivist) calls for a *general* assessment of the relative merits of the theories of the two jurists. Naturally, in a question of this sort you would devote, roughly equal parts of your answer to each of the principal features of the two models. Starting, perhaps, with a slightly more detailed discussion of their definitions of 'law' than you would have given in answer to the question just considered, you would show how Austin's definition ('a rule laid down for the guidance of an intelligent being by an intelligent being having power over him') excludes any reference to the concept of sovereignty or State. Bentham's definition (which, in its briefer form, is 'a volition conceived or adopted by the sovereign in a State, concerning the conduct to be observed in a certain case by a certain person or class of persons'), on the other hand, recognises both of these elements.

By confining 'laws properly so called' to the commands of a sovereign (who exists only 'if a determinate political superior, not in the habit of obedience to a like superior, receive habitual obedience from the bulk of a given society, and the society (including the superior) is a society political and independent') Austin bases his idea of sovereignty on the habit of obedience adopted by members of society. The sovereign must, moreover, be 'determinate' for 'no indeterminate sovereign can command expressly or tacitly, or can receive obedience or submission'. This logically leads Austin to exclude from his definition of law, public international law, customary law and much of constitutional law. He presents us with a conception of law which rests on a narrow conception of a sovereign — whose powers are illimitable and indivisible — and who is habitually obeyed.

Bryce (*Studies in History and Jurisprudence*, vol. 2, pp. 51–60) suggested that Austin may have confused the *de facto* sovereign (or the body that receives habitual obedience) with the *de jure* sovereign (or the law-making body). As Dias points out (*Jurisprudence*, p. 348), the Crown in Britain receives allegiance from its subjects, while the Crown in Parliament is the supreme law-making body. When he refers to the uncommanded commander who makes laws,

Austin means the *de jure* sovereign. Other criticisms relate, of course, to the fact that by denying that the sovereign's power could be limited or divided, Austin (a) relegates large portions of constitutional law to 'positive morality', (b) ignores the possibility of limitations on the sovereign through disabilities rather than duties or by special procedures such as entrenchment, and (c) overlooks the possibility of vesting sovereignty in more than one body.

Bentham, on the other hand, offers a far more pragmatic conception of a sovereign which he defines as 'any person or assemblage of persons to whose will a whole political community are (no matter on what account) supposed to be in a disposition to pay obedience; and that in preference to the will of any other person'. This enables Bentham to entertain the idea of a sovereign that, unlike Austin's, is not necessarily determinate. It is therefore possible for Bentham to explain the continuity of legal systems where the sovereign dies or the sovereign body is in recess. Austin is driven to the view that when Parliament has been dissolved, sovereignty resides with the Queen, the Lords and the electorate. But, on this view, it is impossible to distinguish the commander from the commanded: it renders his general theory of sovereignty even more suspect. Bentham, however, allows that the sovereign's authority may be divided, he may even adopt the commands of his predecessor or a person to whom he has delegated his law-making power.

You would also examine the differences between the two writers in their attitude to sanctions (see above) and you would be entitled to treat this subject in less detail than you would have done in the context of a question explicitly focused on sanctions.

Having considered the particular differences, you may legitimately indulge in some general reflections about the two theories. Despite the superiority of Bentham's account, you may wish to refer to some of its limitations. Professor Raz (*The Concept of a Legal System*, p. 10) identifies a number of defects in Bentham's analysis of sovereignty, including the fact that it does not:

(a) fully explain *divided* sovereignty,

(b) account for the *relationship* between the various powers which constitute the single sovereign power,

(c) explain *how* sovereignty can be limited by the law,

(d) explain how to decide whether a certain legal power is *part* of a sovereign power.

You will add to this list yourself.

FURTHER READING

Austin, John, *The Province of Jurisprudence Determined and the Uses of the Study of Jurisprudence* (London: Weidenfeld & Nicolson, 1954).

Bentham, Jeremy, *A Fragment on Government; or, A Comment on the   Commentaries*, 2nd ed. (London: W. Pickering, 1823).

Bentham, Jeremy, *An Introduction to the Principles of Morals and Legislation*, ed. J. H. Burns and H. L. A. Hart (London: Athlone Press, 1970) (The Collected Works of Jeremy Bentham, ed. J. H. Burns).

Bentham, Jeremy, *Of Laws in General*, ed. H. L. A. Hart (London: Athlone Press, 1970) (The Collected Works of Jeremy Bentham, general ed. J. H. Burns).

George, Robert P. (ed.), *The Autonomy of Law: Essays on Legal Positivism* (Oxford: Clarendon Press, 1995).

Hamburger, Lotte, and Hamburger, Joseph, *Troubled Lives: John and Sarah Austin* (Toronto; London: University of Toronto Press, 1985).

Hart, H. L. A., *Essay on Bentham: Studies on Jurisprudence and Political Theory* (Oxford: Clarendon Press, 1982).

Jori, Mario (ed.,), *Legal Positivism* (Aldershot: Dartmouth, 1992).

Morison, W. L., *John Austin* (London: Edward Arnold, 1982).

Postema, Gerald J., *Bentham and the Common Law Tradition* (Oxford: Clarendon Press, 1986).

Waldron, Jeremy (ed.), *Nonsense upon Stilts: Bentham, Burke and Marx on the Rights of Man* (London: Methuen, 1987).

4 MODERN LEGAL POSITIVISM: HART AND KELSEN

Modern 'positivism', is generally associated with the work of two brilliant, but very different, legal philosophers: H. L. A. Hart and Hans Kelsen. Though they do — as legal positivists — subscribe to the view that an analytical distinction must be maintained between law and morality, between 'is' and 'ought' (*sein* and *sollen*), their starting-points, methodology and conclusions bear little resemblance to each other. As Professor MacCormick succinctly puts it (*H. L. A. Hart*, p. 26): 'Hart is a Humean where Kelsen is a Kantian' (a piquant quotation I recently invited students to 'discuss' in an examination; a useful, though difficult, recent essay attempts to show that Kelsen is not a full-blown Kantian: Alida Wilson, 'Is Kelsen really a Kantian?', in *Essays on Kelsen*, ed. R. Tur and W. Twining). The meaning and consequences of this distinction (which implies, of course, a reasonable understanding of the theories of Hume and Kant) should become clear in a moment.

HART

There can be little doubt that Professor H. L. A. Hart is the leading contemporary legal philosopher. Almost single-handedly, he has succeeded in applying the techniques of analytical (and especially linguistic) philosophy to the study of law. His work (largely, but by no means exclusively, *The Concept of Law*, published in 1961) has clarified the meaning of legal concepts, the manner in which we use them, and even the way we think about law and the legal system. A second edition, which includes a 'postscript' by Hart (much of which is devoted to a response to Dworkin's views (see chapter 6)) was published in 1994. Page references here are to the first edition, unless otherwise stated.

Despite its importance (and its readability) few students actually read *The Concept of Law* or, at any rate, the whole of it. This is unfortunate for there are few better methods of familiarising yourself with (what are still) the central questions of jurisprudence. And Hart's reflections are set out so elegantly, coherently and clearly that by reading it you will gain more than an 'understanding of law, coercion, and morality as different but related social phenomena' (as Hart, in his preface, modestly describes the aim of the book). Moreover, it is no exaggeration to say that *The Concept of Law* has been used as a springboard by several legal theorists (Raz, Finnis, Dworkin, MacCormick) and has provided the inspiration for many more. If you simply cannot read the entire book, you should, *at the very least*, read chs 4, 5 and 6. And I strongly recommend Neil MacCormick's *H. L. A. Hart* (the major part of which is devoted to an analysis of *The Concept of Law*) as a reliable and sympathetic account of Hart's contribution to legal theory.

Hart as Legal Positivist

Although he is unquestionably a positivist (particularly in the sense of maintaining, for analytical purposes, the separation of law and morality) Hart acknowledges the 'core of indisputable truth in the doctrines of natural law' (*The Concept of Law*, p. 146). You will see in chapter 5 that one of the hallmarks of the natural law tradition (attacked by Bentham and Austin) is the view that such a separation cannot be sustained. How is it then that the leading contemporary positivist concedes that there is a 'minimum content' of natural law? The answer is that Hart's positivism (though it follows very much in the tradition of classic English legal positivism, especially as developed by Bentham) is a far cry from the largely coercive picture of law painted by his predecessors. For Hart, law is a *social* phenomenon: it can only be understood and explained by reference to the actual social practices of a community. Hence his formulation of the 'minimum content' of natural law is a recognition of the fact that in order to survive as a community certain rules must exist. These are a consequence of the 'human condition' (he is strongly influenced here by David Hume) which Hart sees as exhibiting the following fundamental characteristics:

'Human vulnerability':	We are all susceptible to physical attacks.
'Approximate equality':	Even the strongest must sleep at times.
'Limited altruism':	We are, in general, selfish.
'Limited resources':	We need food, clothes and shelter and they are limited.
'Limited understanding and strength of will':	We cannot be relied upon to cooperate with our fellow men.

Because of these limitations there is a necessity for rules which protect persons and property, and which ensure that promises are kept. But, despite this view, Hart is *not* saying that law is *derived from* morals or that there is a necessary conceptual relationship between the two. Nor is he suggesting that if we accept his 'minimum content' of natural law this will guarantee a fair or just society.

You should be able to discuss the validity (e.g., are we really 'approximately equal' — what of minority groups, women, children?) and the completeness (e.g., what about sex?) of this analysis and be in a position to relate it to the general subject of natural law (see chapter 5).

Another important feature of Hart's positivism is the so-called Hart-Fuller debate concerning the 'morality of law'. This is something of an old chestnut in jurisprudence, and continues to appear in examination papers. You should therefore have a good grasp of the arguments. The subject of the debate (must law be moral to be law?) raises the wider controversy that still rages between the theories of natural law and positivism. Its importance warrants its separate treatment, and it is therefore briefly considered in the next chapter.

Law and Language

An important element in much of Hart's writing is the *linguistic* analysis of law. The influence of the work of (amongst others) the philosophers Gilbert Ryle and J. L. Austin (not to be confused with the jurist, John Austin) is apparent in *The Concept of Law* (in the preface to which J. L. Austin's aphorism that we may use 'a sharpened awareness of words to sharpen our awareness of the phenomena' is quoted) and other works by Hart (notably his inaugural lecture 'Definition and theory in jurisprudence' (1954) 70 LQR 37). The relationship between law and language pervades much of his thinking about law; this gives rise to questions such as: what does it *mean* to have a 'right'?, what is a 'corporation' or an 'obligation'? For Hart we cannot properly understand law unless we understand the conceptual context in which it emerges and develops. He argues, for instance, that language has an 'open texture': words (and hence rules) have a number of clear meanings, but there are always several 'penumbral' cases where it is uncertain whether the word applies or not.

Thus no set of rules can provide predetermined answers to every case that may arise. This does not mean, however (contrary to the claims of the American realists, see chapter 7), that the meaning of words is completely arbitrary and unpredictable. In most cases judges have little difficulty in simply applying the appropriate rule — without any need to call in aid moral or political considerations. The importance Hart attaches to language is sometimes criticised as being somewhat one-dimensional: language is obviously important, critics have conceded, but when a model of law as a system of rules (see below) is attacked (e.g., by realists) it is not the law's linguistic uncertainty that is the target, but the process of precedential legal reasoning. It is argued that this process cannot be adequately accounted for by postulating a model of judicial decision-making that treats it as merely the laying down of rules which bind subsequent courts.

Law as a System of Rules

Most students experience little difficulty in grasping the general features of Hart's system which may be represented in the simple diagram in figure 4.1.

Figure 4.1   Hart's system of rules

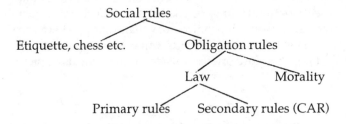

All societies have *social rules*. These include rules relating to morals, games etc., as well as *obligation rules* which impose duties or obligations. The latter may be divided into moral rules and legal rules (or *law*). As a result of our human limitations there is a need for obligation rules in all societies: the 'minimum content of natural law' (see above). Legal rules are divisible into *primary rules* and *secondary rules*. The former proscribe 'the free use of violence, theft and deception to which human beings are tempted but which they must, in general, repress if they are to coexist in close proximity to each other' (*The Concept of Law*, p. 89). Primitive societies have little more than these primary rules imposing obligations. But as a society becomes more complex, there is a need to change the primary rules, to adjudicate on breaches of them, and to identify which rules are actually obligation rules.

hese three requirements are satisfied in each case in modern societies by the introduction of three sorts of *secondary rules*: rules of change, adjudication and recognition (CAR). Unlike primary rules, the first two of these secondary rules do not generally impose duties, but usually confer power. The rule of recognition, however, does seem to *impose duties* (largely on judges). This is considered further below.

In order for a legal system to exist, two conditions must be satisfied. First, valid obligation rules must be generally obeyed by members of the society, and, secondly, officials must accept the rules of change and adjudication; they must also accept the rule of recognition 'from the *internal point of view*'.

This is a bird's-eye view of Hart's picture of a legal system. Some of its more important (and controversial) features are now briefly examined.

Social Rules

Hart rejects John Austin's conception of rules as commands and, indeed, the very idea that rules are phenomena that consist merely in externally observable activities or habit. Instead he asks us to consider the *social* dimension of rules, namely the manner in which members of a society *perceive* the rule in question, their *attitude* towards it. This 'internal' aspect (see below) distinguishes between a rule and a mere habit. Thus, to use his example (*The Concept of Law*, pp. 55–6), chess players, in addition to having similar *habits* of moving the queen in the same way, also have a 'critical reflective attitude' to this way of moving it: they regard it as a *standard* for all who play chess; each 'has views' about the propriety of such moves. And they manifest these views in the criticism of others and acknowledge the legitimacy of such criticism when received from others. In other words, in order to explain the nature of rules we need to examine them from the point of view of those who 'experience' them, who pass judgment on them or, to use the language of hermeneutics, from the conceptual framework of the agent. It is particularly in respect of Hart's approach to the nature of rules that, though he is unashamedly positivist, Hart is to be distinguished from Austin and Bentham. He is concerned to demonstrate that far more significant than commands, sovereignty and sanctions, is the *social* source of legal rules: they are a manifestation of our actual behaviour, our words and our thoughts.

He also uses the concept of a 'rule' to distinguish between 'being obliged' and 'having an obligation'. The Austinian model cannot explain why if you are threatened by a gunman who orders you to hand over your money or he will shoot you, that though you may be *obliged* to comply, you have no *obligation* to do so — because there is no *rule* imposing an obligation on you (*The Concept of Law*, p. 80).

In the 'second edition' of *The Concept of Law* (p. 255), Hart acknowledges that the existence of social rules requires more than its general acceptance by most members of a group. He recognises the relevance of Ronald Dworkin's distinction between conventions and concurrent practice. The former involves acceptance which is dependent upon its acceptance by *others*. In this sense, the rule of recognition (see below) is conventional. On the other hand, 'the shared morality of a group' consists in a 'consensus of independent *convictions* manifested in the concurrent practices of the group' (p. 255). This point is made in a brief but useful review of the new edition of Hart's classic by David Lyons in (1995) 111 LQR 519, 521. Watch the journals for more reviews of the book, and articles which analyse Hart's revisions to his theory.

Secondary Rules

It is important that you understand the nature and function of secondary rules — which play a leading role in Hart's system. Students often have difficulty in respect of the three types of rules that Hart describes (i.e., in sorting out how the CAR works!) and the relationships between them.

Rules of change: confusion sometimes arises as a result of Hart's use of this form of rule in *two* contexts. Rules of change are required in order to facilitate legislative or judicial changes to both the primary rules and certain secondary rules (e.g., the rule of adjudication, below). This process of change is regulated by *rules* (secondary rules) which confer power on individuals or groups (e.g., Parliament) to enact legislation in accordance with certain procedures. These rules of change are also to be found in 'lower-order' secondary rules which confer power on ordinary individuals to change their legal position (e.g., by making contracts, wills etc.). Thus power-conferring secondary rules of change appear to have *two* meanings in Hart's model.

Rules of adjudication: certain rules confer competence on individuals to pass judgment mainly in cases of breaches of primary rules. This power is normally associated with a further power to punish the wrongdoer or compel the wrongdoer to pay damages. Further rules are required in this connection (e.g., someone is under a duty to imprison the wrongdoer).

The rule of recognition is essential to the existence of a legal system (and is considered further below). It determines the criteria by which the validity of the rules of a legal system are decided. As pointed out above, unlike the other two types of secondary rules, it appears, in part, to be *duty-imposing*: it requires those who exercise public power (particularly the power to adjudicate) to follow certain rules. This gives rise to an element of circularity (identified by MacCormick, *H. L. A. Hart*, pp. 108–9) for the criteria for recognising the validity of certain rules necessarily include — as a criterion of validity — the valid enactment of rules by the legislature in exercising its power conferred by the rule of change. But the rule of recognition presupposes the existence of judges whose duties are laid down by the rule of recognition. And these judges are empowered by a rule of adjudication. But this rule of adjudication is valid only if it satisfies some criterion of the rule of recognition. And, as just stated, the rule of recognition *presupposes* judges. And the existence of judges presupposes a rule of adjudication! 'Which member of this logical circle of rules', asks Professor MacCormick, 'is the ultimate rule of a legal system?' Think about it!

The Rule of Recognition

Pointing to the serious limitations of the classic legal positivist theory of sovereignty (see page 48), particularly the idea that legal authority is expressed in terms of a habit of obedience, Hart instead contends that rules are valid members of the legal system only if they satisfy the criteria laid down by the rule of recognition. This secondary rule is a crucial aspect of Hart's model and you would be well advised to give it your closest attention. Not only is it important in its own right (as the centre-piece of Hart's positivism), but it provides the target of attack for several non-positivists (notably Professor Dworkin) when they come to analyse, for instance, the judicial function (see page 116ff).

Comparing it to the standard metre bar in Paris (the definitive standard by which a metre is measured), Hart says that the validity of the rule of recognition cannot be questioned: 'It can neither be valid nor invalid but is simply accepted as appropriate for use in this way' (*The Concept of Law*, pp. 105–6). In the United Kingdom, he argues, the rule of recognition is 'what the Queen in Parliament enacts is law.' But the question of whether there is a *single* rule of recognition, whether it includes the doctrine of precedent (as it surely must) and whether there are several, perhaps graded rules of recognition is one which has not been adequately elaborated by Hart and which has generated considerable discussion.

Students generally find this the most perplexing aspect of the whole of Hart's theory. They often take the concept too literally. Hart certainly claims that for every developed legal system there is an 'ultimate rule of recognition' whose validity cannot be questioned and whose existence depends solely on the fact that it is accepted by officials 'from the internal point of view'. But Hart is not saying that the rule of recognition is merely a single rule or set of rules which, as if by some magical incantation, can supply the answer to the question: which rules are legal rules? It is more complex than that. The rule of recognition contains a set of different criteria of recognition which interact with each other in a variety of ways. A useful exercise I give students is to attempt to set out the rule of recognition for a particular jurisdiction (which has certain constitutional and institutional features). I don't do this any longer because, in his book, *H. L. A. Hart* (p. 110) Professor MacCormick has done it for us. And far better! This is his fictitious rule of recognition for a State with a written constitution:

The judicial duty is to apply as 'valid law' all and only the following:

(i)   Every provision contained in the constitution of 1950, save for such provisions as have been validly repealed by the procedures set in Article 100 of that constitution, but including every provision validly added by way of constitutional amendment under Article 100;

(ii)   Every unrepealed Act of the Legislature validly enacted under, and otherwise consistent with, the provisions of the constitution of 1950;

(iii)   Every provision by way of delegated legislation validly made under a power validly conferred by any unrepealed Act of the Legislature;

(iv)   Every ruling on any question of law made by the Supreme Court or the Court of Appeal established by the Constitution of 1950, save that the Supreme Court may reverse any of its own prior rulings and those of the Court of Appeal, and the Court of Appeal may reverse its own prior rulings; and save that no judicial ruling inconsistent with any provision covered by criteria (i), (ii), or (iii) is valid to the extent of such inconsistency;

(v)   Every rule accepted as law by the custom and usage of the citizens of the State, either by way of general custom or local and particular custom, such being applicable either generally or locally so far as not inconsistent with (i)-(iv) above; and

(vi)   Every rule in force in the State prior to the adoption of the Constitution of 1950, save for any such rule inconsistent with any rule valid under (i)-(v) above.

But this, you may cry, is simply a roll-call of the 'sources' of law. Surely, the rule of recognition is more complex (and less obvious) than that! To this there are, I think, two answers. First, the connection between any 'acid test' of law and the 'sources' of law is a necessary and indeed inescapable one. It is clear that in applying the criteria of legal validity, a court (for it is normally courts that are called upon to decide such questions) is bound to accord validity to the enactments of the legislature, the judgments of courts etc. It would be curious if this were otherwise. But the rule of recognition is more: it is 'a common, public standard of correct judicial decision' (*The Concept of Law*, p. 112) which is binding *only if accepted by the officials in question*. Secondly, this is more than a *list* of formal standards of validity; in Hart's theorem this fictitious rule of recognition is actually a single rule which comprises six criteria ranked in order of importance. And each of them exerts complex mutual interrelations with one another.

The Existence of a Legal System

It has already been seen that it is Hart's view that a legal system may be said to 'exist' only if valid (primary) rules are obeyed and officials accept the rules of change and adjudication. In Hart's words: 'The assertion that a legal system exists is ... a Janus-faced statement looking both to obedience by ordinary citizens and to the acceptance by officials of secondary rules as critical common standards of official behaviour' (*The Concept of Law*, p. 113). It is not clear whether these conditions are being postulated by Hart as a historical or developmental thesis (i.e., primitive societies eventually develop by virtue of the emergence of secondary rules), or whether it is a purely hypothetical model to illustrate the function of these rules or as a heuristic device by which to recognise the existence of a legal system — as J. W. Harris puts it (*Legal Philosophies*, p. 111):

If a country is in a state of turmoil and the political scientist is trying to assess whether it has that social grace commonly known as 'law', wheel in the patient and apply this two-pronged stethoscope — 'Are your primary rules generally observed?' 'Do your officials accept your secondary rules?'

Hart is not suggesting that members of society need 'accept' the primary rules or the rule of recognition; it is only the *officials* who need to adopt an 'internal point of view'. He acknowledges that if a legal system does not receive widespread acceptance it would be both morally and politically objectionable. But these moral and political criteria are not identifying characteristics of the notion of 'legal system'. The validity of a legal system is therefore independent from its efficacy. A completely ineffective rule may be a valid one — as long as it emanates from the rule of recognition. Nevertheless, in order to be a valid rule, the legal system of which the rule is a component must, as a whole, be effective.

The 'Internal Point of View'

It is important to grasp precisely what Hart means by this ubiquitous phrase (which appears in numerous guises throughout *The Concept of Law*). Let him speak for himself in a passage (*The Concept of Law*, p. 56) that is worth studying closely:

What is necessary is that there should be a critical reflective attitude to certain patterns of behaviour as a common standard, and that this should display itself in criticism (including self-criticism), demands for conformity, and in acknowledgements that such criticism and demands are justified, all of which find their characteristic expression in the normative terminology of 'ought', 'must', and 'should', 'right' and 'wrong'.

This 'internal' aspect of rules serves, of course, to distinguish social rules from mere group habits. You will notice, too, the emphasis on the language ('normative terminology') that is generated by the presence of rules. But a question that has been raised is whether by 'accepting' secondary rules, officials must 'approve' them. The better view is that acceptance does not mean approval. In other words, certain judges in a wicked legal system (say, apartheid South Africa) may abhor the rules they are required to apply; this would nevertheless satisfy Hart's conditions for a legal system to exist. There is also a distinction between *accepting* the rules and *feeling bound* by them: see the discussion of the views of Alf Ross in chapter 7.

The Judicial Function

In developing his theory of a legal system as a 'union of primary and secondary rules', Hart seeks to reject both the strictly formalist view (with its emphasis on judicial precedents and codification) and the rule-scepticism of the American realist movement (see chapter 7). In so doing, he strikes something of a compromise between these two extremes: he (naturally) accepts that laws are indeed rules, but he recognises that in arriving at decisions, judges have a fairly wide discretion. And he is, in any event, driven to this conclusion by virtue of the rule of recognition: if there is some 'acid test' by which judges are able to decide what are the valid legal rules, then where there is *no* applicable legal rule or the rule or rules are uncertain or ambiguous, the judge must have a strong discretion to 'fill in the gaps', in such 'hard cases'. The extent to which judges *do* have a discretion to decide — almost as they please — what the law is in these cases has, of course, become one of the most hotly contested subjects in contemporary jurisprudence (and hence popular examination question fodder; it is discussed at greater length in chapter 6).

I have already mentioned that Hart recognises that, as a consequence of the inherent ambiguity of language, rules have an 'open texture' (e.g., what is a 'vehicle'?) and, are, in some cases, vague (e.g., what is 'reasonable care'?). He therefore has no difficulty in accepting the proposition that in 'hard cases' judges *make* law. They will, of course, be guided by various sources (e.g., persuasive cases from foreign jurisdictions), but, in the end, the judge will base his decision on his own conception of fairness or justice. Whether this is a valid way of describing the judicial function is examined in chapter 6.

An 'Essay in Descriptive Sociology'?

In his preface to *The Concept of Law*, Hart says the book may be viewed in these terms. And the extent to which this is a justifiable claim is a matter that has attracted the attention of both jurists and social scientists (see, e.g., M. Krygier (1982) 2 Oxford J Legal Stud 155), as well as the occasional examiner. Lloyd (*Introduction to Jurisprudence*, p. 344) prefers to regard it as 'an essay in analytical jurisprudence', and Professor Twining finds it difficult to support the claim 'not because it is wrong or misleading, but because the idea of a descriptive sociology of law is not developed in *The Concept of Law* nor in Hart's other writings' ((1979) 95 LQR 557, 579). You could not do justice to an examination question on this subject unless you had undertaken a fairly rigorous preparation; see chapter 8 on the sociology of law.

Critique

It would be impossible to consider here the prodigious literature that Hart's work has excited. Nor could any student be expected to read even one tenth of it. So relax! But you may be absolutely certain that your examination will contain at least one question (and probably several more) which require a thorough understanding of *The Concept of Law* and probably also the later reflections of its author in the 1994 edition. Some of the criticisms that have been made of Hart's thesis have been referred to above, there are many more (e.g., Is the 'internal point of view' an oversimplification? Can people have an 'internal' attitude to rules of which they are unaware? Does Hart's system of rules ignore the concept of an institution? Is his anthropological evidence descriptive or analytical?), and the most important and influential critique of all is considered in chapter 6.

Do not be content (as many students are) to memorise and reproduce the bare bones of Hart's theory. Your examiner will be looking for more than a simplified sketch of primary and secondary rules. If you follow the advice in chapter 1 you ought to be able to have a solid grasp of the main arguments of *The Concept of Law* and (an aspect all too often neglected in examination answers) the *positivist* tradition that it represents and develops. You must also be familiar with the principal criticisms that have been made on the thesis (from a variety of standpoints) and be able to say whether and why you consider these attacks to be justified. In all your answers, but more so in writing about this particular jurist, you must exhibit a 'critical reflective attitude'. For a lively example, see A. C. Hutchinson, 'A Postmodern's Hart: Taking Rules Sceptically' (1995) 58 MLR 788.

KELSEN

Of all the legal theorists you will study in your course, Hans Kelsen (1881–1973) is probably the least understood (not only by students) and most misrepresented. Much of this is due to his use of fairly difficult and abstract conceptual language which, especially to those unfamiliar with the Continental approach to philosophy, is not always congenial. Very few doubt his remarkable facility for critical exposition and inquiry, indeed, to Lloyd (*Introduction to Jurisprudence*, p. 271), 'No single writer . . . has made a more illuminating analysis of the legal process'. His pure theory of law has become as important (if not nearly as influential) as Hart's theory, and represents what Dias calls 'the most refined development to date of analytical positivism' (*Jurisprudence*, p. 258).

To the extent that he insisted on the separation of law and morals, what 'is' (*sein*) and what 'ought to be' (*sollen*), Kelsen may legitimately be characterised as a 'positivist', but he is a good deal more. The pure theory is a subtle and profound statement about the way in which we should understand law. And we should do so, he argues, by conceiving it to be a system of 'oughts' or *norms*. But Kelsen acknowledges that the law consists not merely of norms, but 'is made up of legal norms and legal acts as determined by these norms' (*General Theory of Law and State*, p. 39). In other words, legal norms (which include judicial decisions and legal transactions such as contracts and wills) when *acted upon* also describe actual human conduct. Even the most general norms describe human conduct. Thus:

... Kelsen's observation that the legal scientist is not concerned with human conduct but is only concerned with norms may have obscured from view the important point that so far as human conduct features in a norm as condition or consequence such conduct falls four-square within the concerns of the Kelsenian legal scientist.... Kelsen permits of a greater degree of reference to actual human conduct than is sometimes perceived by those who would label his contribution as 'sterile'. (Tur and Twining (eds), *Essays on Kelsen*, pp. 23–4.)

Indeed, it has been argued that Kelsen's attempt to understand and explain the 'science of the mind and of meaning and of values as instantiated in actual human societies' is 'the only jurisprudence ever to take sociology seriously' (R. Tur, 'The Kelsenian Enterprise' in Tur and Twining (eds), *Essays on Kelsen*, p. 150 at p. 182). He was, it has been suggested, 'engaging in sociology when writing his *Pure Theory*, notwithstanding his indignant denials' (Sawer, *Law in Society* (Oxford, 1965), p. 5, quoted by Tur). The validity or otherwise of these claims should become clearer in the course of the following pages in which, I confess, I have 'drawn on' parts of my essay 'One country, two *Grundnormen*? The Basic Law and the basic norm' in R. Wacks (ed.), *Hong Kong, China and 1997: Essays in Legal Theory*.

You will read (and be lectured to) about Kelsen's 'neo-Kantianism': as a follower of the great 18th-century philosopher, Immanuel Kant, Kelsen espouses the view that objective reality can be comprehended only by the application of certain formal categories like time and space. These categories do not 'exist' in nature: we use them in order to make sense of the world. Equally, to understand 'the law' we require similar formal categories, in particular the *Grundnorm* or basic norm which lies at the heart of the legal system (see below).

Kelsen's project is thus a fairly ambitious one. He seeks, to use his own words, to raise jurisprudence 'to the level of a genuine science'. His theory is described by Richard Tur as 'a thoroughgoing attempt to develop an epistemology for jurisprudence. It is a recipe for legal knowledge.' ('The Kelsenian enterprise', in Tur and Twining (eds), *Essays on Kelsen*, pp. 149–83, 157). The ingredients are, however, often far from straightforward. And the result is not to everyone's taste.

Unadulterated Law

Few students have difficulty in grasping Kelsen's insistence on excluding the 'impurities' of morality, history, politics, sociology etc. If we are to arrive at a *scientific* (as opposed to a subjective, value-laden) theory of law, says Kelsen, we need to restrict our analysis to the 'norms' of positive law: those 'oughts' which provide that if certain conduct (X) is performed, then a sanction (Y) should be applied by an official to the offender. If X then Y. The theory therefore rules out all that cannot be *objectively* known: the social purpose of law, its political functions etc. Law has only one function: the monopolisation of force.

Kelsen's pursuit of a 'science of law' is premised on the claim that an account of law can be disinfected from 'elements of psychology, sociology, ethics, and political theory' (*Pure Theory of Law*, p. 1):

> This adulteration is understandable, because [these] disciplines deal with subject-matters that are closely connected with law. The pure theory of law undertakes to delimit the cognition of law against these disciplines, not because it ignores or denies the connection, but because it wishes to avoid the uncritical mixture of methodologically different disciplines ... which obscures the essence of the science of law and obliterates the limits imposed upon it by the nature of its subject-matter. (Loc. cit.)

By 'norms' Kelsen means that 'something *ought* to be or *ought* to happen, especially that a human being ought to behave in a specific way' (*Pure Theory of Law*, p. 4). Thus the statement 'the door ought to be closed' or a red traffic-light are both norms. But a norm, in order to be *valid* (that is binding), must be authorised by another norm which, in turn, is authorised by a higher norm in the system. The separation between law and morality means that the validity of legal norms can flow only from another *legal*, as opposed to a *moral* norm. Kelsen is profoundly *relativistic*: he rejects the notion that there are values 'out there'; all norms are relative to the individual or group under consideration. This point is well explained by Professor Raz who shows that Kelsen is not a sceptic (that is, he does not take the view that all normative statements are necessarily *false*), he is a relativist or subjectivist:

> Normative statements can be true or false. It is merely that their truth depends on the existence of relativistic rather than absolute values: 'relativistic ... positivism does not assert that there are no values, or that there is no moral order, but only that the values in which men actually believe are not absolute but relative values' (*What is Justice?*, p. 179). (J. Raz, 'The purity of the pure theory', in Tur and Twining (eds), *Essays on Kelsen*, p. 79 at p. 87.)

As Raz remarks, a conspicuous difficulty with this form of relativism is its assumption that any sincere moral statement I make about myself must be true; because I *believe* that there is a norm requiring me to perform a certain act such a norm *exists* and my statement is *true*. By the same process of reasoning insincere moral statements about myself are always false. And normative statements I make about *others* are true only if they conform to *their* beliefs about themselves. 'Thus', concludes Raz, 'it is true that a racist should behave in a racist way' (ibid., p. 88). This is clearly unacceptable.

Nevertheless Kelsen's relativist, value-free theory of law seeks to locate legal science in a world free of the 'impurities' of social science. It provides, in Stewart's words:

> ... the basic forms under which meanings can be known scientifically as legal norms — which will have a content, although the particular content is empirically contingent, and which, once determined as having a particular content, can be morally evaluated. Far from being an attempt to exclude considerations of experience, content, and justice, the pure theory is intended to make attention to them more rigorously possible. (I. Stewart, 'Kelsen and the exegetical tradition' in Tur and Twining (eds), *Essays on Kelsen*, p. 123 at p. 128.)

The hierarchy of legal norms that forms a legal system is ultimately traced back to the *Grundnorm* or basic norm of the legal system. Its nature, function and relationship to other norms will be examined later.

The law consists of norms used as a 'specific social technique' by politicians to determine how individuals ought to behave so as to promote social order and peace. This technique consists in the acts of will of individuals authorised by the law to create norms which render the behaviour of individuals lawful or unlawful by providing *sanctions* for failure to comply with the norms. Thus legal norms differ from other norms in that they prescribe a sanction. The legal system is founded on State coercion; behind its norms is the threat of force.

This distinguishes the tax collector from the robber. Both demand your money. Both, in other words, require that you *ought* to pay up. Both exhibit a *subjective* act of will, but only the tax collector's is *objectively* valid. Why? Because, says Kelsen, the subjective meaning of the robber's coercive order is not interpreted as its objective meaning. Why not? Because 'no basic norm is presupposed according to which one ought to behave in conformity with this order' (*Pure Theory of Law*, p. 47). And why not? Because the robber's coercive order lacks the 'lasting effectiveness without which no basic norm is presupposed'. This illustrates the fundamental relationship in Kelsen's theory between validity and effectiveness which is discussed below.

Legal science, according to Kelsen, restricts its analysis to the 'norms' of positive law: those 'oughts' which provide that if certain conduct (X) is performed, then a sanction (Y) should be applied by an official to the offender. If X then Y. The theory therefore rules out all that cannot be *objectively* known: the social purpose of law, its political funcitons etc. Law has only one function: the monopolisation of force.

Kelsen's reduction of all legislation to this form is widely regarded as unacceptably narrow. The *form* of law is given primacy over its *meaning*. It presumes (which, of course, Kelsen is content to do) that law is essentially coercion; many would want to argue that law has other functions, for example, regulatory purposes.

Other critics seek to show that Kelsen accords unwarranted importance to the role of sanctions in law. It results in a lopsided analysis of legal duty not only because a statute may impose duties *without* necessarily providing a sanction, but because, on the other hand, certain conduct may be made the condition of a sanction even though it is not the subject of a *duty*. Thus J. W. Harris points out that to measure effectiveness we need to know the content of the norm, i.e., the nature of the duty involved. As he puts it, 'The concept of 'duty' must . . . stand on its own feet, as something distinct from the concept of sanction. A theory of law must define duty and sanction separately' (*Legal Philosophies*, p. 67).

A Hierarchy of Norms

Kelsen represents a legal system as a complex series of interlocking norms which progress from the most general 'oughts' (e.g., sanctions ought to be effected in accordance with the constitution); to the most particular or 'concrete' (e.g., Philip is contractually bound to mow Elizabeth's lawn). Each norm in this hierarchical system draws its validity from another (higher) norm. The validity of all norms are ultimately based on the *Grundnorm* (see below).

This systemic, hierarchical model of law provides also the explanation for the dynamic creation of legal norms. The membership of norms in the legal system is determined by other norms in the hierarchy. Law is created by facts (for example, a judicial decision) which convey normative force from the authorising norm to the authorised norm. The authorising norm being valid and capable of endowing law-creating acts with status to create law, the norm so created is also valid. Law-creating acts thereby confer validity from one norm to another (see Raz, in Tur and Twining (eds), *Essays on Kelsen*, p. 95).

As has been pointed out, the validity of each norm is dependent on a higher norm in the system whose validity is in turn dependent upon a higher norm in the system and so on. A point is eventually reached beyond which this climbing cannot go. This is the basic norm or *Grundnorm*. All norms flow from it in increasing levels of 'concreteness': the basic norm expresses an 'ought' at the highest level of generality. Below it, in the hierarchy of norms, is the historically first constitution. Below it are laws enacted (by the legislature or judiciary) which are more 'concrete', all the way down to the most concrete, individualised norm such as: 'the bailiff is empowered to seize the property of the defendant who has been found by a court to be liable to the plaintiff and who is unable to pay what he owes'. The coercive act of the bailiff (or the prison warder in incarcerating a prisoner) is the ultimate stage in the progression from general basic norm to particular individuated norm.

The Grundnorm

Since, by definition, the validity of the *Grundnorm* cannot depend on any other norm it must be presupposed. What does this mean? Kelsen seems to be saying (and this is a matter of some controversy) that we need this assumption in order to understand the legal order. As he puts it, disclaiming any originality:

> By formulating the *Grundnorm*, we do not introduce into the science of law any new method. We merely make explicit what all jurists, mostly unconsciously, assume when they consider positive law as a system of valid norms and not only as a complex of facts, and at the same time repudiate any natural law from which positive law would receive its validity. That the *Grundnorm* really exists in the juristic consciousness is the result of a simple analysis of actual juristic statements. The *Grundnorm* is the answer to the question: how — and that means under what condition — are these juristic statements concerning legal norms, legal duties, legal rights, and so on, possible? (*General Theory of Law and State*, p. 117.)

This is a lucid statement of the role Kelsen assigns to his basic norm: it exists, but only in the 'juristic consciousness'. It is an assumed construct which facilitates an understanding of the legal system by the legal scientist, judge or lawyer. But it is not chosen arbitrarily; it is selected by reference to whether the legal order as a whole is 'by and large' efficacious. Its validity depends on efficacy (see below).

The presupposed basic norm, as Stewart puts it:

> is the nodal point at which the *pure* part of legal science passes over into the *empirical* part; on the *pure* side, the basic norm stands in a relation of validity to the specific and generic formulations of the presupposition 'basic norm' and through them to the pure theory as a whole, while on the *empirical* side it stands in a relation of validity to the remainder of the legal order; its validity on the *pure* side cannot be questioned from the *empirical* side, since it is the condition of possibility, furnished by the *pure* side for the *empirical* side. ('Kelsen and the exegetical tradition', in Tur and Twining, *Essays on Kelsen*, p. 123 at p. 132, emphasis added.)

In other words, the validity of the basic norm rests, not on another norm or rule of law, but is assumed — for the purpose of purity. It is therefore a hypothesis, a wholly formal construct, a fiction. It 'presents itself ... not as a guess or hypothesis about the reality behind the law but explicitly as a methodological maxim, a norm of method which is ontologically neutral'. (Tur and Twining, *Essays on Kelsen*, p. 170.)   Consider Kelsen's religious analogy:

A father addresses to his son the individual norm, 'Go to school'. The son asks his father, 'Why should I go to school?' That is, he asks why the subjective meaning of his father's act of will is its objective meaning, i.e., a norm binding for him — or, which means the same thing, what is the basis of the validity of this norm. The father responds: 'Because God has commanded that parents be obeyed — that is, He has authorised parents to issue commands to children'. The son replies: 'Why should one obey the commands of God?' What all this amounts to is: why is the subjective meaning of this act of will of God also its objective meaning — that is, a valid norm? or, which means the same thing, what is the basis of the validity of this general norm? The only possible answer to this is: because, as a believer, *one presupposes that one ought to obey the commands of God*. This is the statement of the validity of a norm that must be presupposed in a believer's thinking in order to ground the validity of the norms of a religious morality. This statement is *the basic norm of a religious morality*, the norm which *grounds the validity of all the norms of that morality* — a *'basic' norm*, because no further question can be raised about the basis of its validity. The statement is not a positive norm — that is, not a norm posited by a real act of will — but a norm *presupposed* in a believer's thinking. ('The function of a constitution' translated by I. Stewart, in Tur and Twining (eds), *Essays on Kelsen*, p. 112, emphasis added.)

Kelsen's *Grundnorm* may therefore be an attempt to answer a more fundamental (perhaps the *most* fundamental) question of legal theory: why is law obeyed? His complex and controversial reply was: because legal norms are objectively valid. And they derive their ultimate validity from the *Grundnorm*, a neo-Kantian transcendental-logical condition of the interpretation of law-creating acts of wills as objectively valid legal norms. (On Kelsen's neo-Kantianism see below.) It has two principal functions. First, it helps to distinguish between the demands of a robber and those of the law (see above), that is, it makes it possible to regard a coercive order as objectively valid. Secondly, it provides an explanation for the coherence and unity of a legal order. All valid legal norms may be interpreted as a non-contradictory field of meaning.

What if I do not 'accept' the basic norm of the legal system? Suppose I consider the system immoral or unjust? Does the basic norm supply a *normative* or moral justification for law? The better view is that this is not Kelsen's purpose. He employs the idea of normativity in a *legal* sense only. Nevertheless, it is important, as Professor Raz demonstrates (Tur and Twining (eds), *Essays on Kelsen*, pp. 91–7), to clarify precisely the nature of Kelsen's claim. Statements about the law may be 'committed', that is, they state what the law *ought* to be. Such moral statements are, of course, excluded by positivists like Raz from the proper realm of legal theory, and Kelsen's purity is bought at the cost of such exclusion:

... legal theory to remain pure cannot study the law insofar as it is embedded in the moral beliefs of one person or another. That would violate the sources thesis [which claims that the identification of the existence and content of law does not require or resort to any moral argument] by making the identification of the law dependent on a particular set of moral beliefs. To be pure, legal theory must strictly adhere to the sources thesis and identify law by social facts only. Hence to describe it normatively it must non-committally or fictiously accept the basic norm of the legal man, that is, the Kelsenian basic norm, for it is the only one to give validity to the *empirically established* law and to nothing else. This, then, is the sense in which the basic norm is the scientific postulate of legal thought. (Tur and Twining (eds), *Essays on Kelsen* p. 95.)

It is important to recognise, therefore, that Kelsen's conception of normativity is a narrow one. He repeatedly eschews moral absolutes. His theory, he says, 'cannot answer questions as to whether a particular law is just, or what is justice, because they cannot be answered scientifically at all' (*What is Justice?*, p. 266). Such relativism strips his normativity of its usual moral connotations. This is not always grasped by commentators, though it is easy to see why this confusion should arise; it is often supposed that the 'ought' in the question whether an immoral law 'ought' to be obeyed is the same as the 'ought' in Kelsen's question whether the law 'ought' to be obeyed. The latter enquiry is, for him, expunged of moral considerations: it is a matter of determining whether the basic norm is valid; if it is the law 'ought' to be obeyed.

The *Grundnorm* has two main features. First, it is presupposed. But, in Kelsen's words:

The basic norm is ... not a product of free invention. It refers to particular facts existing in natural reality, to an actually laid down and effective constitution and to the norm-creating and norm-applying facts in fact established in conformity with the constitution. ('The function of a constitution', translated by I. Stewart, in Tur and Twining (eds), *Essays on Kelsen*, p. 115.)

Secondly, it has no content. It is a purely formal category. Kelsen formulates the basic norm as follows:

Coercive acts ought to be performed under the conditions and in the manner which the historically first constitution, and the norms created according to it, prescribe. (In short: One ought to behave as the constitution prescribes.) (*Pure Theory of Law*, p. 201.)

In *General Theory of Law and State*, he gives the following version:

> Coercive acts ought to be carried out only under the conditions and in the way determined by the 'fathers' of the constitution or the organs delegated by them. (*General Theory of Law and State*, pp. 115–16.)

The basic norm's supposed 'neutrality' suggests that there is no *logical* reason why the basic norm of, say, a socialist legal system cannot be the basic norm of a capitalist one. Kelsen says: '... any kind of content might be law. There is no human behaviour which, as such, is excluded from being the content of a legal norm' (*Pure Theory of Law*, p. 198). And: 'The validity of a positive legal order cannot be denied because of the content of its norms' (*Pure Theory of Law*, p. 267).

Kelsen insists that his basic norm is unrelated to the political ideology of the legal system in question. As Honoré puts it:

> Legal theory has to be able to deal not merely with the law of democratic societies, but with dictatorships and one-party States. Many of the societies whose laws form the subject-matter of legal theory ... are non-democratic. Of course different legal systems are bound to have different basic norms; at the very least they must be different in that they refer to the history or circumstances of different societies. But if the point of view of legal theory is itself to be a coherent one ... these basic norms must be consistent with one another. Legal theory cannot simultaneously entertain the hypothesis, in relation to one system, that only laws proceeding from democratic institutions are valid and, in relation to another, that only laws proceeding from Marxist institutions are valid. (*Making Law Bind*, 'The Basic Norm of a Society', pp. 98–9.)

Kelsen does, however, concede:

> A communist may, indeed, not admit that there is an essential difference between an organisation of gangsters and a capitalist legal order which he considers as the means of ruthless exploitation. For he does not presuppose — as do those who interpret the coercive order in question as an objectively valid normative order — the basic norm. He does not deny that the capitalist coercive order is the law of the State. What he denies is that this coercive order, the law of the State, is objectively valid. The function of the basic norm is *not* to make it possible to consider a coercive order which is by and large effective as law, for ... a legal order is a coercive order by and large effective; the function of the basic norm is to make it possible to consider this coercive order as an objectively valid order. ('A reply to Professor Stone' (1965) Stan L Rev 1144.)

But, one is bound to say, by the same token, a 'capitalist' may be just as prone to deny that a socialist legal order is objectively valid. By Kelsen's own admission, this does not matter. However, as J. M. Eekelaar has argued ('Principles of revolutionary legality' in A. W. B. Simpson (ed.), *Oxford Essays in Jurisprudence*, 2nd ser., pp. 27–30), it neglects the distinct social phenomena that differentiate the two societies.

To be fair, Kelsen (somewhat contradictorily) acknowledges that 'Even an anarchist, if he were a professor of law, could describe positive law as a system of valid norms, without having to *approve* of this law' (*Pure Theory of Law*, p. 218 n, emphasis added). So, as Eekelaar puts it, 'a Communist professor might presuppose a capitalist basic norm in explaining a capitalist legal system' (loc. cit.). And the reverse would hold too. One way out of this dilemma is to *take neutrality seriously*. The notions of a 'capitalist basic norm' or a 'socialist basic norm' are themselves problematic if the basic norm is a purely *formal* construct. We might therefore seek instead a basic norm which is in some way independent of specifically ideological significance. Another solution is to reject Kelsen's pursuit of the will-o'-the-wisp of a basic norm of the legal system and instead postulate some general 'basic norm of society'. This is Professor Honoré's suggestion (*Making Law Bind*). He acknowledges the need for a 'basic norm' of some kind, if we are to 'take law seriously'. He proposes a 'platitudinous basic norm' which 'will appear plausible to a variety of people living in societies with different social and political structures' (ibid., p. 111). He suggests: 'the members of a society have a duty to co-operate with one another'. It admirably captures a principle so bland that it cannot fail to win universal approbation.

Nevertheless its purpose is not, as far as I understand it, to *authorise* the process of norm-creation (as Kelsen's *Grundnorm* seeks to do) but to justify every law: it therefore operates to fix the *content* of legal norms — however broadly.

Validity, Efficacy and Revolution

For Kelsen the *efficacy* (or effectiveness) of the whole legal order is a condition of the *validity* (or legitimacy) of every norm within it. In other words, implicit in the very existence of a legal system is the fact that its laws are generally obeyed. As Kelsen says:

> It cannot be maintained that, legally, men have to behave in conformity with a certain norm, if the total legal order, of which that norm is an integral part, has lost its efficacy. The principle of legitimacy is restricted by the principle of effectiveness. (*General Theory of Law and State*, 119.)

In *The Pure Theory of Law* he puts the matter plainly: 'Every by and large effective coercive order can be interpreted as an objectively valid normative order' (p. 217). But how is this to be measured? How do we *know* whether laws are actually being obeyed rather than ignored? How do we test whether the law is, in Kelsen's phrase, 'by and large' effective? Are, for example, one's motives for disobeying the law relevant?

J. W. Harris suggests that we might relate the number of laws in the system to the number of times that the specified sanctions have been or are likely to be applied. The ratio between the official acts and the acts of disobedience would provide an index of effectiveness (*Legal Philosophies*, p. 103). What Kelsen seems to be suggesting, therefore, is that for the legal order to be valid it is not necessary that every law be obeyed, but that there should be general adherence to the *Grundnorm*. Nor does a legal order cease being valid merely because a single norm losses its effectiveness. But if an individual legal norm is generally ineffective (because, e.g., it is applied only occasionally), it does not lose its validity. If, however, it is *never* applied, it may cease to be valid.

An obvious difficulty arises: the extent to which a legal order is effective is primarily an empirical matter. Yet the pure theory spurns 'sociological' enquiries of this kind. Moreover, the *reasons* for the effectiveness of the law (its rationality, morality etc.) must similarly be excluded by Kelsen.

If the validity of a legal order depends on the effectiveness of its basic norm, it follows that when that basic norm of the system no longer attracts general support, it may be supplanted by some other basic norm. This is precisely what occurs after a successful revolution. According to Kelsen when the new laws of the revolutionary government are effectively enforced, lawyers presuppose a new *Grundnorm*. This is because the *Grundnorm* is not the constitution, but the presupposition that the new situation ought to be accepted in fact.

And this aspect of Kelsen's theory has been applied by courts in various jurisdictions which have undergone revolutions: the coup in Pakistan in 1958 (see *The State* v *Dosso* PLD 1958 SC 180; 553, overruled 14 years later by the Supreme Court which rejected Kelsen's view in *Jilani* v *Government of Punjab* PLD 1972 SC 670), the Ugandan coup in 1965 (see *Uganda* v *Commissioner of Prisons, ex parte Matovu* [1966] EA 514), the Rhodesian UDI in 1965 (see *Madzimbamuto* v *Lardner-Burke* (1968) 2 SA 284 and see the decision of the Privy Council in [1969] 1 AC 645), and, most recently, in *Mitchell* v *Director of Public Prosecutions* [1986] AC 73 (concerning the revolution in Grenada).

In all these decisions, the courts cited a passage from Kelsen which covers this very state of affairs, and (in all but the second Pakistani case) appear to have held that validity is a function of efficacy. It should, however, be noted that the essential criterion of validity is what *the courts* regard as valid. In other words, in the hiatus between the overthrow of the old regime and its effective replacement by the new one, there is no longer a *Grundnorm*;

nevertheless courts may continue to apply 'laws' which the courts recognise by reference to their *own* criterion of validity.

Thus in *Madzimbamuto* v *Lardner-Burke* the court held that the revolutionary 1965 constitution was effective, yet for more than two years the Rhodesian courts had accepted the validity of certain of the revolutionary post-UDI 'laws' — even though they refused to recognise the legality of the revolutionary 1965 constitution. It is hard to see how this could be explained in simple Kelsenian terms. It suggests, says Dias (*Jurisprudence*, p. 366), that effectiveness is not the criterion of the *Grundnorm*, but what *courts* are prepared to accept as the basis of validity. It shows, too, that the validity of a law does not necessarily derive from an effective *Grundnorm*, but rather what *courts* are willing to accept as valid. Dias concludes (p. 367) that:

> Kelsen's theory does not apply in revolutionary situations, in which case it ceases to be a 'general theory'; or, if general, it ceases to be true. In settled conditions it teaches nothing new; in revolutionary conditions, where guidance is needed, it is useless, for the choice of a *Grundnorm* is not dictated inflexibly by effectiveness but is a political decision, as Kelsen has admitted.

To some extent the Grenada Court of Appeal in *Mitchell* v *Director of Public Prosecutions* [1988] LRC(Const) 35 seems to have accepted this view. Haynes P (at pp. 71–2) was reluctant to regard the revolutionary government as legal unless it complied with four conditions: (a) a successful revolution must have taken place, i.e., the government is firmly established administratively; (b) the government is in effective control, i.e., there is by and large conformity with its mandates; (c) such conformity was due to popular support not mere tacit submission to coercion; and (d) the regime must not be oppressive or undemocratic.

It would clearly be a good idea to read these decisions for yourself and refer to them when answering a question which requires an analysis of this aspect of the pure theory. Ask yourself the question whether Kelsen's theory may properly be used by judges to legitimate legal systems on the sole basis of their efficacy.

Is efficacy the sole criterion employed by courts? What of other considerations such as 'justice'? John Eekelaar ('Principles of revolutionary legality' in A. W. B. Simpson (ed.), *Oxford Essays in Jurisprudence*, 2nd ser., p. 29) argues that effectiveness is merely *one* of several criteria of the legal justification of a revolution; he suggests eight other factors (including legitimate disobedience to improper laws, necessity, the principle that a court should not allow itself to be used as an instrument of injustice, and the right to self-determination and the unacceptability of racial discrimination). Some would assert that the application of these kinds of criteria involve the courts in making 'political' judgments, but it is hard to see how this can be avoided even if they ostensibly confine themselves to questions of effectiveness. Others suggest that merely by remaining in office, a judge gives tacit support to the effective legal order.

Kelsen defines a revolution (*General Theory of Law and State*, p. 117) as that which 'occurs whenever the legal order of a community is nullified and replaced by a new order ... in a way not prescribed by the first order itself'. Another definition he provides is 'every not legitimate change of [the] constitution or its replacement by another constitution' (*Pure Theory of Law*, p. 209). If some *unlawful* or *unconstitutional* act is required to create a new, valid legal order then a peaceful transfer of sovereignty implies no change in the basic norm. 'A revolution is neither a necessary nor a sufficient condition for anything that should be described as a change in the identity of the State or the legal system' (J. M. Finnis, 'Revolutions and the continuity of law' in A. W. B. Simpson (ed.), *Oxford Essays in Jurisprudence*, 2nd ser., p. 75).

When does this come about? As we have seen, effectiveness is, for Kelsen, a condition of validity. In the words of J. W. Harris:

> The *Grundnorm* does not change the moment the revolutionaries shoot the King ... the *Grundnorm* changes when legal scientists make a new basic presupposition; but, as legal scientists, they must do this when the legal norms which are by and large effective within a territory can only be interpreted as a consistent field of meaning if a new *Grundnorm* (authorising a new ultimate source of law) is presupposed. ('When and why does the *Grundnorm* change?' [1971] CLJ 103 at p. 119.)

In short, then, Kelsen's theory fails to account for the acceptability or otherwise of the new legal order. Such explanations lie — inevitably — beyond the horizons of a rule-bound landscape. In the end questions about the validity of law must also be questions about its legitimacy. This is a question of a profoundly practical kind. 'To say this' as John Finnis puts it:

> is not to provide an answer to any concrete problem about the identity of any society or legal system. It is simply to say that the problem for the jurist is the same as the problem for the historian or for the good man wondering where his allegiance and his duty lie. From neither perspective is the thesis of discontinuity, as expressed by Kelsen, persuasive or acceptable. ('Revolutions and continuity of law', in A. W. B. Simpson (ed.), *Oxford Essays in Jurisprudence*, 2nd ser., p. 75.)

International Law

Kelsen regards international law as 'law' in the same sense as domestic law, though he concedes that the international legal order is a 'primitive' system which lacks many of the institutions (especially for the enforcement of sanctions) to be found in domestic systems. He insists, however, on the need to conceive of both as a single, unified whole. This is based, he argues, on the fact that States recognise that each other's legal systems have equal force. This, in turn, suggests that they acknowledge the existence of a basic norm which is superior to the basic norm of their individual domestic legal systems. But what, asks Kelsen, provides the source of this notion of equality? It must come from a superior basic norm which, in the international context, takes the form of customary practice adopted by States expressed in normative language and backed by the threat of coercion: war and reprisals. But Dias detects a shift in the meaning of the basic norm here:

> With reference to municipal law ... the *Grundnorm* has to possess some basis in fact, namely, a minimum of effectiveness. It would seem that with reference to international law the *Grundnorm* is a pure supposition lacking even this basis. Assuming that a monist legal theory has to be offered to account for the present state of international society, then one way of explaining the assertion of equality by States would be by hypothesising a norm superior to that of each national order from which equality might be said to derive. It is open to doubt, however, whether even an attempt at a monist explanation is worthwhile, for one is entitled to question whether there is any *Grundnorm* which commands the necessary minimum of effectiveness demanded by Kelsen's theory. (*Jurisprudence*, p. 371.)

In other words, international relations are dictated by self-interest and fear. And, as Dias shows, appeals by revolutionary governments to ground the legitimacy of their regime in the fact that it has received international recognition have been given short shrift by courts (see *Jilani* v *Government of Punjab* PLD 1972 SC 139).

Kelsen's monism is frequently attacked also on the ground that it leads him to reject the possibility of a conflict between the norms of domestic law, on the one hand, and international law, on the other. In seeking to present a unified system of norms, he provides an analogy between an unconstitutional statute and a statute that contravenes the norms of international law. The former is valid until it is declared unconstitutional; it may, moreover, remain valid in circumstances where no procedure exists to declare it void. Nevertheless those who passed the statute may be subject to sanctions. Equally, in the latter case, a statute in apparent breach of a norm of international law is valid though its passage may be the subject of sanctions (reprisals and war) under international law:

> The relationship of international law to a norm of national law which ... is contrary to international law, is the same as the relationship of the

constitution of a national legal order, which, for example in its provisions concerning fundamental rights, determines the content of future statutes to a statute which violates fundamental rights and is therefore considered to be unconstitutional — if the constitution does not provide for a procedure in which statutes, because of their unconstitutionality, may be abolished, but contains only the provision that certain organs may be tried in court personally for their part in the establishment of the 'unconstitutional' statute. International law determines the content of the national legal order in the same way as the constitution, which does not establish a judicial control of the constitutionality of statutes, determines the contents of future statutes. (*Pure Theory of Law*, p. 331.)

This ingenious comparison rests on somewhat special, not to say atypical, circumstances and, in any event, the alleged 'conflict' between domestic and international law posited by Kelsen is unlikely to lead to the sorts of consequences he suggests. As one commentator points out, the more plausible result of the condemnation of a State for passing legislation in violation of international law is either that the State will recognise the existence of the international law on the point in issue (in which case it will argue that the statute is not in breach of it) or it will declare itself not bound by the particular norm of international law. In neither case will the international community regard the statute as valid. (G. Hughes, 'Validity and the Basic Norm' (1971) 59 Cal L Rev 695 at p. 711.)

What is the basic norm of this unitary world of domestic and international law? Kelsen says the unity of the system may rest on the primacy of domestic law or, alternatively, on the primacy of international law. Either is acceptable; it is a matter of ideology. If the latter is adopted (which seems to be his preferred view), it is necessary both to specify the basic norm of the international legal order and its domestic counterpart must stipulate that it is inferior to the supra-national presupposed norm, 'the 'constitution' of international law in a transcendental-logical sense'. (*Pure Theory of Law*, p. 216.) Kelsen defines the basic norm of international law as follows:

'States — that is, the governments of the States — in their mutual relations ought to behave in such a way'; or: 'Coercion of State against State ought to be exercised under the conditions and in the manner, that conforms with the custom constituted by the actual behaviour of the States'. (*Pure Theory of Law*, p. 216.)

It is also necessary to substitute the domestic basic norm with one which recognises the validity of international law. As Kelsen says:

... the reason for the validity of the individual national legal order can be found in positive international law. In that case, a positive norm is the reason for the validity of this legal order, not a merely presupposed norm. [This] norm of international law ... usually is described by the statement that, according to general international law, a government which, independent of other governments, exerts effective control over the population of a certain territory, is the legitimate government; and that the population that lives under such a government in this territory constitutes a 'State' in the meaning of international law.... Translated into legal language: A norm of general international law authorises an individual or a group of individuals, on the basis of an effective constitution, to create and apply as a legitimate government a normative coercive order. (*Pure Theory of Law*, pp. 214–15.)

This is all very well as a description of the criteria employed by international law to establish the rights and duties of states, but Kelsen presents it as a justification for the validity of domestic legal systems. This is considerably less compelling. As Professor Hughes argues:

It is one thing to say that there is a system of international order which recognises for certain basic purposes any effective government as a participant in the system. Such a statement speaks only to the organs of international order. But it is a different matter to say that the reason for the *validity* of a *national* system is a norm of *international* law which somehow legitimises any effective, coercive order. Such a statement seems rather to speak to citizens of each State, telling them that because of a superior, supra-national norm, the system under which they live properly commands their respect so long as it can apply coercion effectively. Under Kelsen's position, if a citizen asks why a rule of the system under which he lives is to be regarded as valid, the ultimate answer would be that a norm of international law so provides because the system under which he lives is able to organise coercion effectively. Such an answer manages at once to be both dangerous and silly. It is dangerous because it appears to invest effective coercion with disproportionate value; it is silly because no one has ever been persuaded that the mere presence of effective coercion is sufficient to answer all inquiries about the validity of an order. [Apartheid] South Africa is a good example, for it is for some purposes recognised as a participant in the international system of order simply because it is an effective coercive government in a certain piece of territory. But a South African black would certainly not agree that the system under which he lives is valid because it monopolises effective coercion. Kelsen's presentation fails to distinguish between these quite different questions. (59 Cal L Rev 695 at p. 713, emphasis added.)

Yet even here Kelsen's positivism is less than pure. His conception of international law as constituting a legal order, albeit a primitive one, seems frequently to advance less of an analytical than an ideological position. It is an expression of hope rather than a statement of fact or theory. In a number of his works (notably *Law and Peace*, *Principles of International Law*, and *The Law of the United Nations*) Kelsen advocates an evolutionary theory of international law which envisages a progression towards the centralisation of sanctions by the international community. As Professor Bull comments:

> Kelsen's doctrine that in international society there is a 'force monopoly of the community' strains against the facts. It is one of the most salient features of the modern international system that in it force is the monopoly not of the community but of the *sovereign States* of which it is made up. Kelsen's approach, like so much that was written by experts on international law and organisation in that period, was the product of wishful thinking. (Tur and Twining (eds), *Essays on Kelsen*, p. 329, emphasis added.)

The 'idealist and progressivist assumptions' (ibid., p. 336) that underlie his attempts to incorporate international law within a coherent, unified system of norms betray the limits of a theory which aspires to scientific inquiry in circumstances where the realities of power politics cry out for analysis and understanding.

Kelsen and Kant

The German philosopher, Immanuel Kant (1724–1804), developed a theory of knowledge which, like Hume, attacked metaphysics and sought to replace it with an explanation of knowledge based upon the categories we use in thinking about our experience. To summarise the essence of his theory very briefly, Kant attempted to show that our a priori knowledge (that is, knowledge that is not derived from experience but is necessary and universal) falls into two groups: analytic and synthetic. The first consists of statements or judgments the truth of which can be established without reference to experience (e.g., 'a green leaf is green'). Synthetic judgments, on the other hand, contain, as the predicate of the judgment, some information which is not contained in the subject (e.g., 2 + 2 = 4): the judgment is a synthesis of two separate notions, one of which is the subject about which the other, the predicate, is asserted.

To explain what we can know, Kant employs two notions: first, 'the forms of intuition' by which we make a priori judgments (we impose them on everything we encounter: all things must have temporal and geometrical features) and, secondly, certain organising principles, or 'categories' which enable us to make judgments about things we encounter in the world (they include causality, accident, substance, and possibility). These two notions facilitate knowledge of the phenomenal world (i.e., the world we actually experience, as opposed to the noumenal or non-empirical world). But such knowledge is limited to the form, not the content, of the phenomenal world. Its content is determined by transcendental inquiries: they attempt to determine from our experience and judgments what their necessary features must be.

Kant was pessimistic about the prospect of metaphysical knowledge about reality beyond the world of experience. Our a priori understanding is limited to things we can actually experience. Nor can such understanding be inferred from what we know of the phenomenal world to the noumenal world. For Kant such inferences or applications are 'antinomies': conclusions which can be both proved and shown to be false. I argue that the world must have had a beginning in time; you argue that it cannot have. We cannot demonstrate conclusively which of two opposing arguments is 'true'. We cannot know whether the noumenal world has any of the features of the phenomenal world.

In developing his pure theory of law, Kelsen explicitly acknowledges the influence of Kant and he is frequently described as a neo-Kantian. In particular, his empirical and rationalist approach to law would seem to place him firmly in the Kantian epistemological tradition:

> Pure reason is the faculty of knowledge a priori. The critical philosophy reveals that knowledge is necessarily a synthesis of a priori form and a posteriori data. Consequently the *Pure Theory of Law* is not a book of knowledge but a book about knowledge. As a prolegomenon to all future jurisprudence which aspires to be scientific it must necessarily relate to the forms of knowledge and not provide legal knowledge itself. (R. Tur in Tur and Twining (eds), *Essays on Kelsen*, p. 160.)

Yet in his pursuit of purity and, hence, his denial of any equation of law and 'justice', Kelsen parts ways with a Kantian ethics. Thus, while Kant conceived of law as part of morals, Kelsen repudiates such impurity. Their similar, though different, approaches to the basic norm are well described by Richard Tur:

> [Kant's basic norm] is an impure material 'ought' from which normative conclusions may be drawn by logical deduction. This conflicts not only with the Kelsenian formulation of the basic norm as a logical, formal 'ought' providing no inference ticket to material normative conclusions, but also Kant's own critical philosophy. For Kant that knowledge is 'pure' which contains 'no admixture of anything empirical'. The distinction between form and content is central to Kant's critical enterprise. Kant holds

that his formal category cannot tell us a priori what effects causes actually have in empirical reality ... Kelsen holds that his formal category cannot tell us what consequences conditions have in the normative sphere. In both cases, therefore, it is a contingent matter of *fact* which provides the content of judgments, be they causal or normative. If one regards the Kantian epoch in the history of ideas as the critical synthesis of empiricism and rationalism then it is the absolutist, natural law ethics which falls to be discarded and the relativist epistemology, retained. This is Kelsen's option. (R. Tur and W. Twining, 'Introduction', in *Essays on Kelsen*, p. 7, emphasis added; see H. Steiner, 'Kant's Kelsenianism', in Tur and Twining (eds), *Essays on Kelsen*, p. 65.)

It is therefore important to recognise the limitations of Kelsen's neo-Kantianism. In particular, Kelsen does not accept Kant's argument that practical reason is the source of norms. For Kelsen, moral judgments and values are not susceptible of rational knowledge. And he also rejects the material nature of Kant's 'ought': Kelsen's 'ought' is completely formal in nature.

Some would go further and deny a Kantian essence in Kelsen's theory. Alida Wilson argues that, notwithstanding Kelsen's explicit acknowledgement to Kant, the pure theory is informed by Kantian ideas considerably less than is generally believed. She concentrates her analysis on Kelsen's use of the concept of *Zurechnung* (usually translated as 'imputation'). Briefly, she challenges Kelsen's assumption that his a priori category of *Zurechnung* in the normative context is analogous to Kant's category of causation. When he attempts to apply Kant's method beyond the phenomenal world:

... the charge against him is not merely that he endeavours to use the Kantian intellectual instrument and fails; not merely that he overlooks a prime fact about Kant's categories, that is, their definition in terms adapted to our understanding of natural phenomena; but rather that he supposed it possible to employ Kant's method on intellectual ground where he had debarred himself from so doing. For, if we bar argument from the 'is' statement to a statement or prescription in terms of 'ought', it is hard to see how any useful connection could be found between such concepts as are involved a priori in our knowledge of what is and the type of concepts involved a priori in the normative view of the world. That is to say, talk of *analogy* between causality and *Zurechnung* is of no help with morality and law, if we insist that the essence of each of these is its normative character. (A. Wilson, 'Is Kelsen really a Kantian?', in Tur and Twining (eds), *Essays on Kelsen*, p. 56. Cf. H. Steiner, 'Kant's Kelsenianism', in Tur and Twining (eds), *Essays on Kelsen*, p. 65, Stanley L. Paulson, 'The neo-Kantian dimension of Kelsen's pure theory of law' (1992) 12 Oxford J Legal Stud 311.)

Whether or not Kelsen succeeds in applying the Kantian method is ultimately a futile question; the pure theory falls to be evaluated in its own right. Does his non-cognitivist, relativist account of the normative basis of law have explanatory power? Is the presupposed transcendent *Grundnorm* a satisfactory heuristic device by which the unity and (following a revolution) the validity of the legal system may be understood? And so on.

Democracy and the Rule of Law

By refusing to recognise the State as an independent entity placed above the law, Kelsen effectively equates the State and the legal system. The institutions, powers and functions of the State are defined by the law; their identity is determined by legal norms. He therefore concludes:

> If the identity of State and law is discovered, if it is recognised that the law — the positive law, not the law identified with justice — *is* this very coercive order in which the State appears to a cognition which is not mired in anthropomorphic metaphors but which penetrates through the veil of personification to the man-created norms, then it is simply impossible to justify the State through the law; just as it is impossible to justify the law through the law.... And then the attempt to legitimise the State as governed by law, as a *Rechtsstaat*, is revealed as entirely useless because... every State is 'governed by law' in the sense that every State is a legal order. This, however, represents no political value judgment. (*Pure Theory of Law*, pp. 318–19.)

In other words, Kelsen firmly rejects any Hegelian absolutist super-State and in so doing, exposes the coercive nature of law stripped of the sort of moral legitimacy provided by natural law theories. (But see I. Stewart, in Tur and Twining (eds), *Essays on Kelsen*, p. 145, who argues that Kelsen 'tried to counter the State-absolutist substitute by constructing a basis, through an analogy, in a natural-scientific kind of objectivism'. Stewart believes Kelsen failed in this attempt and that the pure theory, along with legal positivism in general, is merely 'one of the frayed ends of iusnaturalism' (pp. 145–6). Not every legal order is a *Rechtsstaat* (a democratic State governed by the rule of law which provides legal security), but little is required for a State to be a legal order: 'A relatively centralised, autocratic coercive order which, if its flexibility is unlimited, offers no legal security is a legal order too; and ... the community, constituted by such a coercive order, is a legal community and as such, a State' (*Pure Theory of Law*, p. 319). And the equation of law and State is also the break between between fact and value:

From the point of view of a consistent legal positivism, law, like the State, cannot be comprehended otherwise than as a coercive order of human behavious. The definition says nothing about the moral value or justice of positive law. Then the State can be juristically comprehended no more and no less than law itself. (*Pure Theory of Law*, p. 319.)

Kelsen's unwillingness to elevate the State above the law constitutes an important statement of his recognition of the need for controls over arbitrary power. For Professor Cotterrell a 'major reason why he refuses to accept the State as an entity above law is because, when it is recognised as such, appalling things can be done in its name' (*The Politics of Jurisprudence*, p. 113).

Critique

As with Hart, the writings of Kelsen have provoked a considerable outpouring of critical literature. Both Professor Raz (*The Concept of a Legal System*, especially ch. 5, and *The Authority of Law*, especially ch. 7) and J. W. Harris (*Law and Legal Science*) have subjected the key elements of the pure theory to rigorous analysis. Raz is unconvinced that Kelsen has developed the positivism of Austin and Bentham. As he puts it (in a passage from *The Concept of a Legal System*, p. 95, that is worthy of close scrutiny):

Kelsen remains faithful to the principle of origin: The identity of a legal system, as well as the membership of a law in a system, is determined solely by the facts of its creation, by its origin. But the source of unity is no longer one legislative body, it is one power-conferring norm. The basic norm replaces the sovereign, otherwise nothing has changed.

These two theorists tend to venture into territory which the average student of jurisprudence is likely to find fairly impenetrable and which he or she may not legitimately be expected to traverse. Nevertheless, I have always suggested that students *attempt* to read their work in order to assist their understanding of their legal theories. And even if this occasionally has the opposite effect, it may assist you to develop your ability to present your own arguments (especially in the examination) in a more refined, sophisticated (though not, I hope, similarly inaccessible) style (see chapter 2). I recommend that you do the same even though I cannot say that my expectations have always been fulfilled.

Kelsen's theory did not remain static and he attempted to modify or revise it over the years. For a useful account of these developments, see Michael Hartney's introduction to his recent translation of Kelsen's *General Theory of Norms*. Yet there seem, generally speaking, to be four main kinds of criticism that have been levelled at various strands of the pure theory. You should be able to discuss them (at greater length and in greater depth than the following outline). First is the assault on the very notion of a 'pure' theory itself: is it really possible (let alone desirable) to exclude from a model of law social and political factors? Harold Laski described it as an 'exercise in logic but not in life'. It is even arguable that the concept of efficacy, by which Kelsen sets so much store can be measured only by reference to the very sociological considerations which he is so determined to exclude. Secondly, the *Grundnorm* as the progenitor of all other norms (even, in Kelsen's view, in the case of international law: and you should be familiar with his ambitious claims in this area) has been attacked largely on the ground that its existence cannot explain the validity of what Dworkin calls 'non-rule standards', i.e., policies and principles (see chapter 6).

Thirdly, Kelsen's reduction of all legislation to the form 'If X then Y' (where X is a certain form of conduct and Y is a sanction) is widely regarded as unacceptably narrow. The *form* of law is given primacy over its *meaning*. It presumes (which, of course, Kelsen is content to do) that law is essentially coercion; many would want to argue that law has other functions. It minimises, as Dias (*Jurisprudence*, p. 373) points out, the regulatory function of law. A fourth kind of assault seeks to show that Kelsen accords unwarranted importance to the role of sanctions in law. It results in a lopsided analysis of legal duty not only because a statute may impose duties *without* necessarily providing a sanction, but because, on the other hand, certain conduct may be made the condition of a sanction even though it is not the subject of a *duty*. (See J. W. Harris's octopus example (*Legal Philosophies*, p. 66), and consider his point (p. 67) that to measure effectiveness we need to know the content of the norm, i.e., the nature of the duty involved. As he puts it, 'The concept of 'duty' must ... stand on its own feet, as something distinct from the concept of sanction. A theory of law must define duty and sanction separately.')

THE EXAMINATION

In addition to answering specific questions on Hart and Kelsen (or particular aspects of their theories) and comparisons between their theories (or specific aspects of them), you should be able to answer questions that require a comparison between, say, Kelsen and Bentham. It would therefore be sensible to draw a line down the middle of a page and, in point form, compare all possible permutations (Austin v Bentham, Austin v Hart, Austin v Kelsen, Bentham v Hart, Hart v Dworkin etc.). You should also be in a position to answer the (more difficult) general question which asks for an analysis of the nature of legal positivism (which would draw on the theories of all four jurists considered in this and the previous chapter): this is a matter that is more conveniently (and more logically) considered in the context of the general 'debate' between positivists and natural lawyers (see chapter 5).

It is fairly common to find examination questions calling for a comparison between a single aspect of the theories of Hart and Kelsen. Consider the following question:

What are the principal differences between Hart's rule of recognition and Kelsen's *Grundnorm*?

Since neither of these concepts would make sense in the absence of a brief account of the theories of which they are each an essential part, a few opening paragraphs might be devoted to describing in general terms Hart's system of rules and Kelsen's pure theory as well as the essential positivism that they share. Your outline of Kelsen ought to include reference to:

(a) The purported 'purity' of the theory.
(b) The nature and function of the *Grundnorm* (in brief).
(c) The relationship between validity and effectiveness.

A concise description of the fundamental features of Hart's theory should include:

(a) Law as a system of rules.
(b) Secondary rules (with an emphasis on the rule of recognition).
(c) The 'internal point of view'.
(d) The minimum conditions for a legal system to exist.

When I say 'brief' or 'concise' I mean that you should confine yourself to the bare essentials. I have found this to be a perennial problem among examinees. There is frequently a tendency (a consequence of insecurity?) to devote large tracts of the answer book to discussing a subject which *in the context of the question set* calls only for a rough sketch. There is an important distinction to be drawn between the approach to be applied in a question requiring a detailed analysis of a particular issue (such as the present question) and one requiring a general discussion of a topic. Thus if you were answering a question on 'legal positivism' your treatment of, say, Hart would be significantly different from the manner in which you would discuss his theory in the present context. This sounds too obvious to require stating. But many is the candidate who (either out of a desperate bid to impress the examiner or because of a simple failure to read the question carefully) expends wasted time and energy in providing a long exegesis on matters which are not relevant to the question posed. It is important, therefore, as pointed out in chapter 2, that you learn (and even prepare) your material in such a way as to equip you to answer questions of *both* sorts: Hart (or Dworkin or Olivecrona) *at large* and Hart (or Kelsen or Llewellyn) *in detail*.

The essence of this question is, of course, a detailed analysis *and comparison* between the rule of recognition and the *Grundnorm*. The next stage should therefore be to provide a closer description of both concepts. Your discussion of the rule of recognition should include the following features:

(a)   Its function in Hart's system of rules: as a test of validity.
(b)   Its imposition of duties upon officials.
(c)   Its definition (and problems associated therewith).
(d)   Criticisms (e.g., Dworkin).

Your account of the *Grundnorm* ought to include:

(a)   Its nature (a meta-legal presupposition etc.).
(b)   Its function: efficacy and validity.
(c)   Its place in the hierarchy of norms.
(d)   Criticisms (e.g., Raz).

You may now proceed to *compare* the essential elements in both constructs. In particular, you might point to the main differences between them which may be tabulated (for the purpose of simplicity — not for the examination) as in figure 4.2.

Figure 4.2 The rule of recognition and Grundnorm compared

RULE OF RECOGNITION	GRUNDNORM
Does not depend on any aspect of coercion for its validity.	Based on coercion.
Its existence is a matter of fact.	A logical presumption of the 'juristic consciousness'.
Its function is to enable one to identify rules.	Functions to validate the constitution.
It may include several criteria of validity.	There is only one *Grundnorm*.
It imparts validity to rules within a legal system by recognising primary and secondary rules.	It imparts validity to a normative order, and is also the source of all norms.
It provides the unity in a legal system.	It enables the legal scientist to interpret all valid legal norms as a non-contradictory field of meaning.
Its own validity (which is meaningless in this context) cannot be demonstrated; it simply exists.	Pre-supposed in terms of efficacy, therefore it must be valid.
No necessary connection between the validity and efficacy of a rule (unless the rule of recognition contains such a provision amongst its criteria).	Its choice is not arbitrary and depends on the principle of efficacy.

This is a very general comparison. It would be a good idea to add to it yourself. You might round off your answer by pointing to the (superficial) similarity between the two concepts in respect of their attempt to postulate some test by reference to which the validity of laws are measurable, but how their fundamentally different approaches lead them to offer essentially different accounts, of which the rule of recognition and the *Grundnorm* are central features.

You are also very likely to be asked to 'compare' the views of Hart and Dworkin in respect of the judicial function, the model of rules versus the model of rules plus principles and policies, and so on. A question of this sort is briefly considered in chapter 6. I cannot emphasise too strongly the importance of your having *prepared* for such questions in the manner already described.

Still, it is possible that you may be asked to analyse a very specific aspect of Hart's theory (e.g., the rule of recognition, his 'internal aspect', his concept of 'validity' etc.) or Kelsen's (e.g., its 'purity', the *Grundnorm*, his concept of 'validity' etc.). Your answer will, of course, require much greater attention to detail than in the previous kind of question considered above.

FURTHER READING

Detmold, M. J., *The Unity of Law and Morality: A Refutation of Legal Positivism* (London: Routledge & Kegan Paul, 1984).

Fuller, Lon Luvois, *The Morality of Law*, rev. ed. (New Haven, Conn; London: Yale University Press, 1969).

Gavison, Ruth, (ed.), *Issues in Contemporary Legal Philosophy: The Influence of H. L. A. Hart* (Oxford: Clarendon Press, 1987).

George, Robert P. (ed.), *The Autonomy of Law: Essays on Legal Positivism* (Oxford: Clarendon Press, 1995).

Hacker, P. M. S., and Raz J. (ed.), *Law, Morality and Society: Essays in Honour of H. L. A. Hart* (Oxford: Clarendon Press, 1977).

Harris, J. W., *Law and Legal Science: An Inquiry into the Concepts Legal Rule and Legal System* (Oxford: Clarendon Press, 1979).

Hart, H. L. A., *The Concept of Law* (Oxford: Clarendon Press, 1961).

Hart, H. L. A., *The Concept of Law*, 2nd ed. by P. A. Bulloch and J. Raz (Oxford: Clarendon Press, 1994).

Hart, H. L. A., *Essay in Jurisprudence and Philosophy* (Oxford: Clarendon Press, 1983).

Hart, H. L. A., *Essays on Bentham: Studies on Jurisprudence and Political Theory* (Oxford: Clarendon Press, 1982).

Jori, Mario (ed.), *Legal Positivism* (Aldershot: Dartmouth, 1992).

Kelsen, Hans, *General Theory of Law and State*, transl. Anders Wedberg (Cambridge, Mass: Harvard University Press, 1949) (20th Century Legal Philosophy Series, vol. 1).

Kelsen, Hans, *General Theory of Norms*, transl. M. Hartney (Oxford: Clarendon Press, 1991).

Kelsen, Hans, *Introduction to the Problems of Legal Theory*, transl. Bonnie Litschewski Paulson and S. L. Paulson (Oxford: Clarendon Press, 1992).

Kelsen, Hans, *Pure Theory of Law*, transl. Max Knight (Berkeley and Los Angeles: University of California Press, 1967).

Kelsen, Hans, *What is Justice? Justice, Law and Politics in the Mirror of Science* (Berkeley and Los Angeles: University of California Press, 1957).

Raz, Joseph, *The Concept of Legal System: An Introduction to the Theory of Legal System*, 2nd ed. (Oxford: Clarendon Press, 1980).

Tur, Richard, and Twining, William (eds), *Essays on Kelsen* (Oxford: Clarendon Press, 1986).

Wacks, Raymond (ed.), *Hong Kong, China and 1997: Essays in Legal Theory* (Hong Kong: Hong Kong University Press, 1993).

5 NATURAL LAW

It is not difficult, in my experience, for teachers of jurisprudence to convince their students of the deficiencies or, at any rate, the limitations of legal positivism. No great sophistry or sophistication is required to demonstrate the simple proposition that the 'external' point of view may offer an incomplete explanation of the complex phenomenon of law. And many students, in turn, blandly accept that legal positivism is 'crude' or 'outmoded' or simply 'nonsense'. Beware of such rash judgments! Attack positivism by all means, (and you will more than likely be invited to do so in your examination) but be sure to show *why* you regard the positivist account as inadequate. Never make assumptions.

WHAT IS WRONG WITH LEGAL POSITIVISM?

This deceptively facile question is at the core of much jurisprudential debate. It is therefore crucial that you have a good grasp of why and how the positivist approach has been subjected to criticism. Broadly speaking, I think the assault on legal positivism takes six forms. They are related, but each has a slightly different starting-point and method of attack.

The first rejects the very project of a value-free account of law. It argues that the emergence of legal positivism coincided with 19th-century capitalism; it therefore represents and expresses a particular *ideology*. Such critics point not only to the formalism that lies at the heart of positivism (the separation between 'is' and 'ought'), but also to the essential individualism that the theory assumes. This view is further explored in chapter 9.

Secondly, it is claimed that the central idea of *validity* cannot be neutral. So, it is urged, the attempts to base validity on sovereignty (Austin), efficacy (Kelsen) or even the 'internal point of view' and 'critical reflective attitude' (Hart) fail to take account of the *values* that underpin legal validity or explain why the law is regarded as valid.

Thirdly, the related concepts of *authority* and *discretion* are attacked. You will recall how Hart suggests (after rejecting Austin's 'gunman' theory and Kelsen's *Grundnorm*) a *neutral* theory of authority. He gives the example of the rules of a game. They are not moral, but they nevertheless define a practice in terms of which 'rights', 'duties' and so on are *accepted*: the participants obey an authority (e.g., the referee in a chess match) because they accept the *rules* of the game. Hart shows that the acceptance of rules from an 'internal point of view' leads to a need for secondary rules of change, adjudication and recognition which, in turn, necessitate authority. There is, therefore, no necessary connection between authority (or law) and morality. For Hart it is thus possible for moral questions to be excluded from the definition of law. But (as we shall see) this means that when a judge is required to make a decision on a matter where there is a 'gap' in the law, he exercises a strong discretion. And in so doing, it is argued by certain critics, moral questions *do* enter into the determination of what is law. Ronald Dworkin, the leading contemporary critic of legal positivism, would deny that judges have a strong discretion and thus goes even further in repudiating the separation between law and morality (see chapter 6).

Fourthly, it is argued, rules, commands or norms do not fully explain reality. These are, it is said, abstract concepts which provide only a formal scheme of the operation of law and the legal system. Can we, say, understand the judicial role without an explanation of the relationship between the judiciary and the legislature? In other words, don't we require a theory of democracy to explain law?

Fifthly, there is said to be a *necessary* connection between law and morality. The best known version of this assault on legal positivism is Professor Lon Fuller's book *The Morality of Law*. You will almost certainly devote some of your jurisprudence course to the so-called Hart-Fuller debate. Although this is one of the old chestnuts of legal theory, you would be well advised to understand its central terms (well analysed by R. Summers in his recent book *Lon F. Fuller*). Be sure to note the problem of the 'grudge informer' which exercises both Hart and Fuller. In a nutshell, Fuller seeks to show that law has an 'internal morality' which consists of the following eight desiderata:

(a) generality,
(b) promulgation,
(c) non-retroactivity,
(d) clarity,
(e) non-contradiction,

(f)   possibility of compliance,
(g)   constancy, and
(h)   congruence between declared rule and official action.

If a system does not conform with any one of these principles, or fails substantially in respect of several, it could not be said that 'law' existed in that community. (See Fuller's sad tale of the unhappy reign of Rex.) Thus Fuller refuses to regard the 'law' of the Third Reich as law, a view rejected by Hart who prefers the simple utilitarian position that 'laws may be law but too evil to be obeyed'. It is arguable that *compliance* with Fuller's 'internal morality' is no guarantee of a just order; the apartheid South African legal system probably satisfied all eight principles — though Fuller argued that its apartheid legislation 'reveals a gross departure from the demands of the internal morality of law' on the ground that this legislation defines race arbitrarily.

Fuller's position is essentially that law is a 'purposive enterprise, dependent for its success on the energy, insight, intelligence, and conscientiousness of those who conduct it'. To count as an instance of that enterprise it must fulfil certain moral requirements. (He does not, however, make clear precisely how his eight principles are *moral*.) A similar, though more complex case for the non-separation of law and morals has recently been made by M. J. Detmold in his book *The Unity of Law and Morality*. For him (p. 54):

Hart's mistake . . . was to try to run two incompatible analyses together: the analysis of sociological statements, where existence can be separated from bindingness and thus from moral statements; and the analysis of internal normative statements, where it cannot. *The Concept of Law* suffers throughout from a failure to separate these things.

This is a bold, provocative claim (and the book is replete with them), but it is one that Detmold attempts to substantiate with largely philosophical evidence which is at once dense and difficult. Serious students will want to look at this book (especially chapters 2 to 6).

Sixthly, it is argued (often by students!) that despite its claim to the contrary by its adherents, legal positivism does *not* promote clear thinking about law. Modern positivists, it is sometimes said, have developed a highly complex, technical and occasionally barely comprehensible account of law. For all their brilliance, the works of Joseph Raz are frequently inaccessible to all but professional jurisprudes.

These six attacks on legal positivism do not constitute a comprehensive statement of the antipositivist tradition, but they do, I think, give you its major strands. Please add to it.

But legal positivism itself was, as we have already seen, a reaction against the philosophy of natural law which, since Greek times, has exercised a considerable influence on ethics and law.

WHAT IS NATURAL LAW?

'The best description of natural law', according to one leading natural lawyer, 'is that it provides a name for the point of intersection between law and morals' (A. Passerin D'Entrèves, *Natural Law*, p. 116). There is an unquestionable tension between 'is' and 'ought'; theories of natural law attempt to resolve this. Its principal claim — put simply — is that what naturally *is, ought* to be. But this apparently uncomplicated proposition has been widely misunderstood and misinterpreted (not least by students of jurisprudence).

It is important that you have a good grasp of the historical development of natural law theory. A very useful reader is *Natural Law*, edited (in two volumes) by John Finnis, in the International Library of Essays in Law and Legal Theory, published by Dartmouth in 1991. Most accounts of natural law to which you may be referred in your course normally sketch the 'development' of natural law thinking, starting with the Greeks and the Romans, through the religious teachings of St Thomas Aquinas and its secular (and political) adaptation by Grotius, Hobbes, Locke, Rousseau and Blackstone. The decline of natural law theory in the 19th century (the rise of legal positivism after the attack by Hume) are then described — often to demonstrate that the 'debate' between natural lawyers and legal positivists, while important, is inconclusive. You will then be told of the 'revival' of natural law in the 20th century. In most examination questions about natural law, candidates are expected to exhibit a knowledge of these developments, but too many merely reel off these historical 'developments' (which they have committed to memory) without demonstrating a real understanding of what questions natural lawyers have sought to answer.

It is therefore perhaps preferable (and less tedious) to consider the matter 'backwards', as it were. Instead of tracing the genesis of the theory and its application to various ethical and legal questions over the centuries, consider the *character* of the natural law enterprise. There is no better starting-point for this approach than John Finnis's book *Natural Law and Natural Rights*. It is a central claim of Finnis that anyone who tries to explain law, makes assumptions, willy-nilly, about what is 'good'. As he puts it (p. 3):

> It is often supposed that an evaluation of law as a type of social institution, if it is to be undertaken at all, must be preceded by a value-free description and analysis of that institution as it exists in fact. But the development of modern jurisprudence suggests, and reflection on the methodology of any social science confirms, that a theorist cannot give a theoretical description and analysis of social facts, unless he also participates in the work of evaluation, of understanding what is really good for human persons, and what is really required by practical reasonableness.

This constitutes an important challenge to the alleged 'objectivity' of legal positivism. But it also represents an incisive philosophical starting-point of the natural law approach. It suggests that when we are discerning what is *good*, we are using our intelligence differently from when we are discerning what *exists*. In other words, if we are to understand the nature and impact of the natural law project, we must recognise that it yields 'a different logic' (p. 34). Whatever you make of Finnis's own interpretation of Aquinas and his general theory (see p. 83ff.), I think it is important that you bear in mind that the philosophy of natural law cannot sensibly be 'contrasted with' legal positivism as so many jurisprudence examinations require candidates to do. It is essential to acknowledge (and *say* that you do) that, while the questions they pose may be similar, their method of analysis is different. This is not to defend the natural law position; it merely signifies that you have understood its essence.

It would be illusory to seek or attempt a 'definition' of natural law, but I think Cicero's more or less Stoic pronouncement (*De Re Publica*, bk 3, ch. 22, sect. 33) contains the three main components of any natural law philosophy:

> True law is right reason in agreement with Nature; it is of universal application, unchanging and everlasting.... It is a sin to try to alter this law, nor is it allowable to attempt to repeal any part of it, and it is impossible to abolish it entirely.... [God] is the author of this law, its promulgator, and its enforcing judge.

It stresses natural law's:

(a)   universality and immutability;
(b)   its standing as a 'higher' law, and
(c)   its discoverability by reason (it is in this sense 'natural').

Any answer to an examination question requiring an account of natural law should — at the very least — incorporate these three elements.

THE DEVELOPMENT OF NATURAL LAW PHILOSOPHY

There is some truth in the observation by Alf Ross (the Scandinavian realist, see chapter 7) that 'like a harlot, natural law is at the disposal of everyone' (*On Law and Justice*, p. 261). The theory has been employed to justify both revolution and reaction.

During the sixth century BC, the Greeks described human laws as owing their importance in the scheme of things to the power of fate which controlled everything. This conservative view could be (and presumably was) used to justify and feature (however evil) of the status quo. By the fifth century BC, however, it was acknowledged that there might be a conflict between the law of nature and the law of man. With Aristotle there is less reference to natural law than to the distinction between natural and conventional justice. It was the Stoics who were especially attracted to the notion of natural law where 'natural' meant in accordance with *reason*. The Stoic view informed the approach adopted by the Romans (as expressed by Cicero) who recognised (at least in theory) that laws which did not conform with 'reason' might be regarded as invalid.

It was, however, the Catholic Church that really gave expression to the full-blown philosophy of natural law as we understand it today. As early as the fifth century, St Augustine asked, 'What are States without justice, but robber bands enlarged?' (*City of God*, bk 4, iv). (More than one student has misquoted this as 'rubber bands enlarged'!) In about 1140 Gratian published his *Decretum*, a collection of some 4,000 texts dealing with numerous aspects of church discipline which he sought to reconcile. His work begins by declaring, in keeping with the medieval conception of natural law: 'Mankind is governed by two laws: the law of nature and custom. The law of nature is contained in the scriptures and the gospel.' But he goes on to say: 'Natural law overrides customs and constitutions. That which has been recognised by usage, or recorded in writing, if it contradicts natural law, is void and of no effect.'

Of course, the leading exposition of natural law is by the Dominican, Thomas Aquinas (1225–74) whose principal work *Summa Theologica* contains the most comprehensive statement of Christian doctrine on the subject. He distinguishes between four categories of law, as illustrated in table 5.1.

Table 5.1 Aquinas's four categories of law

1. *Lex aeterna* (eternal law)	Divine reason — known only to God. God's plan for the Universe. Man needs this law without which he would totally lack direction.
2. *Lex naturalis* (natural law)	Participation of the eternal law in rational creatures. Discoverable by *reason*.
3. *Lex divina* (divine law)	Revealed in the scriptures (God's positive law for mankind).
4. *Lex humana* (humanly posited law)	Supported by reason. Enacted for the common good. Necessary because the *lex naturalis* cannot solve many day-to-day problems. Also, people are selfish; compulsion is required to force them to act reasonably.

For Aquinas human posited law draws its power to bind from natural law. His 'definition' of natural law (above) speaks of participation of the eternal law in rational ceatures (*participatio legis aeternae in rationali creatura*). I must confess that I did not understand this description until I read John Finnis's explanation. Aquinas does not mean 'participation' in the normal sense of the word. As Finnis explains (*Natural Law and Natural Rights*, p. 399):

> For Aquinas, the word *participatio* focally signifies two conjoined concepts, causality and similarity (or imitation). A quality that an entity or state of affairs has or includes is participated, in Aquinas's sense, if that quality is *caused by* a *similar* quality which some other entity or state of affairs has or includes in a more intrinsic or less dependent way.
>
> Aquinas's notion of natural law as a participation of the eternal law is no more than a straightforward application of his general theory of the cause and operation of human understanding in any field or inquiry.

His theory of understanding may be very briefly summarised as follows: Aquinas (following Plato and Aristotle) postulates a 'separate intellect' which causes in us our own power of insight. Humans (as opposed to animals) 'participate' in natural law in this sense: we are able to grasp the essential principles of natural law i.e., human nature's Creator's intelligent and intelligible plan for human flourishing. But we grasp it not by any kind of direct knowledge of the divine mind, but rather: 'all those things to which man has a natural inclination, one's reason naturally understands as good (and thus as 'to be pursued') and their contraries as bad (and as 'to be avoided')' (*Summa Theologica*, pt 2, 1st pt, question 94, art. 2).

His analysis of natural law distinguishes between primary and secondary principles; the former may be supplemented by new principles, but not subtracted from. The latter may, in exceptional circumstances, be susceptible to change. But he does not tell us on what *basis* this distinction is drawn: which principles are primary? Nor does he explain how the secondary principles are *derived* from the primary ones.

But by far the most important position adopted by Aquinas (and one which, according to Finnis, has been widely misconstrued) is that a 'law' which fails to conform to natural or divine law is not a law at all. This is normally expressed in the maxim *'lex iniusta non est lex'* (an unjust law is not law). It appears that Aquinas himself never made this assertion, but merely quoted St Augustine. Certainly Plato, Cicero and Aristotle expressed similar sentiments, but it is a proposition that is most closely associated with Aquinas. Read Finnis, *Natural Law and Natural Rights*, pp. 363–6, for a powerful refutation not only of the view itself but also the suggestion that Aquinas held it in the naive sense in which most textbooks now present it.

What Aquinas seems to have said was that laws which conflict with the requirements of natural law lose their power to bind morally. In other words, a government which abuses its authority by enacting laws which are unjust (unreasonable or against the common good) forfeits its right to be obeyed — *because it lacks moral authority*. Aquinas calls any such law a 'corruption of law'. But he does not suggest that one is always justified in *disobeying* it, for though he says that if a ruler enacts unjust laws 'their subjects are not obliged to obey them', he adds 'except, perhaps, in certain special cases when it is a matter of avoiding 'scandal' (i.e., a corrupting example to others) or civil disorder (*Summa Theologica*, I/II, 96, 4). This is a far cry from the radical claims sometimes made in the name of Aquinas which seek to justify disobedience to law.

By the 17th century in Europe, the exposition of entire branches of the law (notably public international law) purported to be founded on natural law. Hugo de Groot (1583–1645), or Grotius as he is generally called, is normally associated with the secularisation of natural law. In his influential work *De Jure Belli ac Pacis* he asserts that even if God did not exist (*'etiamsi daremus non esse Deum'*) natural law would have the same content. This proved to be an important basis for the developing discipline of public international law, though exactly what Grotius means when he postulates his *etiamsi daremus* idea is not entirely clear. (For differing interpretations contrast D'Entrèves, *Natural Law*, pp. 53–6, and Finnis, *Natural Law and Natural Rights*, pp. 43–4.) I have always thought that he means that certain things are 'intrinsically' wrong — whether or not they are decreed by God; for, to use Grotius's own analogy, even God cannot cause two times two not to equal four. In saying this, however, he is not denying the existence of God (as is sometimes suggested); he is stressing that what is right or wrong are matters of natural fittingness, not of arbitrary divine *fiat*.

In England the high-water mark of natural law was reached in the 18th century with Sir William Blackstone's *Commentaries on the Laws of England*. Blackstone (1723–80) commences his great work by adumbrating classical natural law doctrine — in order, it has been argued (see D. Kennedy, 'The structure of Blackstone's *Commentaries*' (1979) 28 Buffalo LRev 205), to sanctify English law by this appeal to God-given principles. But, while he makes various claims about positive law deriving its authority from natural law and being a nullity if it conflicts with it, these assertions do not actually inform Blackstone's analysis of the law itself. It was, of course, this attempt to clothe the positive law with a legitimacy derived from natural law that attracted the criticism (one might even say the wrath) of Bentham who described natural law as, amongst other things, 'a mere work of the fancy'.

NATURAL LAW IN POLITICAL PHILOSOPHY

Aquinas is associated (as we saw) with a fairly conservative view of natural law. But natural law has been used to justify revolutions (especially the

American and the French) on the ground that the law infringed individuals' *natural rights*. Thus in America the revolution against British colonial rule was based on an appeal to the natural rights of all Americans, in the lofty words of the Declaration of Independence of 1776, to 'life, liberty and the pursuit of happiness'. As the Declaration puts it, 'We hold these truths to be self-evident, that all men are created equal, that they are endowed by their Creator with certain unalienable rights'. Equally stirring sentiments were incorporated in the French *Déclaration des droits de l'homme et du citoyen* of 26 August 1789 which speaks of certain 'natural rights' of mankind.

The *political* application of natural law theory is bound up with various 'contractarian' theories which conceive of political rights and obligations in terms of a *social contract*. This 'contract' is not an agreement in a strict legal sense, but contains the idea that only with his consent can a person be subjected to the political power of another. It continues to have a hold on the thinking of contemporary liberal theorists, most notably John Rawls (see chapter 9). Some teachers of jurisprudence refer only in passing to the thoughts of the leading social contractarians (Hobbes, Locke and Rousseau) either in the present context or when they are discussing the revival of such theories in the work of Rawls. They are, of course, not, strictly speaking, jurists, but they have exercised such an important influence on social and political as well as legal theory that you ought — at the very least — to be familiar with the essentials of their respective views. You will find useful summaries in *Lloyd's Introduction to Jurisprudence*, pp. 101–108 (and extracts from their leading works at pp. 137–44).

For present purposes it will suffice to give only the briefest outline of each of their analyses of natural law and the social contract. You would, however, be well advised to spend some time reading about these important theorists or, better still, consulting their own works.

For many students *Thomas Hobbes* (1588–1679) is swiftly identified with his aphorism that life is 'solitary, poor, nasty, brutish and short', though more than one examination candidate has rendered this as 'nasty, *British* and short'. (He lived an extraordinarily *long* life and was something of a fitness fanatic!) What he actually said (in his famous work, *Leviathan*) was that this was the condition of man *before the social contract*, i.e., in his natural state. Natural law teaches us the need for self-preservation: law and government are required if we are to protect order and security. We therefore need, by the social contract, to surrender our natural freedom in order to create an orderly society. Hobbes, it is now widely thought, adopts a fairly authoritarian philosophy which places order above justice. In particular, his theory (indeed, his self-confessed objective) is to undermine the legitimacy of revolutions against (even malevolent) government.

For Hobbes every act we perform, though ostensibly kind or altruistic, is actually self-serving. Thus when I give a donation to charity, it is in fact a means of enjoying my power. In his view any account of human action, including morality, must acknowledge our essential selfishness. In *Leviathan* (a book that Oxford University publicly burnt as a seditious tract!) he wonders how we might behave in a state of nature, before the formation of any government. He recognises that we are essentially equal, mentally and physically: even the weakest has the strength to kill the strongest.

This equality, he suggests, generates disagreement. And we tend to quarrel, he argues, for three main reasons: competition (for limited supplies of material possessions), distrust, and glory (we remain hostile in order to preserve our powerful reputations). As a consequence of our propensity toward disagreement, Hobbes concludes that we are in a natural state of perpetual war of all against all, where no morality exists, and all live in constant fear:

> In such condition, there is no place for industry, because the fruit thereof is uncertain; and consequently no culture of the earth, no navigation, nor use of the commodities that may be imported by sea; no commodious building, no instruments of moving and removing such things as require much force; no knowledge of the face of the earth, no account of time, no arts, no letters, no society; and which is worst of all, continual fear and danger of violent death; and the life of people, solitary, poor, nasty, brutish, and short.

Until this state of war ceases, everyone has a right to everything, including another person's life. Hobbes argues that from human self-interest and social agreement alone, one can derive the same kinds of laws which natural lawyers regard as immutably fixed in nature. He re-defines traditional moral terms (such as right, duty, liberty and justice) so as to reflect his account of self-interest and the social contract. In order to escape the horror of the state of nature, Hobbes concludes peace is the first law of nature:

> That every person ought to endeavour peace as far as he has hope of obtaining it; and when he cannot obtain it, that he may seek and use all helps and advantages of war; the first branch of which rule contains the first and fundamental Law of Nature, which is, To seek peace and follow it; the second, the sum of the right of nature, which is, By all means we can, to defend ourselves.

The second law of nature is that we mutually divest ourselves of certain rights (such as the right to take another person's life) so to achieve peace. This mutual transferring of rights is a contract and is the basis of moral duty. I undertake to forfeit my right to steal your property in return for a similar promise from you. In this way we transfer these rights to each other and hence fall under a duty not to steal from each other. For purely selfish reasons we mutually transfer these and other rights, for this will terminate the state of war between us. Such contracts, he concedes are not generally binding, for, if I live in fear that you will breach your side of the bargain, no genuine agreement exists.

Hobbes derives his laws of nature deductively: from a set of general principles, more specific principles are logically derived. His general principles are:

(1)   that people pursue only their own self-interest,
(2)   the equality of people,
(3)   the causes of quarrel,
(4)   the natural condition of war,
(5)   the motivations for peace.

From these five principles he derives the two laws mentioned above, as well as several others. He is under no illusion that merely concluding can secure peace. Such agreements need to be honoured. This is Hobbes's third law of nature.

Hobbes acknowledges too that since we are selfish we are likely, out of self-interest, to breach contracts. I may break my agreement not to steal from you when I think I can evade detection. And you know this. The only certain means of avoiding this breakdown in our mutual obligations, he argues, is to grant unlimited power to a political sovereign to punish us if we violate our contracts. And again it is for purely selfish reasons (ending the state of nature) that motivates us to agree to the establishment of an authority with the power of sanction. But he insists that only when such a sovereign exists can we arrive at any objective determination of right and wrong.

Hobbes supplements his first three Laws of Nature with several other substantive ones such as the fourth law (to show gratitude toward those who comply with contracts). He concludes that morality consists entirely of these Laws of Nature which are arrived at though the social contract. This is, as you will have noticed, a rather different rendition of natural rights from that espoused by classical natural law. But his account might be styled a modern view of natural rights, one that is premised on the basic, the mundane right of every person to preserve his own life: a free-market version of natural rights. But one that may have a message for us in our turbulent world.

A different position is adopted by *John Locke* (1632–1704) who argued that far from being the nightmare portrayed by Hobbes, life before the social contract was almost total bliss! One major defect, however, was that in this state of nature property was inadequately protected. For Locke, therefore (especially in *Two Treatises of Civil Government*), it was in order to rectify this flaw in an otherwise idyllic natural state that man forfeited, under a social contract, some of his freedom. Strongly reminiscent of Aquinas's central postulates. Locke's theory rests on an account of man's rights and obligations under God. It is a fairly complex attempt to explain the operation of the social contract and its terms, but be sure to have — at least — a grasp of two important precepts in Locke's theory. First, its *revolutionary* nature: when a government is unjust or authoritarian, Locke acknowledges the right of 'oppressed people' to 'resist tyranny' and overthrow the government: 'a tyrant has no authority'. Secondly, he attaches considerable importance to man's right to *property*: God owns the earth and has given it to us to enjoy; there can therefore be no right of property. But by mixing his labour with material objects, the labourer acquires the right to the thing he has created. This view exercised an important influence on the framers of the American constitution with its emphasis upon the protection of property. Locke has thus been at once hailed as the source of the idea of private ownership and vilified as the progenitor of modern capitalism. For Locke, the state exists to preserve the natural rights of its citizens. When governments fail in this task, citizens have the right — and sometimes the duty — to withdraw their support and even to rebel. Though strongly influenced by Hobbes, he rejected his view that the original state of nature was 'nasty, brutish, and short', and that individuals through a social contract surrendered — for their self-preservation — their rights to a supreme sovereign who was the source of all morality and law. The social contract, in his view, preserved the natural rights to life, liberty, and property, and the enjoyment of private rights: the pursuit of happiness — engendered, in civil society, the common good.

Whereas for Hobbes natural rights are logically prior and natural law is derived from them, Locke derives natural rights from natural law, that is from reason. While Hobbes discerns a natural right of every person to every thing, Locke's natural right to freedom is circumscribed by the Law of Nature and its injunction that we should not harm each other in 'life, health, liberty, or possessions'.

Locke espoused a limited form of government: the checks and balances among branches of government and the genuine representation in the legislature would, in his view, minimise government and maximise indvidual liberties.

Natural law plays less of a central role than does the social contract in the works of *Jean-Jacques Rousseau* (1712–78). More metaphysical than either Hobbes or Locke. Rousseau's conception of the social contract (in *Social Contract*) rests on the idea that it represents an agreement between the individual and the community by which he becomes part of what Rousseau calls the 'general will'. There are, in Rousseau's theorem, certain natural rights that cannot be removed, but, by investing the 'general will' with total legislative authority, the law could infringe upon these rights. As long as government represents the 'general will' it may do almost anything.

Rousseau, while committed to participatory democracy, is also willing to invest the legislature with virtually untrammelled power by virtue of its reflecting the 'general will'. It has become trite to remark that he is therefore a paradox: a democrat and yet a totalitarian.

THE DECLINE OF NATURAL LAW IN THE 19TH CENTURY

Broadly speaking, two principal developments contributed to this decline. First, the rise of legal positivism (considered in chapter 3), and secondly, noncognitivism in ethics (see page 106). You will not need to be reminded of the assault on natural law led, in particular, by Bentham who was scathingly dismissive of Blackstone's espousal of natural law. For Bentham the assertion that human law derives its validity from natural law was a means of fending off the sort of criticism of the law that he so skilfully made. Yet even Blackstone was unable to provide an actual *instance* of the law of England being regarded as invalid because it conflicted with natural law. It is sometimes thought, therefore, that Bentham was attacking a paper tiger. Moreover, the reply of natural lawyers (and not merely natural lawyers: see chapter 6) is that when we make a statement about the law we are normally also making a statement about morality. The question of what is the law is inextricably bound up with moral considerations. As Finnis puts it (*Natural Law and Natural Rights*, p. 290):

> The tradition of natural law theorising is not concerned to minimise the range and determinacy of positive law or the general sufficiency of positive sources as solvents of legal problems.
> Rather, the concern of the tradition ... has been to show that the act of 'positing' law (whether judicially or legislatively or otherwise) is an act which can and should be guided by 'moral' principles and rules; that those moral norms are a matter of objective reasonableness, not of whim, convention, or mere 'decision'.

The second development generally associated with the decline of natural law is the proposition that in moral reasoning there can be no rational solutions: we cannot *objectively* know what is right or wrong (noncognitivism in ethics). It was David Hume (1711–76) who, in his *Treatise of Human Nature*, first remarked that moralists seek to derive an *ought* from an *is*: we cannot conclude that the law should assume a particular form merely because a certain state of affairs exists in nature. Thus the following syllogism, according to this argument, is *invalid*:

> All animals procreate (major premise).
> Human beings are animals (minor premise).
> Therefore humans *ought* to procreate (conclusion).

Facts about the world or human nature cannot be used to determine what *ought* to be done or not done.

Finnis agrees with Hume that arguments of the above type are invalid. He refutes the claim that classical natural law theory (as expounded by Aristotle and Aquinas) ever sought to derive an 'ought' from an 'is' in this way. Read Finnis, *Natural Law and Natural Rights*, pp. 33–42, for a powerful defence of this position.

THE REVIVAL OF NATURAL LAW THIS CENTURY

A number of factors have contributed to a reawakening of natural law theory in the 20th century. Without providing a comprehensive account of this development here, the following six factors (in no particular order) seem to constitute the major landmarks in this evolution:

(a)   The post-war recognition of *human rights* and their expression in declarations such as the Charter of the United Nations, the Universal Declaration of Human Rights, the European Convention on Human Rights, the Declaration of Delhi on the Rule of Law of 1959. Natural law is conceived of, not as a 'higher law' in the constitutional sense of invalidating ordinary law, but as a *yardstick* against which to measure positive law. Thus the Universal Declaration of Human Rights speaks of its terms merely as a 'common standard of achievement' (or, in the French text, a 'common ideal to be achieved').

(b)   The impact of the *Nuremberg trials* which established the principle that certain acts constituted 'crimes against humanity' regardless of the fact that they did not offend against specific provisions of the positive law. The judges in these trials did not appeal explicitly to natural law theory, but their judgments represent an important recognition of the principle that the law is not necessarily the sole determinant of what is right.

(c)   The *neo-Kantianism* of Rudolf Stammler (1856–1938) and Giorgio Del Vecchio (1878–1970) who developed the idea of natural law 'with a variable content' (its principles are relativistic and evolving), and Gustav Radbruch (1878–1949) who, until the horrors of the Nazi regime, was a legal positivist, and then advanced the argument that 'the idea of law can be nothing but the achievement of justice ... [which] like virtue, truth and beauty is an absolute value'. Radbruch is discussed by Professors Hart and Fuller in (1958) 71 Harv LRev 593 and 630 respectively — the so-called Hart-Fuller debate. (For a very useful analysis of Radbruch's thoughts see B. v. D. van Niekerk (1973) 90 SALJ 234.) These jurists were neo-Kantian in the sense that they developed, in different ways, theories of law as 'justice' which envisaged the historical realisation of a community of rational, autonomous agents.

(d)   The *neo-Thomism* now best known to English-speaking lawyers in the works of John Finnis (see below).

(e)   The development of *constitutional safeguards* for human or civil rights in various jurisdictions (e.g., the American Bill of Rights and its interpretation by the United States Supreme Court, especially the Warren Court in the 1950s; the West German Basic Law.

(f)   The natural law theory of Lon Fuller (in *The Morality of Law*, especially ch. 3, and (1958) 71 Harv LRev 630) and Hart's 'minimum content of natural law' (in *The Concept of Law*, ch. 9, and (1958) 71 Harv LRev 593). See chapter 4.

This is merely a sketch. You will obviously have examined the terrain in greater detail.

JOHN FINNIS

Though he disclaims originality, and describes his book as 'introductory' Finnis's *Natural Law and Natural Rights* constitutes a major restatement of classical natural law theory that is, I think, unique in its application of analytical jurisprudence to a body of doctrine usually considered to be its polar opposite. Again, there is no substitute for reading the original (though parts of the book are heavy going), a long extract from which may be found in *Lloyd's Introduction to Jurisprudence*, pp. 163–84. You should not only be in a position to state Finnis's seven 'basic forms of human flourishing' and his nine 'basic requirements of practical reasonableness' (which most students find little difficulty in memorising and scrawling down). Note that Lloyd pays far too little, if any attention to the latter. It is important to grasp the *purpose* of this enterprise. In particular, it represents a rejection of Hume's conception of practical reason which holds that every reason for action is merely ancillary to our *desire* to attain a certain objective. Reason merely informs us how best to achieve our desires; it cannot tell us *what* we *ought* to desire. Instead, Finnis adopts an Aristotelian starting-point: *what constitutes a worthwhile, valuable, desirable life?* His list of seven 'basic forms of human flourishing':

1   Life
2   Knowledge
3   Play
4   Aesthetic experience
5   Sociability (friendship)
6   Practical reasonableness
7   'Religion'

is an attempt to answer that question. Combined with his nine 'basic requirements of practical reasonableness':

1 The active pursuit of goods
2 A coherent plan of life
3 No arbitrary preference among values
4 No arbitrary preference among persons
5 Detachment and commitment
6 The (limited) relevance of consequences: efficiency within reason
7 Respect for every basic value in every act
8 The requirements of the common good
9 Following one's conscience

these constitute the universal and immutable 'principles of natural law'.

Finnis argues that this approach accords with the general conception of natural law espoused by Thomas Aquinas. It does not, he claims, fall foul of the noncognitivist strictures of Hume (see above) for these objective goods are *self-evident*; they are not deduced from a description of human nature. So, for example, 'knowledge' is self-evidently preferable to ignorance. And even if one were to seek to deny this (how often is one tempted to assert that 'ignorance is bliss'?), it could only be done by accepting that one's argument is a useful one; one is therefore accepting that knowledge is indeed good! You thus apparently fall into the trap of self-refutation. Some critics have, however, responded that in arguing against the proposition that knowledge is an objective good you could be accepting that knowledge is valuable when put to a certain *use* (i.e., instrumentally), but that when it consists in the acquisition of useless information it is not necessarily an objective good (see N. E. Simmonds, *Central Issues in Jurisprudence*, p. 66).

Do not simply swallow Finnis's assumptions unthinkingly. You will gain considerably more from a critical reading of his analysis (even if you finally come to agree with it) than from committing to memory his seven basic goods plus nine basic requirements of practical reasonableness as if it were a mathematical formula. Many students have found, for instance, Finnis's model of the family to be idealised, his politics too conservative, his basic goods too restrictive (doesn't the common good require the 'right to *work*'?). Finnis has conceded, in later writings, that his third basic good should have been: skilful performance in *work* or play. But do not lose sight of his general project. The quotation from Finnis on page 99 illustrates, I think, his purpose: to understand 'what is really good for human persons'. For Finnis, before we can pursue human goods we require a *community*. This explains his view (mentioned above) that unjust laws are not simply nullities, but — because they militate against the common good — lose their direct moral authority to bind. Similarly, it is by an appeal to the common good that Finnis develops his conception of justice. For him principles of justice are no more than the implications of the general requirement that one ought to foster the common good in one's community. The basic goods and methodological requirements are clear enough to prevent most forms of injustice; they give rise to several absolute obligations with correlative absolute natural rights:

> There is, I think, no alternative but to hold in one's mind's eye some pattern, or range of patterns, of human character, conduct, and interaction in community, and then to choose such specification of rights as tends to favour the pattern, or range of patterns. In other words, *one needs some conception of human good, of individual flourishing in a form (or range of forms) of communal life that fosters rather than hinders such flourishing.* One attends not merely to character types desirable in the abstract or in isolation, but also to the quality of interaction among persons; and one should not seek to realise some patterned 'end-state' imagined in abstraction from the processes of individual initiative and interaction, processes which are integral to human good and which make the future, let alone its evaluation, incalculable. (*Natural Law and Natural Rights*, pp. 219–20, emphasis added.)

This important passage encapsulates much of the essence of Finnis's conception of natural rights including the rights not to be tortured, not to have one's life taken as a means to any further end, not to be lied to, not to be condemned on knowingly false charges, not to be deprived of one's capacity to procreate, and the right 'to be taken into respectful consideration in any assessment of what the common good requires' (p. 225).

Remember that a crucial element in Finnis's explanation of natural law is his insistence that its first principles are (contrary to the widely held view *not* deductively inferred from facts, speculative principles, metaphysical propositions about human nature or about the nature of good and evil, or from a teleological conception of nature. *They are not derived from anything; they are underived.* Aquinas, according to Finnis, makes it clear that each of us 'by experiencing one's nature, so to speak, from the inside' grasps 'by a simple act of non-inferential understanding' that 'the object of the inclination which one experiences is an instance of a general form of good, for oneself (and others like one)' (p. 34). For Aquinas, to discover what is morally right is to ask, not what is in accordance with human nature, *but what is reasonable.*

This restatement of classical natural law theory has been (and will continue to be) considerably influential. Finnis brings his impressive scholarship to bear on a subject that has for too long been surrounded in mystery and generalisation. There have, inevitably, been a number of criticisms made of Finnis's views. Some have claimed that his interpretation of Thomist philosophy is mistaken; he has replied, and the argument continues. More importantly, there is a question mark that, for some critics, hangs over Finnis's account of *law*. Thus for Lloyd (*Introduction to Jurisprudence*, p. 127):

> Finnis is a social theorist who wants to use law to improve society. His arguments for law thus, not surprisingly, centre on its instrumental value. The focal meaning of law concentrates on what it achieves, not what it is. As a result of this orientation we are left with the suspicion that Finnis gives us no substantial reason why social ordering through law is the most appropriate way of organising political life, that it has, in other words, the greatest moral value.

I am not sure that this is a fair criticism, but it would be a provocative quotation for use in an examination question.

THE EXAMINATION

It would not be unreasonable to expect an examination question which invites you to consider the nature, development and influence of natural law. Indeed, it would be an odd examiner who omitted this subject from his paper altogether. Even more likely, however (and more interesting), is a question that calls for an analysis of the differences between natural law and positivism — either in general or with reference to specific practical issues (such as disobedience to unjust laws). Knowing what questions to expect is, of course, the least problematic aspect of the beleaguered jurisprudence student's life! Far more challenging is to know how to *answer* the questions! More has probably been written on the natural law/legal positivism dichotomy than on any other subject in legal theory. Faced with this prodigious literature, how should you prepare for the examination?

You will, of course, have attended all lectures on the subject (and prepared for them in the manner I suggested in chapter 1). If you have read the materials mentioned in the course of this chapter, as well as any other texts which your lecturer has recommended, you will wish to prepare a summary of the principal aspects of legal positivism and natural law. You will also (I hope) have read chapters 3 and 4 of this book. This much is obvious. But an immediate problem presents itself: when called upon to write an essay on the natural law/legal positivism debate, you will be expected to discuss these theories *at a different level of generality* than if you were answering a question on, say, Hart's concept of law. It would be absurd (and impossible) if you were to attempt to discuss the *general* theory of legal positivism in the detail that you would discuss, say, Hart's version of it. Similarly, you would not approach a general discussion of natural law with the same attention to detail that you would give to a question on Finnis. It is therefore essential that you are equipped to answer *both* types of question.

The essay that requires a detailed analysis of a particular jurist or even a concept within his theory (e.g., the *Grundnorm*) is, I think, less difficult than the kind we are considering now. You will, in this sort of essay, be expected to identify the salient issues that advance your argument or comparison. It will not be especially helpful, therefore, in a question requiring an analysis of the Hart-Fuller debate, for you to spend pages explicating Hart's primary and secondary rules or Fuller's 'inner morality' of law. You will, of course, want to *mention* these elements in outlining their general account of law, but you would reserve a detailed exposition for a question which was confined to the specifics of their respective legal theories. Naturally, this is a matter of individual judgment; there are no hard and fast rules. I can only tell you that one of the chief complaints of jurisprudence examiners is that vast quantities of 'irrelevant' material are dished up (often quite accurately and intelligently written) in response to questions which are quite explicit in what they require.

I suggest that you organise your material in such a way that you do not have to spend valuable time during the examination sorting out what is relevant to a particular question. The most efficient method of doing this is to *prepare* notes on each of the major issues that arise when comparing the two theories. You might, for instance, divide the subject under the following headings:

(a)   Source and validity of law.
(b)   This is/ought dichotomy.
(c)   Unjust laws: Hart-Fuller.
(d)   Unjust laws: disobedience.
(e)   Common ground.

This may not enable you to answer *any* question posed (we must leave some room, for the examiner's imagination and ingenuity) but it will certainly facilitate a readier and more realistic method of coping with what is, after all, an artificial three-hour test of your understanding.

Suppose that the question merely quotes a general statement (such as Dias's view that in the controversy between natural law and legal positivism on the relation of law to morality, the two sides have been 'shadow-boxing on different planes') and asks you whether you agree. This might be read as an invitation to discuss *every* feature of this debate. Resist such an interpretation. When in doubt assume a *narrow* construction (see chapter 2). Instead of diving headlong into a panoramic exposition of even the *relevant* points of disagreement identified above, consider carefully whether you can either support or refute the sentiments expressed in the quotation. In what respects might it be said that the pugilists are merely 'shadow-boxing'? Are you able to show that they do genuinely join issue? If so, can you demonstrate the manner and form of this disagreement (e.g., in their different approaches to the study of law)? What *practical* consequences flow from the dispute? You need to be selective; by all means *mention* the practical issues you regard as important (e.g., Nazi laws, disobedience to law) but *tell the examiner* that, in your opinion, for example, the different positions adopted by the two theories constitutes a *real* point of conflict in respect, say, of the moral attitude to law. You may then show how and why this is so by considering in some detail the different perspectives of, say, Finnis and Raz, on this question (usefully reviewed by R. Gavison (1982) 91 Yale LJ 1250). Concede (to illustrate how balanced and thoughtful you are) that in certain respects, say, their approaches to the rule of law, the two accounts have more in common than they have in conflict.

A useful starting-point for any such comparison is Professor Raz's identification (in *The Authority of Law*, p. 37 ff.) of three principal claims made by positivists and attacked by natural lawyers:

(a)   The *'social thesis'*: that law may be identified as a social fact, without reference to moral considerations.

(b)   The *'moral thesis'*: that the moral merit of law is neither absolute nor inherent, but contingent upon 'the content of the law and the circumstances of the society to which it applies'.

(c)   The *'semantic thesis'*: that normative terms such as 'right' and 'duty' are not used in moral and legal contexts in the same way.

Raz accepts only the 'social thesis'. He does so on the basis of the three accepted criteria by which a legal system may be identified: its efficacy, its institutional character and its sources. From all three, moral questions are excluded. Thus, the institutional character of law means simply that laws are identified by their relationship to certian institutions (e.g., the legislature). Anything (however morally acceptable) not admitted by such institutions is not law, and vice versa. For Raz it is a stronger version of the 'social thesis' (the 'sources thesis') that is the essence of legal positivism. His principal justification for the sources thesis is that it accounts for a fundamental function of law, namely, the setting of standards by which we are bound, in such a way that we cannot excuse our non-compliance by challenging the rationale for the standard.

It is largely upon his acceptance of the social thesis (and his rejection of the moral and semantic theses: see Raz, *The Authority of Law*, p. 155 ff.) that Raz builds his argument that there is no general moral obligation to obey the law. In arriving at this conclusion he rejects three common arguments made for the moral authority of law. First, it is often argued that to seek (as positivists do) to distinguish between law and other forms of social control is to neglect the *functions* of law; and because functions cannot be described in a value-free manner, any functional account of law must involve moral judgments — and so offend the social thesis. Raz shows that, while law does indeed have certain functions, his own analysis of them is value-neutral.

Secondly, it is frequently claimed that the *content* of law cannot be determined exclusively by social facts: so, for example, since courts inevitably rely on explicitly moral considerations, they insinuate themselves into what the law *is*. Raz, though he acknowledges that moral concerns do enter into adjudication, insists that this is unavoidable in any source-based system. But it does not, in his view, establish a case against the source thesis. Finally, it is sometimes suggested that one of the characteristics of law is that it conforms to the ideal of the rule of law. This, it is argued, demonstrates that the law is moral. Raz refutes this proposition by arguing that while conformity to the rule of law reduces the abuse of executive power, it does not confer an independent moral merit upon the law. For him the rule of law is a *negative* virtue for the risk of arbitrary power is created by the law itself. Raz therefore concludes (*The Authority of Law*, p. 233 ff.) that even in a just legal system there is no prima facie duty to obey the law.

The legal positivism of Raz may be contrasted with the natural law theory espoused by Finnis who (as we have seen) bases his conception of law on the requirements of practical reasonableness. Yet there are several respects in which the apparently conflicting theories of legal positivism (*à la* Raz) and natural law (*à la* Finnis) share a common ground. Four examples will suffice here. First, as Finnis himself acknowledges, his approach is informed by the tradition of analytical jurisprudence. Secondly, they both seek to examine and justify the authority of law. Thirdly they both subscribe to the view that there is no prima facie moral obligation to obey an unjust law. Fourthly, they both accept the importance of the ideal of the rule of law.

There are, of course, a number of important differences between the two approaches. For a recent perceptive comparison see D. Beyleveld and R. Brownsword, 'The practical difference between natural-law theory and legal positivism' (1985) 5 Oxford J Legal Stud 1 (a careful working-through of this essay is an excellent means of advancing — and testing — your understanding of the principal features of both standpoints, their differences and similarities). Three instances will suffice here. First, at the most general level, legal positivists contend that there is no necessary connection between law and morality (see the discussion of Hart in chapter 4 above). Natural lawyers, of course, reject this view. Secondy, most positivist accounts of law tend to be descriptive and analytical, while natural lawyers are concerned, in the main, with evaluating society and law. This leads, thirdly, to different views concerning the relationship between practical reason and the moral point of view as an aspect of practical reason (and this may have a number of practical consequences). A good, short (and eminently readable) account of this question is Neil MacCormick's essay, 'Contemporary legal philosophy: the rediscovery of practical reason' (1983) 10 J Law & Soc 1.

This is merely a rough sketch of some of the possible issues you may pursue in answering a question of this kind. There are, of course, stronger and weaker versions of both approaches, and your account should acknowledge these gradations (which cannot be discussed here). You will, I hope, have noticed that the emphasis in the suggested answers is on fairly specific discussion of ideas or jurists. Few things are more irritating to an examiner than to be told (as if it were a revaluation!) that 'natural law is different from positivism' followed by a tedious recital of banal facts ('Hart is a leading positivist') without a proper examination of how this 'difference' is manifested both conceptually and in practice. You *cannot* provide an exhaustive account of the debate (even *outside* of the examination) so be *selective* — always *telling* the examiner that you will confine your analysis to X, Y and Z.

And the X, Y and Z are really up to you. Be sure to demonstrate that you have a sound grasp of the two theoretical positions, but then develop your answer in a way that reflects your own interests and, of course, preparation (see page 16 ff.). You may want to look at the problem of the grudge-informer (as explored by Hart and Fuller; you will find a good exposition of the issue in J. Finch, *Introduction to Legal Theory*, ch. 3) or the problems of obedience to law (see J. Harris, *Legal Philosophies*, ch. 16) or the question of the moral position of a judge in an unjust legal system (which I have attempted to examine in 'Judges and injustice' (1984) 101 SALJ 266 and 'Judging judges' (1984) 101 SALJ 295) and in an essay 'Judges and moral responsibility' in W. Sadurski (ed.), *Ethical Dimensions of Legal Theory*. Don't waffle. Be specific.

FURTHER READING

Aquinas, Thomas, Saint, *Summa Theologica* in *Selected Political Writings*, transl. J. G. Dawson, ed. P. D'Entrèves (Oxford: Basil Blackwell, 1970 (Reprint of 1959 ed.)).

Aristotle, *Nichomachean Ethics*, transl. H. Rackham (London: William Heineman, 1938) (Loeb Classical Library).

Augustine, Saint, *City of God*, transl. W. C. Greene (London: William Heinemann, 1960) (Loeb Classical Library).

Augustine, Saint, *Confessions*, transl. W. Watts (London: William Heinemann, 1912) (Loeb Classical Library).

Cicero, M. T., *De Re Publica*, transl. C. W. Keyes (London: William Heinemann, 1928) (Loeb Classical Library)

Detmold, M. J., *The Unity of Law and Morality: A Refutation of Legal Positivism* (London: Routledge & Kegan Paul, 1984).

Finnis, John (ed.), *Natural Law* (Aldershot: Dartmouth, 1991).

Finnis, John, *Natural Law and Natural Rights* (Oxford: Clarendon Press, 1980).

Fuller, Lon Luvois, *The Morality of Law*, rev. ed. (New Haven, Conn; London: Yale University Press, 1969).

George, Robert P. (ed.), *The Autonomy of Law: Essays on Legal Positivism* (Oxford: Clarendon Press, 1995).

George, Robert P. (ed.), *Making Men Moral: Civil Liberties and Public Morality* (Oxford: Clarendon Press, 1993).

George, Robert P. (ed.), *Natural Law Theory: Contemporary Essays* (Oxford: Clarendon Press, 1994)

Hacker, P. M. S., and Raz, J. (eds), *Law, Morality and Society: Essays in Honour of H. L. A. Hart* (Oxford: Clarendon Press, 1977).

Hobbes, Thomas, *Leviathan*, ed. M. Oakeshott (Oxford: Basil Blackwell, 1960).

Hume, David, *A Treatise of Human Nature*, ed. L. A. Selby Bigge, 3rd ed. rev. by P. H. Nidditch (Oxford: Clarendon Press, 1978).

Locke, John, *Two Treatises of Government*, ed. P. Laslett (Cambridge: Cambridge University Press, 1964).

MacCormick, Neil, *H. L. A. Hart* (London: Edward Arnold, 1981).

Passerin D'Entrèves, Alessandro, *Natural Law: An Introduction to Legal Philosophy*, 2nd ed. (London: Hutchinson, 1970).

Summers, Robert S., *Lon L. Fuller* (Stanford, Calif: Stanford University Press, 1984).

6 THE ASSAULT ON LEGAL POSITIVISM: DWORKIN

Since succeeding to Herbert Hart's Oxford chair in jurisprudence, Ronald Dworkin has become by far the most tenacious and articulate critic of legal positivism and, in particular, Hart's own version of it. But he is a great deal more. There is little doubt that he has, almost single-handedly, changed the face of contemporary legal theory. In a wide range of essays (collected in *Taking Rights Seriously*, hereafter called *TRS*) and in *A Matter of Principle* and in his book, *Law's Empire*, he provides not only a stimulating account of law and the legal system, but also an analysis of the place of morals in law, the importance of individual rights (see chapter 11), and the nature of the judicial function. Your jurisprudence course will, almost inevitably, devote a fair amount of time and importance to Dworkin. And you will therefore not be suprised to learn that examiners have a particular fondness for him.

What should you do? A good start would be to read *Law's Empire*. This sounds like a tall order (the book has 453 pages). But, as Dworkin's first comprehensive and systematic account of his theory, it will give you an excellent insight into his exciting (if optimistic) vision of law and provoke you (as it did me) to rethink some of the assumptions we tend to make about law, justice and morality. At the very least, read chs 1, 3, 6, 7 and 11. This chapter will give you the essential elements of Dworkin's theory of law. But, be warned! His is a complex and subtle account which makes unexpected twists and turns into economics, politics and even literary theory. It has, moreover, generated an enormous critical response which has, in turn, evoked spirited defences from Dworkin (and these are often the most illuminating — and entertaining — aspect of Dworkin's writing). A useful collection of criticism (and Dworkin's replies) is M. Cohen, *Ronald Dworkin and Contemporary Jurisprudence* (1983) and Stephen Guest's recent book, *Ronald Dworkin* (1992) is a very helpful discussion of his theory.

A BIRD'S-EYE VIEW

It might be useful if Dworkin's theory — at its most general level — is summarised. I shall then consider some of its more important facets in slightly greater detail. Note that our principal concern here is Dworkin's assault on legal positivism; other aspects of his theory are considered elsewhere (e.g., his argument for 'rights as trumps' is examined in chapter 10).

Dworkin's starting-point might sensibly be regarded as his attack on Hart's model of rules (see chapter 4). You will recall that an article of Hart's faith is the conceptual apartheid of law and morality. For Hart (and other legal positivists) we gain a clearer understanding of law by maintaining, for the purpose of analysis, a separation between the law as it *is* and the law as it *ought* to be. To Dworkin this is unacceptable and, indeed, impossible. This is because law consists not merely of rules (as Hart would have us believe) but also of what Dworkin calls 'non-rule standards'. When a court has to decide a hard case it will draw on these (moral or political) standards — principles and policies — in order to reach a decision. There is no rule of recognition which distinguishes between legal and moral principles. A judge in a hard case therefore must appeal to principles which will include his own conception of what is the best interpretation of the 'great network of political structures and decisions of his community' (*Law's Empire*, p. 245). He must ask 'whether it could form part of a coherent theory justifying the network as a whole' (loc. cit.). In other words, there is always one 'right answer' to every legal problem; it is up to the judge to find it. This answer is 'right' in the sense that it coheres best (or 'fits') with the institutional and constitutional history of the law. Legal argument and analysis is therefore *interpretive* in character.

The theory is premised on Dworkin's concern that the law ought to 'take rights seriously'. If (as Hart claims) the outcome of a hard case turns on the judge's own view or intuition or 'strong discretion', rights are rendered fragile things to be sacrificed by courts at the altar of community interests or other conceptions of goods. If individual rights are to be treated with the respect they deserve, they (i.e., in effect, principles) are to be accorded proper recognition as *part of the law*. This leads Dworkin (*inter alia*) to deny the positivist separation between law and morals; to reject the proposition that judges either do or should *make* law; to argue that judges must seek 'the soundest theory of law' on which to decide hard cases; and to conclude that, since judges (who are unelected officials) do not make law, the judicial role is democratic and prospective.

This is merely the skeleton of the principal features of Dworkin's system. And most students gasp in disbelief (or is it bewilderment?) when they first encounter its provocative claims. Yet many is the student, in my experience, who, after the initial shock and some serious reading of Dworkin, finds himself or herself, if not a hard-line Dworkinian, then certainly sympathetic to the general tenor of the theory.

THE ASSAULT ON POSITIVISM

While his assault on Hart's model of rules provides the springboard for Dworkin's denunciation of legal positivism, in *Law's Empire* he mounts a more comprehensive onslaught on what he calls 'conventionalism' (which includes the 'semantic sting' of positivism). Conventionalism rests on two main claims. First, it argues that law is a function of *social convention* which it then designates as *legal convention*. In other words, it argues that law consists in no more than respecting certain conventions (e.g., decisions of the House of Lords are binding on lower courts). Secondly, it conceives law as incomplete: there are 'gaps' in the law which judges fill by reference to their own predilections — i.e., judges have a 'strong discretion'. In one sense, according to Dworkin, the semantic theories of legal positivists (see chapters 3 and 4) differ from full-blown or 'strict' conventionalism: the former argue that the description of law as convention is recognised and applied *by virtue of the very vocabulary of law*; the latter, however, adopts an *interpretive* conception of law. So semantic theories are linguistic and logical; conventionalists are willing to concede that we need to interpret the behaviour of lawyers and judges in order to determine what they *should* do.

The importance of Dworkin's attack on conventionalism, in general, and legal positivism, in particular, lies in the failure of such theories to provide either a convincing account of the process of law-making or a sufficiently strong defence of individual rights. Consider the important decision of *McLoughlin v O'Brian* [1983] 1 AC 410. You will doubtless recall (from your tort course) that the plaintiff in that case learned, at home, from a neighbour that her husband and four children had been injured in a motor-car accident. The neighbour drove her to the hospital where she found her husband and sons screaming and seriously injured, and was told that her daughter was dead. She suffered nervous shock and sued, among others, the defendant driver whose negligence had caused the accident. As the law stood, a plaintiff could recover damages for nervous shock only where he or she had actually witnessed the accident or arrived on the scene immediately thereafter. The House of Lords, reversing the decision of the Court of Appeal, unanimously held that, despite precedents to the contrary, the plaintiff, Mrs McLoughlin, *could* recover damages for nevous shock. On 'policy' grounds, the Law Lords held that there was nothing in the law to prevent the plaintiff from succeeding.

Though it is not easy to discern the *ratio* of the case (for there are certain differences between the five judgments in their view of the proper role of policy) it is clear that, in formulating the law, the House of Lords arrived at a decision on the basis of what it regarded as the law. Now, according to Dworkin, a conventionalist would say that in this case (which he uses, along with three others, to illustrate his point) there is *no law* and that the judge must therefore exercise a *discretion* and make new law which is then applied *retrospectively* to the parties in the case. For Dworkin, however, '... propositions of law are true if they figure in or follow from the principles of justice, fairness, and procedural due process that provide the best constructive interpretation of the community's legal practice' (*Law's Empire*, p. 225). Thus, in *McLoughlin* v *O'Brian* deciding whether the plaintiff should recover involves deciding whether legal practice is seen in a 'better light' if we assume the community has accepted the principle that people in her position are *entitled* to receive compensation. In other words, in Dworkin's vision of 'law as integrity' (see page 100), a judge must think of himself not (as the conventionalist would have it) as giving voice to his *own* moral or political convictions (or even to those convictions which he thinks the legislature or the majority of the electorate would approve), but 'as an author in the chain of common law' (*Law's Empire*, pp. 238–9). As Dworkin put it (*Law's Empire*, p. 239):

> He knows that other judges have decided cases that, although not exactly like his case, deal with related problems; he must think of their decisions as part of a long story he must interpret and then continue, according to his own judgment of how to make the developing story as good as it can be.

There is, therefore, 'no law beyond the law'; contrary to the positivist thesis, there are no 'gaps' in the law. Law and morals are inextricably intertwined. There cannot therefore be a rule of recognition by which to identify what is 'law'. Nor does law 'as a union of primary and secondary rules' provide an accurate model, for it fails to account for principles and policies. For a spirited defence of the rule of recognition against Dworkin's attack, read Matthew H. Kramer, 'Coming to Grips with the Law (1999) 5 *Legal Theory* 171.

PRINCIPLES AND POLICIES

In addition to rules (which 'are applicable in an all-or-nothing fashion') there are 'principles' and 'policies' which, unlike rules, have 'the dimension of weight or importance'. In other words, if a rule applies, and it is a valid rule, a case must be decided in a way dictated by the rule. A principle, on the other hand, provides a *reason* for deciding the case in a particular way, but it is not a *conclusive* reason: it will have to be *weighed* against other principles in the system. A distinction must, however, be drawn between 'principles' and 'policy'. A *'principle'* is 'a standard to be observed, not because it will advance or secure an economic, political, or social situation, but because it is a requirement of justice or fairness or some other dimension of morality' (*TRS*, p. 22). A *'policy'*, on the other hand, is 'that kind of standard that sets out a goal to be reached, generally an improvement in some economic, political, or social feature of the community' (loc. cit.). Of course, Dworkin rejects any master rule or rule of recognition by which these principles and policies gain admission to the legal system, indeed such a rule would be an impossibility for such standards 'are numberless, and they shift and change so fast that the start of our list would be obsolete before we reach the middle. Even if we succeeded, we would not have a key for law because there would be nothing left for our key to unlock.' (*TRS*, p. 44.)   Principles describe *rights*; policies describe *goals*. It is part of Dworkin's argument for 'taking rights seriously' that he contends that rights have a 'threshold weight' against community goals; this is his theory of 'rights as trumps' (see chapter 10). If we are to respect individual rights, he argues, they must not be capable of being squashed by some competing community goal. The central question in any litigation is whether the plaintiff has a 'right to win'; not whether the community's interests should be satisfied. Thus civil cases are, and should be, decided by reference to *principles*. And even if a judge appears to be advancing an argument of *policy*, we should read him to be referring to *principle* because he is actually deciding the individual *rights* of members of the community. As he puts it (*TRS*, p. 100):

> If a judge appeals to public safety or the scarcity of some vital resource, for example, as a ground for limiting some abstract right, then his appeal might be understood as an appeal to the competing rights of those whose security will be sacrificed, or whose just share of that resource will be threatened if the abstract right is made concrete.

In order to refute the model of rules, Dworkin asks us to consider the American case of *Riggs v Palmer* (1889) 115 NY 506, 22 NE 188. The stark question faced by the court was whether a murderer could inherit under the will of his victim. The will was validly executed and was in the murderer's favour. But the law was uncertain: the *rules* of testamentary succession provided no applicable exception. So, on the face of it, the murderer should have a right to get his money. The New York court held, however, that the application of the *rules* was subject to the *principle* that 'no man should profit from his own wrong'. Hence a murderer could not inherit from his victim. Dworkin argues that this decision demonstrates that, in addition to rules, the law includes *principles*.

HERCULES AND HARD CASES

Having disposed of the model of rules, Dworkin invites us to concentrate our attention on what actually happens in a 'hard case'. We have already seen that these cases, to which no rule is immediately applicable, require the judge, in Dworkin's thesis, to deploy standards other than rules (since, by definition, no rule applies). For this purpose he appoints Hercules, a judge 'of superhuman skill, learning, patience and acumen' (*TRS*, p. 105). Hercules is expected to 'construct a scheme of abstract and concrete principles that provides a coherent justification for all common law precedents and, so far as these are to be justified on principle, constitutional and statutory principles as well' (*TRS*, pp. 116–17). Where the legal materials allow for more than one consistent reconstruction, Hercules will decide on the theory of law and justice which best coheres with the 'institutional history' of his community.

Both Hercules and the notion of a 'hard case' have attracted (as we shall see) a certain amount of criticism. Hercules J is a much misunderstood fellow. Several critics have sought to show that he is both megalomaniac and myth. These allegations will be considered later, but it is important at this stage to recognise Hercules for what he is (or, more accurately, what his creator intended him to be). He is postulated as a hypothetical model; Dworkin does not expect us, save in our imagination, to believe that he inhabits any actual bench. He is a useful *idea* because he sets a standard by which real judges might measure their performance: 'He is more reflective and self-conscious than any real judge need be or, given the press of work, could be' (*Law's Empire*, p. 265). As for the concept of a 'hard case', you should be clear what Dworkin means by such cases. They are those cases which deal with a fundamental proposition of law, the outcome of which lawyers disagree. Some critics have attacked the primacy which Dworkin accords to such cases in describing the judicial function. What about *easy* cases? But a close reading of Dworkin will reveal that, while Hercules may well deploy his grand theory in easy cases, it is in hard cases when such theory really displays its cutting edge. In other words, the idea of the 'hard case' is, like Hercules, a paradigm case which focuses our attention on the judicial role in its most graphic and most important form.

ONE RIGHT ANSWER

The proposition that there is, to every legal problem, only one right answer, never fails to stop students in their tracks. This, they inevitably protest, is nonsense. Surely, they cry, there are at least two possible outcomes, neither of which can be said with any certainty to be the correct one. But (as already pointed out above) Dworkin's model of adjudication points unequivocally to the idea that, in his pursuit of coherence and integrity, Hercules will find the best answer to the legal question before him. That answer will be the right one. And there can be only *one* answer that 'fits' most comfortably; there must therefore be only one right answer. It is only a size 8 shoe that fits my foot. Neither a 7 ½ nor an 8 ½ is the correct size. There is only one right size. If my own analogy seems a little obscure, try Dworkin's: Tal's smile. In the course of a chess tournament one of the players (Tal) smiles inanely at his opponent who (unsmilingly) objects. The referee must decide whether smiling is in breach of the rules of chess. The rule book is silent. He must therefore reflect upon the nature of chess: it is a game of intellectual skill; does this include the use of psychological intimidation? He must, in other words, find the answer that best 'fits' the general theory and practice of chess. To this question there can be only one right answer. A more entertaining (true) chess tournament (see box, on p. 126) raises the same question of principle. And this is equally true of the judge deciding a hard case. What is more, lawyers *accept* that there is only one uniquely correct result to any legal dispute. When giving advice, a lawyer does not say 'This will is neither valid nor invalid'; it is either one or the other. He too, bases himself on an interpretation of the law (precedents, statutes, doctrine) and this enables him to give an answer that best represents the state of the law as he finds and understands it.

THE RIGHTS THESIS

It should be clear by now (and this question is further explored in chapter 10) that Professor Dworkin grounds his legal theory on a version of liberalism which he describes as springing from the proposition that 'government must treat people as equals'. By this he means that it 'must impose no sacrifice or constraint on any citizen in virtue of an argument that the citizen could not accept without abandoning his sense of equal worth' ('Why liberals should care about equality', in *A Matter of Principle*, p. 205). This leads Dworkin (in a series of essays) not only to adopt a liberal position on a number of specific issues (e.g., whether the criminal law should enforce private morality (it should not); whether wealth is a value (it is not); whether reverse discrimination is immoral (it is not)), but also to 'define and defend a liberal theory of law' (*TRS*, p. vii) which informs his assault on positivism, conventionalism, and pragmatism (which he defines as resting on the claim that 'judges do and should make whatever decisions seem to them best for the community's future, not counting any form of consistency with the past as valuable for its own sake' (*Law's Empire*, p. 122)). Pragmatists look to efficiency or justice as the guiding light for judges. None of these theories of law provides an adequate defence of individual rights. It is only 'law as integrity' (see page 126) which supplies a proper buttress against the encroachment by instrumentalism upon individual rights and general liberty.

The extent to which you should familiarise yourself with Dworkin's particular jurisprudence on the wide range of contemporary issues he has

FUNNY OLD WORLD

○ "I would have won the tournament if Ngan's breasts had not led me astray," declared Robert Crowley after being eliminated from the South Australian state chess championships. "Every time she moved a piece, she leaned forward and deliberately flashed her boobies at me, and I lost my concentration. That is the only reason she was able to fork me with her bishop."

Defending her appearance, twenty-four-year-old Miss Ngan Koshnitsky said: "Yes, I like wearing sexy clothes, with revealing tops that show off my cleavage,

but so what? What I wear at tournaments shouldn't be an issue at all. It makes me angry that he didn't think I was good enough to win. I believe most men just can't accept losing against a woman."

But Crowley was unrepentant. "It was only her flesh that beat me. Those clothes were suitable for a disco, not a chess tournament. I did everything I could to resist. I even put my hands across my forehead and turned my head, but that didn't work. If I ever have to play her again, I shall have to consider wearing a wide-brimmed hat." *(Brisbane Courier Mail, 2/4/98. Spotter: Norm Reynolds)*

From *Private Eye*, 1 May 1998.

written about will, of course, depend on the importance attached to them in your course. But they are valuable as practical applications of the rights thesis and therefore, even if they are not explicitly dealt with in your course, your reading at least some of them will give you a better, rounder understanding of Dworkin.

LAW AS LITERATURE

Think of a novel you have recently read. Did you *like* it? Why? What is the author *saying*? What does the novel mean to you? Your answer to these sorts of questions reveal your *interpretation* of the work of art in question. And such interpretation is essentially *constructive*: it seeks to discover the author's *purpose* in writing the book, and to give the *best* account possible. In interpreting a work of art, we are trying to *understand* it in a particular way. We are, moreover, attempting to depict the book (or painting, film, poem) *accurately* — as it really is, not 'through rose-coloured glasses'. We are, in other words, in search of the actual, historical intentions of the author, not foisting our values on the author's creation.

Now, what has all this to do with law? Why this detour into literary theory? Dworkin argues (see especially ch. 2 of *Law's Empire* and 'How law is like literature', in *A Matter of Principle*, p. 146) that law is, like literature, an 'interpretive concept'. Judges are like interpreters of an unfolding novel: they 'normally recognise a duty to continue rather than discard the practice they have joined. So they develop, in response to their own convictions and instincts, working theories about *the best interpretation of their responsibilities under that practice.*' (*Law's Empire*, p. 87; emphasis added.) So, Dworkin seems to be saying, in the same way as you and I might disagree about the *real* meaning intended by a novelist in his work, two judges might disagree about 'the soundest interpretation of some pertinent aspect of judicial practice' (loc. cit.).

If this suggestion strikes you as a little obscure or far-fetched, consider Dworkin's 'courtesy' example (*Law's Empire*, pp. 46–86) which seeks to apply this form of interpretation to a *social* practice. He asks us to imagine a community whose members follow a set of rules which they call 'rules of courtesy'. Various such rules exist requiring, for instance, that peasants doff their caps to nobility. Over a period of time members of the society begin to develop certain attitudes toward these rules: they assume that the rules have a certain *value* (i.e., they serve some purpose) independent of their mere existence, and they regard the requirements of courtesy as flexible — the strict rules need to be adapted or modified to meet changing needs. Once people have made these two assumptions, they have adopted an 'interpretive' view of courtesy: the institution of courtesy ceases to be mechanical. Members of the community now try to impose some *meaning* on it: to view courtesy in its best light, and then to reinterpret it in the light of that meaning. If a philosopher wishes to explain this particular social practice, he would not be assisted by a theory which confined itself to a set of semantic rules which declare the proper use of the word 'courtesy'. He would fall prey to the 'semantic sting'. He can explain it only by 'imposing' a certain structure on [the] community's practice such that particular substantive theories can be identified and understood as subinterpretations of a more abstract idea' (*Law's Empire*, p. 71). In other words, his claim is 'interpretive' rather than semantic: it is not a claim about *linguistic* ground rules that everyone must follow to make sense.

And the same, argues Dworkin, is true of law. Semantic theories (such as those proffered by legal positivists) fail to explain the essence of law. Thus the so-called Hart-Fuller debate concerning whether evil 'laws' are indeed 'laws' (see chapter 5) is sterile if conducted at the *semantic* level: this merely relates to the meaning of 'law' at what Dworkin calls the 'preinterpretive' stage. It becomes a more interesting and important debate at the *interpretive* level, for then the question becomes, not one of mere semantics, but one about the *substance* of law. For someone to claim that Nazi law is not 'law' then represents a 'sceptical interpretive judgment that Nazi law lacked features crucial to flourishing legal systems whose rules and procedures do justify coercion. His judgment is now a special kind of political judgment' (*Law's Empire*, p. 104).

Judges should therefore be thought of as authors engaged in a 'chain novel', each one of whom is required to write a new chapter which is added to what the next co-novelist receives. Each novelist attempts to make a single novel out of the material he receives; he tries to write his chapter in such a way that the final product will appear to be the creation of a single writer. If he is to do this (and he wants to do the best possible job) he must have a view of the novel as it progresses: its characters, plot, theme, genre, objective. He will seek the meaning or layers of meaning in the unfolding work and an interpretation that best explains it. This stimulating analogy is part of Dworkin's vision of 'law as integrity'.

LAW AS INTEGRITY

Hercules is thus a constructive interpreter of the chapters of the law that have been written before him (though, of course, unlike the chain novel analogy, he may have written some of the chapters himself). 'Law as integrity' requires him to ask whether his interpretation of the law could form part of a coherent theory justifying the whole legal system. But where does 'integrity' come in? Dworkin does not 'define' it, but he provides a picture of its significant features:

... law as integrity accepts law and legal rights wholeheartedly.... It supposes that law's constraints benefit society not just by providing predictability or procedural fairness, or in some other instrumental way, but *by securing a kind of equality among citizens that makes their community more genuine and improves its moral justification for exercising the political power it does*.... It argues that rights and responsibilities flow from past decisions and so count as legal, not just when they are explicit in these decisions but also when they follow from the principles of personal and political morality the explicit decisions presuppose by way of justification. (*Law's Empire*, pp. 95–6, emphasis added.)

Thus, at the heart of Dworkin's theory is the age-old problem of the relationship between law and force. Law is inevitably bound up with the extent to which coercion may legitimately be used. This is a continuing theme in legal positivism, natural law and certain social theories (see chapters 3, 4 and 8). Dworkin argues that a society which accepts integrity as a political virtue does so, in large part, in order to justify its moral authority to assume and deploy a monopoly of coercive force. This sounds an echo of certain aspects of Weber's idea of 'legitimate domination' (see chapter 8) to whom Dworkin makes no reference. I say 'in large part' because Dworkin identifies a number of other consequences that flow from the acceptance of integrity, including protection against partiality, deceit and corruption. More importantly, integrity promotes the ideal of self-government and participation in democracy. It is, in short, an amalgam of values which form the essence of the liberal society and the rule of law.

THE ASSAULT ON DWORKIN

Law's Empire has predictably stimulated a lively debate in the literature. For a fairly comprehensive, irreverent (yet serious) critique of the whole Dworkinian enterprise, see Allan C. Hutchinson's entertaining review, 'Indiana Dworkin and Law's Empire' (1987) 96 Yale LJ 637. Cheap shots?

Little in the post-*Empire* attack is new, though the target is a large one. Dworkin's detractors adopt a variety of standpoints from which to launch their assault. They may briefly be summarised under the following heads:

(a) *The attack on Hart*. Professor Hart has described Dworkin's claim that judges do not make law as a 'noble dream' ('American jurisprudence through English eyes: the nightmare and the noble dream', in *Essays in Jurisprudence and Philosophy*, p. 123). I strongly urge you to read Hart's posthumously published 'postscript' to the second edition of *The Concept of Law* which appeared in 1994. It contains a powerful defence of his position against the attack of Dworkin. Other critics have attacked Dworkin's model in three main ways:

(i)   *Rules may incorporate principles.* Some critics (notably MacCormick and Sartorius) have sought to rescue Hart's model of rules by arguing that principles interact with rules, underpinning and qualifying them. Sartorius (while otherwise adopting Dworkin's view in this respect) argues that by 'loosening up a bit' Hart's rule of recognition, to take account of 'general results', it would provide an authoritative standard by which to identify principles as well as rules (*Individual Conduct and Social Norms*, p. 192).

(ii)   *Judges* do *have a discretion.* Dworkin acknowledges that judges have a 'weak' discretion (their decision determines the outcome of a hard case and they have to apply their judgment). But a number of critics reject the idea that judges lack a 'strong' discretion in the sense of having a *choice* between a decision X and decision Y. Some point to the ambiguity of the very concept of discretion (see B. Hoffmaster, 'Understanding judicial discretion' (1982) 1 Law & Philos 21), while others (like Professor Hart) adopt the 'unexciting' middle ground that sometimes judges do and sometimes they don't exercise a discretion! Raz even suggests that Dworkin's views are no different from Hart's! (see J. Raz, 'Dworkin: a new link in the chain' (1986) 74 Calif L Rev 1103, 1115).

(iii)   *Judges* do *rely on policy:* Several critics (notably Professor Greenawalt) deny Dworkin's claim that judges characteristically decide hard cases on grounds of principle rather than policy. The strongest plank of this argument is the proposition that judges give weight to the interests of third parties (i.e., persons who are not parties to the litigation in issue) in hard cases. For instance, Greenawalt argues that certain conduct might be legally justified because the contrary conduct would have violated or risked damage to the established legal rights of nonparties. Thus, the driver of a car who swerves to avoid a baby may argue that if he had not swerved he would have violated the baby's right. On the other hand, it might be argued that certain conduct was *unjustified* because it violated, or risked damage to, the rights of third parties ('Policy, rights, and judicial decision', in Cohen, *Ronald Dworkin and Contemporary Jurisprudence*, pp. 88–118, at p. 97). This argument also raises doubts about Dworkin's distinction between arguments of principle and arguments of policy.

(b)   *The rights thesis.* Dworkin's argument that utilitarianism does not take rights sufficiently seriously is denied by some critics who accuse Dworkin himself of working 'in the shadow of utilitarianism' (Hart, 'Between utility and rights', in *Essays in Jurisprudence and Philosophy*, p. 198, at p. 222). In particular, Hart argues that it does not follow (as Dworkin claims) that if X's liberty is curtailed, this shows that he is not being treated as an equal. For Dworkin counting 'external preferences' is a form of double counting (see chapter 10), a view rejected by Hart and others who are sympathetic to utilitarian versions of justice.

(c)   *A 'hard case' is inadequately defined.* Dworkin describes a hard case (*inter alia*) as one in which lawyers would disagree about rights, where no settled rule disposes of the case, where the rules are subject to competing interpretations. Some critics have complained that this fails to distinguish sufficiently a hard case from an easy one. The strong version of this argument suggests that Dworkin 'is committed to the view that all cases are "hard cases"' (A. C. Hutchinson and J. N. Wakefield, 'A hard look at hard cases' (1982) 2 Oxford J Legal Stud, p. 86, at p. 100). This startling conclusion is arrived at by identifying Dworkin's allegedly circular reasoning that claims:

(i)   In order to discover which cases are 'hard', Hercules must apply the principles recommended by the 'soundest theory'.

(ii)   A 'hard case' is one in which principled (as opposed to syllogistic) reasoning is employed.

(iii)   Principled reasoning must therefore be used to identify those cases which are 'hard cases'.

(iv)   Thus Hercules is committed to the view that all cases are 'hard cases'.

You will find Dworkin's response on page 121 above.

(d)   *Hercules is objectionable.* I mentioned above that critics have had difficulty in accepting Hercules. Four major objections have been voiced:

(i)   *He is a politician.* Some critics charge Hercules with substituting his own political judgment for the politically neutral, correct interpretation of previous decisions.

(ii)   *He is a fraud.* He *thinks* he has discovered the answer to a hard case, but he is fraudulently offering *his* judgment as the judgment of the law.

(iii)   *He is a tyrant.* He arrogantly assumes his conception of the law is correct, though he cannot *prove* his opinion is better than that of those who disagree.

(iv)   *He is a myth.* No real judges can behave in this Utopian style.

Each of these charges against Hercules is deflected by Dworkin (see *Law's Empire*, pp. 258–66, 397–9).

(e)   *The theory travels badly.* A number of commentators point to the limitations of Dworkin's model of law. It seems to be grounded in a liberal democratic (read American) view of society, and therefore runs into a number of difficulties when it is applied to other kinds of communities, especially 'unjust societies'. On the latter, see R. Wacks, 'Apartheid and the judicial conscience: the dilemma of the moral judge in an unjust legal system' (1988)

12 Bull of the Austr Society of Legal Philosophy 221, and R. Wacks, 'Judges and moral responsibility' in W. Sadurski (ed.), *Ethical Dimensions of Legal Theory*.

(f)   *There is no right answer.* Several critics argue that it is not true that to every legal question there is one right answer. Dworkin's claim in support of the right-answer thesis is a fairly complex one (see 'Is there really no right answer in hard cases?' in *A Matter of Principle*, p. 119), but you should have a grasp of its main elements. Note that it may be presented in *two* forms. The *first* argues that the surface linguistic behaviour of lawyers is misleading because it suggests that there is no 'logical space' between the proposition 'this is a valid contract' and the counter-proposition that 'this contract is invalid'. It does not, in other words, contemplate that *both* propositions may be false. And they could be: it might be an 'inchoate' contract. Thus the question whether the contract is valid or invalid may have *no* right answer. The *second* version does not suppose that there is any 'logical space' between the propositions that a contract is valid and that it is invalid. It does not, in other words, suppose that there is any third option. Yet it denies that one of the two possibilities *always* applies — because neither may. Dworkin employs formal logic to express these alternatives. But, as a beleaguered law student, it is unlikely that you will be expected to be a trained logician. You should, however, be able to show whether Dworkin has refuted the claim that there is no right answer.

(g)   *Law is not like literature.* Dworkin's depiction of law as an interpretive concept has been attacked by a number of critics, see for example A. D. Woozley ('No right answer', in Cohen, *Ronald Dworkin and Contemporary Jurisprudence*, pp. 173–81). See, too, Stanley Fish, 'Working on the chain gang: interpretation in law and literature' (1982) 60 Texas L Rev 551, and 'Wrong again' (1983) 62 Texas L Rev 299.

(h)   *Law as integrity is too cosy a view.* The consensual model of society implicit in the ideal that '... we should try to conceive our political community as an association of principle' (*Law's Empire*, p. 411) is likely to draw the fire of those who adopt a conflict model of society or who conceive the rule of law as an elaborate trick to conceal the oppressive nature of 'liberal' society (see chapter 9). Nor will it find favour with those critics who reject the interpretive enterprise as naïve, Utopian or simply wrong. Some regard it as a poor explanation for political obligation: see P. Soper, 'Dworkin's domain' (1987) 100 Harv L Rev 1166, 1183.

(i)   *His definition of 'law' is itself 'semantic'.* For an interesting argument along these lines, see Soper, 'Dworkin's domain', pp. 1171–6.

Needless to say, Dworkin has defended his theory (with characteristic skill) from most of these assaults. You would be well advised to look at his 'Reply to critics' in *Taking Rights Seriously* and 'A reply by Ronald Dworkin' in Cohen, *Ronald Dworkin and Contemporary Jurisprudence*, pp. 247–300. And he will be ready to resist other critics that lie in wait. You will, of course, have your *own* views to add to the list.

THE EXAMINATION

Dworkin's writing spans such a wide range of subjects that it is virtually impossible to predict where an examiner may lay his trap. Nor, of course, should you expect a question to be confined to Dworkin's theory and not require you to compare him with another jurist. In either case you will need a good understanding of the central tenets of the rights thesis, of 'law as integrity', and the other elements considered above.

A number of questions in recent examination papers have sought a critical analysis of *Hercules* and the task Dworkin assigns him in a hard case. A question of this kind would need to incorporate, at least, a discussion of:

(a) The criticism that the proposition that law as a system of rules is deficient in that it fails to account for policies and principles.

(b) The nature of and distinction between policies and principles, and how principles (as expressive of rights) are characteristically deployed by Hercules in 'hard cases' (briefly considered).

(c) The manner in which principle-based adjudication takes rights seriously.

(d) The model of law as a gapless system in which all legal problems have a right answer, i.e., the denial of judicial discretion in the strong sense.

(e) The model of 'law as integrity' and as constructive interpretation.

(f) Criticism of Hercules.

Now, it may seem that an apparently specific question requires you to traverse large tracts of Dworkin's theoretical terrain. To some extent, this is a legitimate criticism (and some examiners place wholly unrealistic demands on candidates). But, by the judicious use of emphasis, you can (and, indeed, should) avoid a wholesale restatement of Dworkin at large. You would, in a question of this kind, concentrate on the *judicial* dimension of Dworkin's theory. Of course, this element cannot easily be severed from the numerous related features of the theory: how, for instance, can you properly discuss Hercules in action without a fairly detailed description of the distinction between principles and policies? The answer is: you cannot — except in an examination! No one (not even Professor Dworkin himself) could, in 34 or even 43 minutes, provide a comprehensive answer to a question of this kind. Your examiner will realise (and you will, in any event, *tell* him) that you are constrained to be selective. While you may only *mention* point (a) and *briefly discuss* (e), you would *analyse in detail* the other points that seem to *you* to relate more directly to the issue in question.

You might, for instance, wish to stress point (d) for in *your judgment* (and that is what the examiner is seeking) Hercules owes his existence to the image of law as a 'gapless system'. Thus you might wish to enlarge on Dworkin's holistic conception of adjudication which requires Hercules to seek consistency and integrity (they are not the same thing: see *Law's Empire*, pp. 219–24) in answering the legal question before him. This encourages him to be 'wide-ranging and imaginative in his search for coherence with fundamental principle' (*Law's Empire*, p. 220). He must treat the law *as if* it were a 'seamless web'. If the plaintiff has a 'background moral right', Hercules will recognise an *institutional* right and, in turn, his *concrete* right against the defendant. But the existence of such a 'background' right will depend on a number of considerations, including the previous decisions of courts faced with similar or analogous problems. This leads to a consideration of the role of the doctrine of precedent in Dworkin's thesis — which has been the subject of some controversy. Essentially Dworkin argues that a precedent may have 'enactment' or 'gravitational' force. The effect on future cases of a judgment or opinion having *enactment* force would be limited to its precise words. A judgment or opinion with *gravitational* force has an influence that falls outside the language of the opinion: it appeals to the fairness of treating like cases alike.

This theory of precedent leads Dworkin back to the crucial distinction between the respective roles of principles and policy in hard cases. In Dworkin's words:

> If an earlier decision were taken to be entirely justified by some argument of *policy*, it would have *no* gravitational force. Its value as a precedent would be limited to its *enactment* force, that is, to further cases captured by some *particular words of the opinion*. (*TRS*, p. 113; emphasis added.)

So, in the case of decisions generated by *policy* (which, of course, are, in Dworkin's view, the proper concern of the legislature rather than the courts), there is no need for consistency. If, for example, the government decides to stimulate the economy and is able to do so, with roughly equal efficiency, by expenditure either on new roads or on housing, road construction firms would have no *right* that the former is done. There is no general argument of *fairness* in respect of government decisions which seek to serve a collective goal.

You may have some difficulty in accepting this view of the judicial process. You would, of course, discuss the various criticisms levelled at the model (see pages 125–7) and add some of your own. You might, for instance, want to question how the theory might work in an unjust or even an undemocratic society. Dworkin argues, as we have seen, from and for a liberal democratic perspective. How well would the theory travel to a fundamentally iniquitous society in which the rights which Hercules would be seeking do *not* figure as part of the law? How, for instance, might Hercules have performed in apartheid South Africa where the 'right answer' on the basis of 'institutional fit' was more than likely to be one that is destructive of rights than protective of them? Dworkin suggests that in a 'wicked society' (and he has in mind Nazi Germany and apartheid South Africa) Hercules may have no choice but to *lie*. If he is to give effect to 'law as integrity', Dworkin seems to be saying, how can Hercules reach a decision which is its very antithesis? But this is a complex matter which raises a number of difficulties (e.g., Is *apartheid* a principle or policy? Can principles be morally evil?) that (by Dworkin's own admission) he has not yet canvassed in any detail. For an attempt to scratch the surface, see R. Wacks, 'Judges and injustice' (1984) 101 SALJ 266. Cf. J. Dugard, 'Should judges resign? — A reply to Professor Wacks' (1984) 101 SALJ 286.

Another difficulty might be mentioned. What is the value of the currency of broad legal concepts of the kind in which Hercules deals? To non-American lawyers, at any rate, it sometimes seems that amorphous concepts should be resisted. Dworkin argues, for instance, that Hercules may, as part of his moral and political armoury, incorporate 'an abstract right to privacy against the State' (*TRS*, p. 117). What does this mean? At a fairly high level of generalisation, we understand the nature of this moral or political claim. But does it give us sufficient guidance as to what it entails *in law*? I am uneasy about this particular concept and the zealous application of it in American law on matters as disparate as abortion and advertising (see R. Wacks, *Personal Information: Privacy and the Law*, ch. 1), but you may be more comfortable with the generous use of this or other concepts ('due process', 'equality') than I am, when it comes to the careful recognition and protection of individual rights by the law.

You would, of course, examine some of the attacks launched upon poor Hercules by various writers (see above) and Dworkin's defence of his ideal judge. References to actual cases (*Riggs* v *Palmer, Spartan Steel & Alloys Ltd* v *Martin & Co. (Contractors) Ltd* [1973] QB 27, *McLoughlin* v *O'Brian*, or, indeed, any 'hard case' you like) would clearly enhance your answer and help to demonstrate instances of Hercules in action.

Consider the following question from a recent (Australian) examination paper:

> 'On the one hand it seems an outrage to our sense of justice to say that judges in hard cases are augmenting or amending the law. On the other hand it is an outrage to our sense of realism to deny it.'
> Discuss, with reference to Hart and/or Dworkin.

The quoted sentiments are clear enough, and the examiner obviously wishes you to discuss the subject of judicial discretion. But I don't like the conjunctive/disjunctive sting in the tail. It is hard to see how you could usefully answer the question by confining yourself to Hart. And to consider *only* Dworkin, though more logical, would be to exclude an important element of the subject of the judicial function, namely, Hart's rule of recognition and the gaps judges close in hard cases. It would be preferable to devote the major part of any question on judicial discretion to an analysis of Dworkin's theory (along the lines just described) — since he has addressed the matter far more directly, and in considerably greater detail, than Hart has. But if you should so organise your answer, will you be penalised for not dividing your discussion *equally* between Hart and Dworkin? It would be a most unreasonable examiner who expected you to interpret his 'and' in this sort of question as denoting a neat division of this kind. So I cannot see that you would be taking any risks in loading your answer in favour of Dworkin's analysis of hard cases, Hercules etc., and then examining the various criticisms levelled at it by Hart (in the context of a brief review of his legal positivism) as well as other writers. But this is not, I fear, an isolated instance of a rather unsatisfactory question which embattled students of jurisprudence are sometimes called upon to answer — or (in consequence of its ambiguity and infelicities of expression) to avoid altogether.

Drawing comparisons between the most significant features of the competing or opposing legal theories of Hart and Dworkin is *implicit* in most questions about law as a model of rules (or various versions of this claim), on the one hand, and the rights thesis (or 'law as integrity'), on the other. But you should also expect to encounter questions which *explicitly* require you to 'compare' Hart's theory (or certain aspects of it) with Dworkin's theory (or certain aspects of it). Again (as I attempted with Hart's rule of recognition and Kelsen's *Grundnorm*, page 93), you should draw a line down a page and attempt to write down all the differences you can think of between the two accounts of law.

So, for starters, you might say that for Hart, law consists of primary and secondary rules; Dworkin includes policies and principles as part of law. Secondly, Hart insists upon, while Dworkin rejects, the separation of law and morality. Thirdly, Hart adopts the 'sources thesis' in the form of a rule of recognition, which Dworkin denies. Fourthly, Dworkin argues that law constitutes a gapless, coherent network, while Hart's system of rules breathes through its gaps. Fifthly, for Hart judges sometimes make law, for Dworkin they can never be said to do so. And so on. Don't stop until you have listed at least 10 more points of differences. You will notice that all these points are related (e.g., Hart's insistence on the separation of law and morality is directly related to his concept of a rule of recognition which is directly related to his view that judges in hard cases may exercise a strong discretion, etc. etc.). And the same is true of the principal elements of Dworkin's theory. It would be surprising if this were *not* so: each jurist is seeking to present a coherent model of law. But, from a student's point of view, it emphasises the need to understand legal theories *as a whole*. It is no good merely to memorise and then, in the examination, randomly list a catalogue of points, without demonstrating the relationship between them. This has its positive side: not only will you have a much better prospect of comprehending legal theories which you approach in this way, they may actually have some *meaning* to you — and they will become far easier to remember. In fact, the greater your understanding, the less you will come to see the examination as a cruel (if not unusual) three-hour memory test.

FURTHER READING

Cohen, Marshall (ed.), *Ronald Dworkin and Contemporary Jurisprudence* (London: Duckworth, 1984).

Dworkin, Ronald, *Law's Empire* (Cambridge, Mass: London: Belknap Press, 1986).

Dworkin, Ronald, *Life's Dominion: An Argument about Abortion and Euthanasia* (London: Harper Collins, 1993).

Dworkin, Ronald, *A Matter of Principle* (Cambridge, Mass; London: Harvard University Press, 1985).

Dworkin, Ronald, *Taking Rights Seriously*, new impression with a reply to critics (London: Duckworth, 1978).

Guest, Stephen, *Ronald Dworkin* (Edinburgh: Edinburgh University Press, 1992).

Hunt, Alan (ed.), *Reading Dworkin Critically* (New York: Berg, 1992).

Marmor, Andrei, *Interpretation and Legal Theory* (Oxford: Clarendon Press, 1992).

Wacks, Raymond, *Personal Information: Privacy and the Law* (Oxford: Clarendon Press, 1989)

Wacks, Raymond, *The Protection of Privacy* (London: Sweet & Maxwell, 1980).

Wacks, Raymond, *Privacy and Press Freedom* (London: Blackstone Press, 1995).

7 LEGAL REALISM

Those who claim allegiance to the flag of legal realism might just as easily be called Sceptics (and they sometimes are) or even Cynics. Indeed, many students (especially after the arduous journey through legal positivism) find that they are in good company. The realists, they are relieved to discover, eschew the ponderous metaphysics which they discern in talk of legal concepts — be they 'commands', 'rules', 'norms' or indeed any construct which has no foundation in 'reality'. If you have been disposed to feel similarly unhappy with the 'formalism' of juristic thinking in the work of Bentham, Austin, Hart or Kelsen, you may well find succour in the movement which is (rather loosely) described as legal realism.

WHAT ARE REALISTS REALISTIC ABOUT?

It is at once apparent that though they are both 'realists' in a general sense, there are important differences (which will be returned to) between the American and the Scandinavian realists. Indeed, Friedmann goes so far as to suggest that any similarity is a purely verbal one. Yet we may legitimately group the two 'schools' together in one important respect: they both declare war on all absolute values (such as 'justice') and they are both empirical, pragmatic and, of course, 'realistic'. Nothing captures this approach better than the (oft-repeated) aphorism by one of the leading exponents of American realism, Oliver Wendell Holmes, which comes at the end of this striking extract from 'The path of the law' (1897) 10 Harv LRev 457, 460–1 (emphasis added):

Take the fundamental question, What constitutes the law? You will find some text writers telling you that it is something different from what is decided by the courts of Massachusetts or England, that it is a system of reason, that it is a deduction from principles of ethics or admitted axioms or what not, which may or may not coincide with the decisions. But if we take the view of our friend the bad man we shall find that he does not care two straws for the axioms or deductions, but that he does want to know what the Massachusetts or English courts are likely to do in fact. I am much of his mind. *The prophecies of what the courts will do in fact, and nothing more pretentious, are what I mean by the law.*

'Well said!' many a student is tempted to cry. 'Enough of this metaphysical nonsense! The law is what the courts say it is!' Or, as the Scandinavian realist, Alf Ross, put it, to invoke 'justice' is equivalent to banging on a table: it is an emotional expression which turns one's demand into an absolute postulate. This 'realism', then, is an impatience with theory, a concern with law 'as it is', and a preoccupation with the actual operation of law *in its social context*. To this extent, therefore, legal realism represents an assault on positivism: it is deeply hostile to the formalism that in their view treats law as a lifeless phenomenon. And yet, realists are — paradoxically — themselves positivists. Their preoccupation with the law 'as it is' and their almost obsessive pragmatism and empiricism mark them as advocates of what Hunt describes as 'a rather simplistic positivism' (A. Hunt, *The Sociological Movement in Law*, p. 43; ch. 3 of Hunt's book is a brief but useful assessment of the essence of American legal realism). But, though they accept, along with the positivists, the need for a scientific analysis of law, the realists reject the single avenue of logic and seek to apply the numerous avenues of scientific enquiry, including sociology and psychology. Realism, in Llewellyn's words, 'is not a philosophy — it is a technology'.

AMERICAN REALISM

The jazz age produced its jazz jurisprudence. The turn of the century saw a rejection of the formalism of Austin, Bentham, Mill and Hume. In its place, the realists sought to put a more sociological account of the 'law in action'. You ought to have a reasonably detailed grasp of the views of the three leading members of the movement: Oliver Wendell Holmes, Karl Llewellyn and Jerome Frank. Your examiner would, however, be impressed to discover (since most students confine themselves in examination answers to the big three) that you are not only aware that there were many *other* important realists, but that you know a little about their work. In particular (though a little knowledge is often a dangerous thing — even in examinations!) it would be useful for you to have a passing knowledge of the writing of some of the following (magnificently named) realists: John Chipman Gray (1839–1915), Herman Oliphant (1884–1939), William Underhill Moore (1879–1949), Arthur Linton Corbin (1874–1966) and Wesley Newcomb Hohfeld (1879–1917; see chapter 10), all of whom were pioneers of the realist movement. Professor William Twining's fine book, *Karl Llewellyn and the Realist Movement*, contains not only a brilliant account of its eponymous hero, but provides a penetrating analysis of the leading protagonists of the movement itself. It is a large work, but serious students will want, at the very least, to glance at it. It will certainly give you a much rounder picture of the genesis, history and contribution of the American realists than the general jurisprudence textbooks.

For present purposes it will suffice to consider briefly the big three. This will be followed by a short consideration of the theory and methodology of the movement and its influence.

A sensible starting-point is Llewellyn's important essay 'Some realism about realism' (1931) 44 Harv LRev 1222, in which he identifies nine 'points of departure' common to the realists. This is a useful statement (by one of the movement's leading exponents) of its 'manifesto' which may be summarised as follows:

(a) The conception of *law in flux*, of moving law, and of judicial creation of law.

(b) The conception of law *as a means to social ends*, and not as an end in itself.

(c) The conception of *society in flux* — faster than law.

(d) The *temporary divorce of 'is' and 'ought' for the purpose of study*.

(e) *Distrust of traditional legal rules and concepts* as descriptive of what courts or people actually do.

(f) *Distrust of the theory that traditional prescriptive rule formulations are the main factor* in producing court decisions.

(g) The belief in grouping cases and legal situations into *narrower categories*.

(h) An insistence on evaluating the law in terms of its *effects*.

(i) An insistence on *sustained and programmatic attack* on the problems of law.

Holmes

Holmes (1841–1935) was very much the intellectual and perhaps even the spiritual father of American realism. Any analysis of his work (that is not confined to his several provocative and colourful maxims about logic, experience, bad men and prophecies) must include at least three central elements. First, Holmes, as a Supreme Court Judge, was (not surprisingly) a profound believer in defining the law by reference to what the courts actually said it was. This is especially evident in his famous address 'The path of the law' which he delivered to law students in 1897. He warned them to distinguish clearly between law and morality: consider what the law is, not what it ought to be (shades of legal positivism). Secondly, in developing this view, he introduces the device of the 'bad man' (see page 134): 'If you want to know the law and nothing else, you must look at it as a bad man, who cares only for the material consequences which such knowledge enables him to predict' (*Collected Legal Papers*, p. 171, quoted by Twining, *Karl Llewellyn and the Realist Movement*, p. 17). Thirdly, Holmes firmly believed that legal developments could be scientifically justified: the 'true science of law', he argued, 'consists in the establishment of its postulates from within upon accurately measured social desires instead of tradition' (*Collected Legal Papers*, pp. 225–6). For him history was less important than economics.

Llewellyn

Karl Nickerson Llewellyn (1893–1962) deserves your closest attention. An extraordinary man (he was a keen and fairly accomplished poet) and scholar, his contribution to American realism was formidable. I urge you to consult Twining's book for a careful and sympathetic portrait, but if this is, as Holmes described the study of Roman law, 'high among the unrealities', you should, at the very least, read the extracts in *Lloyd's Introduction to Jurisprudence* from Twining's book (pp. 723–9) and, needless to say, the generous extracts from Llewellyn's own work (pp. 686–723).

The most significant aspect of Llewellyn's contribution to realism is his *functionalism*. This approach, which runs through his major works, *The Bramble Bush* (1930), *The Cheyenne Way* (with E. A. Hoebel) (1941) and *The Common Law Tradition* (1961), at its simplest, perceives law as serving certain fundamental functions: 'law-jobs'. We should, he argues, regard law as an engine 'having purposes, not values in itself' ('A realistic jurisprudence — the next step' (1930) Colum LRev 431). If society is to survive, certain basic needs must be satisfied; this engenders conflict which must be resolved. Six 'law-jobs' are identified:

(a) adjustment of trouble cases;
(b) preventive channelling of conduct and expectations;
(c) preventive rechannelling of conduct and expectations to adjust to change;
(d) allocation of authority and determination of procedures for authoritative decision-making;
(e) provision of direction and incentive within the group;
(f) 'the job of the juristic method'.

The focal concept of this functionalist account of law is the 'institution' of law which performs various jobs: an institution is, for Llewellyn, an organised activity built around the doing of a job or cluster of jobs. And the most important job the law has is the disposition of trouble cases. As he puts it in *The Bramble Bush* (p. 3):

> This doing of something about disputes, this doing of it reasonably, is the business of law. And the people who have the doing in charge, whether they be judges or sheriffs or clerks or jailers or lawyers, are officials of the law. *What these officials do about disputes is, to my mind, the law itself.*

Though he was later to revise this radical assertion, it captures his preoccupation with law as a 'technology' rather than a 'philosophy'.

In addition to *major* institutions (which are concerned with *fundamental* jobs or job clusters upon which the existence of society depends), there are also *minor* institutions such as *crafts*. These consist of the skills that are held by a body of specialists; the practice of the law is a craft. In *The Common Law Tradition* he applies the concept of a craft to the juristic method of the common law. From your study of Llewellyn's work you will be familiar with his famous distinction between the grand style and the formal style of judicial opinions. The former is 'the style of reason' which is informed by 'policy' considerations, while the latter is logical and formal and seeks refuge in rules of law. He, needless to say, prefers the grand style and the 'situation sense' which is its hallmark. It is not part of his argument that either of these styles are to be found in pure form at any point in history. Instead, he paints a picture in which there is an oscillation between the two. Thus, in the early part of the 19th century, when American law was at its creative height, the grand style was employed. From the middle of the 19th century, however, Llewellyn detects a shift toward the formal style. In the middle of the 20th century, Llewellyn finds evidence of a swing back to the grand style, a development he applauds as 'the best device ever invented by man for drying up that free-flowing spring of uncertainty, conflict between the seeming commands of the authorities and the felt demands of justice' (*The Common Law Tradition*, pp. 37–8).

Llewellyn's work has attracted criticism from a variety of standpoints. Thus, by insisting on the universality of his 'law-jobs', Hunt argues that he 'stumbles into a major theoretical deficiency of functionalism of imposing on disparate phenomena, from different societies and different historical periods, an a priori unity' (*The Sociological Movement in Law*, p. 50). And even Twining concedes that the grand style/formal style dichotomy has its drawback for 'it may be as dangerous and misleading to pigeon-hole judges or courts into styles as it is to lump jurists into schools' (*Karl Llewellyn and the Realist Movement*, p. 212). What are we to understand by 'situation sense', which is the pot of gold at the end of the grand style of judicial reasoning? Note that Llewellyn does not suggest (contrary to Ronald Dworkin: see chapter 6) that there is 'one right answer' to every legal question. Indeed, he devotes a large section of *The Common Law Tradition* (pp. 226–32) to rejecting this idea. The subject is not without difficulty and his concept has been widely misunderstood (see Twining, *Karl Llewellyn and the Realist Movement*, pp. 216–29). According to Llewellyn, the result of a case is to be judged by reference to whether it is '... something which can be hoped, or thought, to look reasonable to any thinking man' (*The Common Law Tradition*, p. 277). There is an element of vagueness and speculation in Llewellyn's analysis here. Or at least that is what it seems to one reader. You will have your own views.

Frank

Jerome Frank (1889–1957) was the most 'radical' of the American realists. He is generally associated with the distinction he drew (first in *Law and the Modern Mind* (1930: the same year as Llewellyn's *The Bramble Bush*), but developed in later works such as *Courts on Trial* (1949)) between 'rule-sceptics' (who include Llewellyn, and who were afflicted with 'appellate court-itis') and 'fact-sceptics' (among whom he counted himself), who were concerned to uncover the unconscious forces that affect the discovery and interpretation of the *facts* of the case. For Frank, most realists, in their preoccupation with appellate courts, missed the important aspect of un-predictability in the judicial process: the elusiveness of *facts*. Thus the various prejudices of judges and jurors ('for example, plus or minus reactions to women, or unmarried women, or red-haired women, or brunettes, or men with deep voices, or fidgety men, or men who wear thick eyeglasses, or those who have pronounced gestures or nervous tics' (*Law and the Modern Mind*, p. xiii) often crucially affect the outcome of a case. Read the extract from *Courts on Trial* in *Lloyd's Introduction to Jurisprudence*, pp. 683–6. The main thrust of Frank's attack was directed against the idea that certainty could be achieved through legal rules. This, in his view, was absurd. If it were so, he argued, why would anyone bother to litigate? Even where there is an applicable rule, one of two opposite conclusions is possible. To illustrate the point he gives the example of the division that existed among members of the Supreme Court in 1917 concerning the validity of a particular statute. In 1923 the court, by a majority, ruled that the statute was invalid. But between these two dates the membership of the court had changed several times. Indeed, had the matter been heard between November 1921 and June 1922, the outcome would have been the opposite. In other words, the answer to the question of the statute's validity turned, not on the certainty of the applicable rule, but on the personnel of the court. We *want* the law to be certain, he suggested, because of our deep need for security and safety which is endemic to children. In the same way as a child places his trust in the wisdom of his father, so we seek in the law and other institutions a similar comforting security. We should, he urged, grow up!

Frank is certainly the most accessible of the realists, indeed, as Twining puts it, '... clever rather than wise, a dilettante intellectual rather than a scholar, a brilliant controversialist, but somewhat erratic in his judgments, in his juristic writings Frank exhibited the strengths and weaknesses of a first-class journalist' (*Karl Llewellyn and the Realist Movement*, p. 379). Few students will complain about this!

The American Realist Method

American realism, as Hunt points out, is powerfully informed by a behaviouralist view of law. This 'behaviour orientation' is evident in the work of all the leading members of the movement. Thus Llewellyn suggests that the focus of study should be 'shifted to the area of contact, of interaction, between official regulatory *behaviour* and the *behaviour* of those affecting or affected by official regulatory *behaviour*' ('A realistic jurisprudence — the next step' (1930) 30 Colum LRev 431, more easily found in Llewellyn, *Jurisprudence: Realism in Theory and Practice*, pp. 3–41, at p. 40, emphasis added). And similar declarations are to be found in the writings of Frank, Oliphant, and Yntema (see Hunt, *The Sociological Movement in Law*, p. 54). What does this mean? Behaviourism concentrates on the attempt to describe and explain *outward manifestations* of mental processes and other phenomena that are not directly observable and measurable. Thus behavioural psychology is concerned principally with the measurement of legal, and especially, judicial *behaviour*. And this is especially evident in the realists' near-obsession with 'prediction'. Have a look at Moore, Underhill et al., 'Law and learning theory: a study in legal control' (1943) 53 Yale LJ 1. The modern development of judicial behaviouralism in the sixties is well described by Glendon Schubert, in his book, *Judicial Behavior*.

It is hard to deny Hunt's observation that in their quest for a 'legal science', the American realists (with the exception of Llewellyn) exhibited a narrow empiricism: 'a vast amount of energy was burnt up in the collection of data' (*The Sociological Movement in Law*, p. 55). According to Hunt, empiricists believe incorrectly that the collection of data is a sufficient condition for the development of a social science method. 'Data collection becomes an end in itself; it becomes a purposeless and undirected activity' (pp. 55–6). And charges of 'naïve realism', 'barefoot empiricism' and, most recently, 'pragmatic instrumentalism' (see R. Summers, *Instrumentalism and American Legal Theory*, p. 20) and 'profound conservatism' (see B. Ackerman, *Reconstructing American Law*) are levelled at the realists from other quarters as well. It would be a good idea for you, in your reading of the leading realists, to consider how valid these criticisms are. What of Lloyd's observation in earlier editions (but omitted from the latest) that 'nothing very startlingly fresh has emerged ... beyond what the reasonably progressive and socially-minded lawyer might already have accepted as axiomatic' (*Lloyd's Introduction to Jurisprudence*, 5th ed., p. 687)? Or Hunt's remark that 'In a very real sense we *are* all realists now if only in the most general context of recognising the need to view law in its social context' (*The Sociological Movement in Law*, p. 59)? The realist challenge to the autonomy of law was certainly an important precursor of the critical legal studies and postmodernist approaches to law and the legal system discussed in chapter 10. The relationship between the realist movement and sociological jurisprudence is also a strong one (see chapter 8). Indeed, in Twining's view:

> ... the main achievement of the realist movement was to concretise sociological jurisprudence.... Perhaps the most important lesson to be learned from a study of realism is a partial answer to the question: What difference can it make in practice to adopt a sociological (or realist or contextual) approach to law? (*Karl Llewellyn and the Realist Movement*, p. 383.)

You cannot therefore see realism in a vacuum. Its connections with psychology, anthropology, economics and sociology are clear enough, but it has even been provocatively suggested (by Professor Twining) that there is more in common between Bentham and Llewellyn than may at first appear. A *rapprochement* of this kind is not only intellectually challenging, but it presents some fertile ground for the more imaginative jurisprudence examiner!

THE SCANDINAVIAN REALISTS

A deep distrust of metaphysical concepts (which was exhibited by both the American realists and legal positivists) reaches its apogee with the Scandinavian realists. In the words of one of its leading (and more accessible) members, Professor Alf Ross (1899–1979), 'all metaphysics are a chimera and there is no cognition other than empirical'. We have already encountered some of the limitations of empiricism; in the case of the Scandinavians, it is not so much that they are empiricists, but that they are more than willing to consign anything that smacks of metaphysics (especially 'justice') to the category of 'meaningless'. This, as Professor Hart points out (in his review of Ross's *On Law and Justice* [1959] CLJ 233, reprinted in Hart, *Essays in Jurisprudence and Philosophy*, p. 161), leads to some 'absurdities':

Surely it is wrong to say ... that the words 'just' and 'unjust' applied to a
legal rule as distinct from a particular decision are 'devoid of meaning'.
When we assert that a rule forbidding black men to sit in the public park is
unjust we no doubt use, as our criterion of just treatment, the unstated
principle that, in the distribution of rights and privileges among men,
differences in colour should be neglected.

Few students will want to dissent from Hart's comment. But it seems to
dispose, far too easily, of the position adopted (and defended with remarkable tenacity) by the Scandinavian realists and, in particular, their founding
father, Axel Hägerström (1868–1939).

Hägerström went so far as to deny that any legal rule could be said to 'exist'.
Such a statement presupposes that things could exist in a non-natural sense.
And this, in his view, is nonsense. Talk of 'rights' and 'duties', is therefore
meaningless since these phenomena are not rooted in actual sense experience,
but are hangovers from primitive law in which they were imbued with magical
significance. His refusal to regard legal concepts as anything more than
fantasies of the mind is at the heart of the philosophies of his leading disciples,
Alf Ross (1899–1979), Karl Olivecrona (1897–1980), and A. V. Lundstedt
(1882–1955). Few examiners expect you to have a detailed knowledge of all of
these jurists, and are likely to be satisfied with a general grasp of the principal
tenets of the two writers (Ross and Olivecrona) who have had a reasonably
influential 'reception' in English-speaking countries. (I must confess that, save
for the inevitable — though entirely unintended — laughs that his book, *Legal
Thinking Revised*, provides, I do not expect my students to spend very much time
attempting to unravel the impenetrable thoughts of Lundstedt. The laughs,
incidentally, come from this jurist's breathtaking arrogance and egotism. Read
the opening pages for some hilarious examples. But, for a sympathetic, and very
useful, analysis (especially of his notion of 'social welfare'), see C. Munro, 'The
Swedish missionary: Vilhelm Lundstedt' [1981] JR 55.)

Essentially, Lundstedt regarded law as little more than the fact of social
existence in organised groups, and the conditions that enable us to coexist.
All metaphysical thinking is rejected. Legal rules are merely 'labels' which,
torn from their context of legal machinery, are meaningless scraps of paper.
It cannot be said that *because* of a certain rule, a legal duty arises, for this is to
support a *metaphysical* or normative relationship which can never be proved.
All jurists (save him) are guilty of a fundamental error: they regard the sense
of justice as inspiring the law, whereas, in fact, the opposite is true. Law is
determined by 'social welfare' (which includes the minimum requirements
of material life, security of person and property, and freedom of action).
Jurisprudence must be a *natural* science based on empiricism.

The most obvious criticism of Lundstedt is that his concept of 'social
welfare' is no less metaphysical than any of the notions he attacks. For

Friedmann there is little new in Lundstedt's view 'except the author's claim to originality' (*Legal Theory*, p. 310).

It is especially the work of Ross that has proved to be of most interest and importance.

Alf Ross

In the light of the impact of his work outside Scandinavia, you would be well advised to look at Ross's leading work, *On Law and Justice*, though there is much of value in *Directives and Norms* and his essay 'Tu-tu' (1957) 70 Harv LRev 812. Useful extracts from all three may be found in *Lloyd's Introduction to Jurisprudence*, pp. 769–81.

Ross (in *On Law and Justice*, pp. 13–18) asks us to imagine a game of chess. A third person is watching the two players. If he is ignorant of the rules, he will probably realise some kind of game is being played, but he will not be able to follow what is happening: the moves mean nothing, there is no connection between them. Social life, argues Ross, is like chess in that many individual actions are connected to a set of common conceptions of rules. It is this consciousness of the rules that facilitates our understanding of (and even our ability to predict) the course of events. The primary rules of chess (e.g., that a pawn may move only forward) are *directives* which are accepted by each player as socially binding: he knows that he can only move his pawns according to the rules, and he knows that if he does not abide by this rule he will be met by a protest by his opponent. If, however, he merely makes a poor move no protest is likely to follow! The primary rules are therefore distinguished from the 'rules of skill contained in the theory'. Ross then asks how we can establish *which* directives govern the game of chess. Merely to watch games being played (i.e., to adopt a behaviourist approach, see page 115) would clearly be inadequate: 'Even after watching a thousand games it would still be possible to believe that it is against the rules to open with a rook's pawn' (*On Law and Justice*, p. 15). The easiest method would be to consult textbooks on chess or rulings given at chess congresses. But this might not be adequate either: such declarations might not be adhered to in practice.

The only way, therefore, to find out which rules govern chess is to adopt an 'introspective method': we need to know which rules are actually felt by the players to be binding on them. And we can test this by watching to see whether such rules are actually effective in the game and are outwardly visible as such. The concept of 'validity' in chess thus contains two elements: the effectiveness of the rule as established by observation, and the extent to which the rules are regarded as binding. Ross recognises, of course, that the rules of chess have no 'reality' apart from the experience of the two players. Thus in the concept 'rule of chess' we have two elements: the experienced ideas of certain patterns of behaviour, and the abstract contents of those ideas (the 'norms' of chess). He concludes that the norms of chess 'are the abstract idea content (of a directive nature) which make it possible, as a scheme of interpretation, to understand the phenomena of chess ... as a coherent whole of meaning and motivation, a game of chess; and, along with other factors, within certain limits to predict the course of the game' (*On Law and Justice*, p. 16).

What has all this to do with law? No one with any degree of perception would seek to reduce the complex concept of law to the level of a game — or would they? Game theory has a reasonably respectable place in economics and other social sciences, and the Cambridge philosopher, Wittgenstein, employed 'language games' as a means of illuminating the use of words. In developing his central idea of 'valid law', Ross argues that the concept 'valid norm of chess' provides a useful model. In the same way as the seemingly random moves of chess acquire a coherence once we apply the 'scheme of interpretation' of the valid norms of chess, many human activities have meaning only when we apply the 'scheme of interpretation' of valid legal norms. Thus he defines 'valid law' as 'the abstract set of normative ideas which serve as a scheme of interpretation for the phenomena of law in action, which again means that these norms are effectively followed, and followed because they are experienced and felt to be socially binding' (*On Law and Justice*, p. 18).

This attempt to exclude metaphysical questions from the determination of 'valid law' is justified by Ross by saying that no one would:

> ... think of tracing the valid norms of chess back to an *a priori* validity, a pure idea of chess, bestowed upon man by God or deduced by man's eternal reason. The thought is ridiculous, because we do not take chess as seriously as law.... But this is no reason for believing that logical analysis should adopt a fundamentally different attitude in each of the two cases. (*On Law and Justice*, p. 18.)

This sideswipe at the theory of natural law is not, however, particularly persuasive. Surely, there is nothing in the rules of chess (as opposed to those of law) which could conceivably *prompt* such an analysis; the players are happy to accept the rules and thus metaphysical questions are irrelevant.

You will have noticed that in drawing this analogy, Ross acknowledges the normative character of law, but uses the term 'directives' to describe legal propositions. He nevertheless insists that such directives refer only to the law *actually in force*; other statements that purport to describe the law (e.g., in legal textbooks) are merely propositions *about* the law, not *of* law. And therefore the study of the rules of law in action consists of assertions even though it is normative — for it is *about* norms.

His notion of 'valid law' is not, however, confined to the issuing of directives. There is, in addition, a 'psychological point of view' (*Directives and*

Norms, p. 90) which is experienced by officials (especially judges) — it is not necessary for the people at large to experience this acceptance of validity. This recognition of the 'internal' aspect of law ought to sound echoes in your mind of Hart's 'critical reflective attitude' (see chapter 4). But Hart has himself (in the essay mentioned above, [1959] CLJ 233, reproduced in his *Essays in Jurisprudence and Philosophy*) pointed to an important distinction between the two: Ross 'misrepresents the internal aspect of rules as a matter of 'emotion' or 'feeling' — as a special psychological 'experience' ' (*Essays in Jurisprudence and Philosophy*, p. 166).

Ross was strongly influenced by Hägerström's logical positivism: the view that statements have meaning only if the propositions they express are capable of proof or verification. This, of course, accounts for Ross's hostility to metaphysical questions. And, more than any of his Scandinavian colleagues, he focuses a good deal of his analysis on judicial behaviour and its predictability. In this respect he seems to be working at the same seam as his American counterparts. But, as J. W. Harris points out, Ross differs from them by his insistence that decisions which concur with pre-existing rules demonstrate that the rules effectively control the decisions: if they did not, they could not be verified. Harris puts the distinction well (*Legal Philosophies*, p. 102):

> Ross and Frank agree that it is my lawyer's business to predict what courts will do; but Frank says that they are to beware of rules as grounds for prediction, whilst Ross says rules 'exist' just because they are good grounds for prediction.

Of course, as several critics have been quick to point out, when *a judge* declares that the law is X *he* is not predicting anything.

Karl Olivecrona

A more radical attack on metaphysics is to be found in Olivecrona's *Law as Fact*, which, as its title suggests, argues that law 'exists' in a *factual* sense only: words are printed on pieces of paper or internalised in people's minds, but their significance is that they form a link in the chain of causation which results in certain courses of behaviour. In simple terms, law is little more than a form of psychology — it is a *symbolic expression* for the fact that the human mind responds in certain ways to various forms of social pressure. Given our psychological make-up and educational conditioning, certain behaviour patterns result. Lawyers and officials read the laws enacted by the legislature and, by virtue of their conditioning, they are induced to act in particular ways: the judge decides X, the policeman enforces X. When a revolution takes place, the revolutionaries seize the legal machinery and exert, through propaganda, psychological pressures on the people. As a result of their conditioning, members of society simply carry on as before. He concedes (with Kelsen) that a monopoly of force is required in order for the psychological basis of law to be *effective*, but suggests that once the new regime is established, the coercive element may be pushed into the background and applied only in exceptional circumstances. In most cases the psychological conditioning suffices. This account of the nature of law also provides Olivecrona with an ingenious explanation of both the origin of law and the relationship between law and morality. Law is, as we have just seen, originally coercive — sanctions are provided for infractions of rules. Individuals are then faced with the choice between compliance and disobedience. In time, this process becomes too onerous for most of us so that both the temptation of committing the act in question, on the one hand, and the fear of the possible sanction, on the other, are sublimated or repressed into our subconscious mind. In our conscious mind we simply retain an imperative *symbol* such as 'You shall not!' The rule has therefore been internalised and there is now normally no need for the threat of coercion. As soon as the idea of, say, stealing, enters our head, an unconditional order rings in our ears: 'Stealing is wrong!' This, of course, implies that the creation of new imperatives assumes that some legal system *already exists*. Hence it is, in his view, a futile enterprise to attempt to trace law to its ultimate source; the origin of law is simply a matter of *fact*. And to the argument that what jurists generally seek is not law's actual historical origin as much as the source of its *validity*, Olivecrona replies that this is a meaningless, metaphysical abstraction which has no foundation in *fact*.

This (somewhat idiosyncratic) account of the genesis of law leads him, secondly, to reverse the usual view that the law reflects moral values. Olivecrona suggests that the law is, in fact, the progenitor of many of our moral standards. We are, at an early age, conditioned into accepting that certain conduct is unlawful — the stamp of 'illegality' lends these rules a particular power. We quickly learn to internalise these rules and they then come to be our standards of morality. But surely, you will want to cry, the reform of our laws often springs from a genuine, unselfish desire to improve the lot of society—morality thereby affecting law rather than the reverse. Olivecrona's reply seems to be that law reformers are moved by enlightened self-interest. He could, I suppose, even claim that they are themselves subjected to the same psychological propaganda issuing from the law — thus completing the vicious circle!

For Olivecrona, rules of law are 'independent imperatives': propositions in imperative form (as opposed to statements of fact) but they do not issue — like commands — from particular persons (cf. Austin and Bentham, chapter 3). He gives the example of the Ten Commandments: it cannot be said that *Moses* is issuing the commands — the words are said to be the commands of God. But, as he puts it in the 1939 edition of *Law as Fact* at p. 43 (the passage seems to be omitted from the second edition of 1971):

In reality the Decalogue is a bundle of imperative sentences, formulated several thousand years ago and carried through the centuries by oral tradition and in writing. *They are nobody's commands, though they have the form of language that is characteristic of a command.*

The rules of law are of a similar character. (Emphasis added.)

This is not, however, a crucial element in his theory as, for him, laws only 'exist' in the sense already described (words on paper or in minds).

Critique

The above is, I need hardly point out, only a sketch of the essential features of the jurisprudence of Ross and Olivecrona. You will have several points of your own (negative as well as positive) to make about their theories — especially after reading their work in the original. As with all the other jurists and their accounts of law in your course, you will want to prepare several such points for use in the examination. I have already suggested some of the possible limitations of Ross's theory. As far as Olivecrona is concerned, there are at least four targets to aim at. First, his psychological hypothesis is presented *a priori* without any empirical proof. Ask a friend who is studying psychology whether the rigours of that discipline would allow the theory to stand — in the absence of proof. Secondly, even if the theory were valid, can descriptions of 'the law' be reduced to statements about the psyches and senses of citizens? Thirdly, Olivecrona's account of the part played by coercion strikes many as somewhat naïve: force is, of course, the background of law (he gives the examples of execution, eviction, imprisonment), but does it really operate in the way he describes? Fourthly, his analysis of the connection between law and morality is, at best, suspect. There are, of course, several other criticisms, that have been levelled at both Olivecrona (e.g., his insistence on formality in law does not always apply in autocratic systems, and his idea of the State as an 'organisation' rules out any form of conceptual thinking) and Ross (e.g., his assertion that a decision is at variance with valid law if future courts are unlikely to follow it misunderstands the doctrine of precedent, and it is too dogmatic to confine experience to what is experienced through the senses — we do experience things morally), but you will need to explore their work more deeply before accepting or rejecting these, and other, attacks.

THE EXAMINATION

You will, almost certainly, be asked at least one question on the general subject of realism. Sometimes, of course, the examiner will explicitly confine the question to the American or realist 'school' (and, if he wishes to be really unfriendly, he may be even narrower than that and ask you to analyse, say, Ross's concept of 'valid law'). But examiners in jurisprudence are, as you have already discovered, of a friendly and kind disposition: questions tend to err on the side of breadth. This may, however, be a mixed blessing for (as discussed in chapter 2) it is easier to know what is expected in a narrow question than in a wide one. As suggested there (and, indeed, throughout this book) you should always *tell* the examiner what you propose to discuss and why you have interpreted the question in this way.

One of the obvious difficulties of questions which allude only to 'realism' is that you will be required to exhibit a knowledge of both the American and Scandinavian versions. This is a very tall order in the space of 34 or even 43 minutes. It will therefore call for an economical and systematic account of the leading theories and theorists of both movements. More often than not, however, a careful reading of the question may reveal a particular bias in favour of one form of realism. Take the following question from a recent LLB examination paper set by an English university law school:

In what ways may the 'realist' be regarded as having developed a 'psychological school of jurisprudence'?

While some of the American realists were strongly influenced by developments in psychology and psychiatry (Jerome Frank drew on Freud and Piaget, and Moore and Oliphant both adopted the methods of behavioural psychology), it is the Scandinavians (and especially Olivecrona) who (as we saw) might be said to have developed a 'psychological school of jurisprudence'. You should, in any event, be uncomfortable about accepting the notion of a 'school' of jurisprudence (see my remarks on page 36 concerning a 'school' of legal positivism) and point to the fragility of this idea.

Your answer would therefore include a brief discussion of the concept of 'realism' and the principal features of the American version, but centre on the psychological theory of Olivecrona which is based on the premise that, to use his words, 'The 'binding force' of the law is a reality merely as an idea in human minds' (*Law as Fact* (1939 ed.), p. 17). The purpose of law-givers is to influence the actions of individuals in society, 'but this can only be done through influencing their minds. How the influence works on the individual mind is a question for psychology.' (Ibid. p. 52.) You would, of course, explain in detail Olivecrona's account of psychological conditioning and its effect on the relationship between law and morality. His analysis of 'independent imperatives' would, for the purpose of answering a question of this kind, warrant only brief mention. Though Ross, in *On Law and Justice*, rejected Olivecrona's 'psychological realism', he does, in his later work, *Directives and Norms*, adopt a form of this approach himself. Whereas, in the first work, he argued that a legal norm was principally directed to courts rather than to citizens, in his later account of 'valid law' he distinguishes between a 'logical' and a 'psychological' point of view: legal rules are indeed directed to officials (and hence the rule 'exists' only in the sense that — logically — it depends on the existence of a rule directed to the officials). In other words, the *primary* rule that certain behaviour is prohibited requires a *secondary* rule specifying what sanction the judge is to apply when faced by such a violation. *Logically*, therefore, there is only *one* set of rules — the *secondary* rules, because primary rules contain nothing that is not already *implied* in secondary rules. However, he concedes that from a *psychological* point of view, there are *two* sets of norms: rules addressed to citizens are 'felt psychologically to be independent entities which are grounds for the reactions of the authorities ... primary rules must be recognised as actually existing norms, in so far as they are followed with regularity and experienced as being binding.' (*Directives and Norms*, p. 92.) A reference to Hart's 'internal aspect' of law as experienced by officials (see chapter 4) would demonstrate that you are able to detect 'connections' between the theories you have studied. Always try to show that you are not merely recounting a well-prepared answer confined to a particular jurist or 'school'. Avoid compartments.

You might therefore legitimately conclude that, though realism, in general, could not be said to have developed a 'psychological school of jurisprudence', the legal theories of the Scandinavian realists, Olivecrona and Ross, are rooted in psychology.

But, while a question of this kind contains clues that may facilitate your limiting the scope of your answer in a sensible way, some questions I have seen on realism are couched in such broad terms that the examiner himself appears to be uncertain what he expects the poor examinee to say. For example, the following question is so broad as to be capable of a considerable number of interpretations:

'In a very real sense we *are* all realists now.' Do you agree?

This might call for an analysis of both the American and Scandinavian movements; it provides very little guidance as to whether you are expected to explore realism in its most generic sense or whether to confine yourself to one version. More difficult is the extent to which the examiner is looking for an account of why it *might* be said (for you are, of course, at liberty to *disagree* with the assertion) that we are, indeed, all realists now. Is he, in other words, seeking a detailed account of the developments *since* the Americans or Scandinavians, or both, presented their views of law? It so happens that the quotation comes from Alan Hunt's *The Sociological Movement in Law* (p. 59) and he is echoing the oft-stated aphorism (which, as far as I know, is unattributed): 'Realism is dead; we are all realists now' which (like Hunt's comment) was uttered in relation to American realism; in fact Hunt's next words are: 'if only in the most general context of recognising the need to view law in its social context'. This suggests that what the examiner had in mind was a consideration of what is frequently thought to be the principal achievement of American realism, which, in Twining's words 'was to concretise sociological jurisprudence' (*Karl Llewellyn and the Realist Movement*, p. 383). This question would therefore seem to call for a review of the American realists and a discussion of the development and contribution of sociological jurisprudence and even the sociology of law (see chapter 8). Yet again, it is evident that the attempt to draw clear boundaries between different legal theories is an imprudent course of action. Of course, it is up to you to interpret any question as you see fit (always saying why and how you have done so), but no examiner will take kindly to your answering a question he hasn't set!

It is not uncommon to find questions which require you to *compare* the two versions of realism. I have already stressed (in chapter 2 and elsewhere) the importance, whenever possible, of drawing comparisons as an excellent way of illuminating and understanding ideas; it also provides a very useful preparation for examinations which frequently invite you to compare concepts, jurists or, as here, 'schools' of legal theory. Certainly the American and Scandinavian realists exhibit more differences of approach than they have in common; indeed, as Friedmann (*Legal Theory*, p. 304) puts it, any similarity between the two movements is a 'purely verbal one'. Broadly speaking, three (related) differences might be identified. First, while the Americans are, in general, pragmatist and behaviourist, emphasising 'law in action' (as opposed to legal conceptualism), the Scandinavians launch a philosophical assault on the metaphysical foundations of law; where the Americans are 'rule-sceptics', they are 'metaphysics-sceptics'. This is sometimes explained by locating American realism within the tradition of English empiricist philosophy, while the Scandinavians are more closely associated with the European tradition of philosophy. The deeper hostility of the Scandinavians to any conceptual thinking about law — especially natural law — may not be unconnected to the absence of any significant Catholic influence in Scandinavia. Secondly, the Americans are far more concerned with courts and their operation, while the scope of the Scandinavians' jurisprudence is far broader, embracing the legal system as a whole. The Americans, thirdly, were more empirically minded than the Scandinavians, who, in Lloyd's words 'appear to rely mainly on argument of an *a priori* kind to justify particular legal solutions or developments' (*Lloyd's Introduction to Jurisprudence*, p. 749). You will have identified other differences for yourself.

FURTHER READING

Holmes, Oliver Wendell, *Collected Legal Papers* (London: Constable & Co., 1920).

Llewellyn, Karl N., *The Bramble Bush* (New York, 1930).

Llewellyn, Karl N., *The Common Law Tradition: Deciding Appeals* (Boston, Mass: Little, Brown & Co., 1960).

Llewellyn, Karl N., *Jurisprudence: Realism in Theory and Practice* (Chicago, Ill; London: University of Chicago Press, 1962).

Llewellyn, Karl N., and Hoebel, E. Adamson, *The Cheyenne Way: Conflict and Case Law in Primitive Jurisprudence* (Norman, Okla: University of Oklahoma Press, 1941) (The Civilization of the American Indian Series, vol. 21).

Lundstedt, A. Vilhelm, *Legal Thinking Revised: My Views on Law* (Stockholm: Almqvist & Wiksell, 1956).

Olivecrona, Karl, *Law as Fact* (London: Oxford University Press, 1939).

Olivecrona, Karl, *Law as Fact*, 2nd ed. (London: Stevens & Sons, 1971).

Ross, Alf, *Directives and Norms* (London: Routledge & Kegan Paul, 1968).

Ross, Alf, *On Law and Justice*, transl. Margaret Dutton (London: Stevens & Sons, 1958).

Summers, Robert S. (ed.), *American Legal Theory* (Aldershot: Dartmouth, 1992).

Summers, Robert S., *Instrumentalism and American Legal Theory* (Ithaca, NY; London: Cornell University Press, 1982).

Twining, William, *Karl Llewellyn and the Realist Movement* (London: Weidenfeld & Nicholson, 1973).

8 THE SOCIOLOGY OF LAW

A sociological account of law normally rests on three closely related claims: that law cannot be understood except as a 'social phenomenon', that an analysis of legal concepts provides only a partial explanation of 'law in action', and that law is merely one form of social control. None of these arguments is especially startling; indeed, we have already seen (in chapter 7) that in their 'revolt against formalism' the American realists (and more recently, the CLS and postmodernist movements) exhibited a profound impatience with traditional legal theory and its preoccupation with the 'law in books'. Thus Alan Hunt is able to describe American realism as 'the bridge between sociological jurisprudence and the sociology of law' (*The Sociological Movement in Law*, p. 37). Your lectures will inevitably deal with both ends of this spectrum, and you will be expected to demonstrate an understanding of how the early sociological jurists (especially Roscoe Pound) laid the foundation of the contemporary, full-blown sociology of law. You will also be referred to the works of the leading sociologists (particularly Durkheim, Weber and Ehrlich) who had a great deal to say about law. And (as if this were not enough!) you will be urged to read important modern empirical and theoretical studies of legal institutions (especially lawyers, courts and the police).

So rapidly has this field developed that many law schools offer courses in 'law and society' and sociology of law. And socio-legal studies is alive and fairly well in Britain (see D. R. Harris, 'The development of socio-legal studies in the United Kingdom' (1983) 3 LS 315). The treatment of the subject of sociological jurisprudence and the sociology of law in the context of (an already crowded) jurisprudence course therefore tends to be of the synoptic variety. Nevertheless, as with every other strand in the fabric of legal theory, nothing you study is ever 'wasted', and, particularly in the case of the sociological approach to law, you will derive considerable benefit from devoting a fair amount of effort to this part of your course. This is not only because (as I happen to believe) all the substantive law subjects which you have studied thus far *belong* in a social context, but because a 'sociological perspective' (see below) will enhance your appreciation of the nature of law and its operation.

The scale of the subject is formidable. Not only is there a prodigious literature generated by 'legal sociologists' (or 'sociologists of law') which is of considerable importance to the 'sociological jurist', but a proper understanding of 'law in society' or 'law as a social phenomenon' requires the adoption (or, at least, a sympathetic grasp) of a 'sociological perspective'. The student of jurisprudence (yet again!) is called upon to don another hat. Not content with his aspiring to be an amateur historian, philosopher, economist and political scientist, his teacher now expects him to become part-time sociologist! Fear not, help is at hand! This chapter will (I hope) identify and clarify the major areas of student difficulty, and there is an especially good recent book, between whose covers you will find a clear, incisive introduction to the theory and practice of sociological approaches to law. All serious students will want to consult (or, better still, own) the latest edition of Roger Cotterrell's *The Sociology of Law: An Introduction*. It contains, in addition, a wealth of suggestions for further reading and a very helpful bibliography. I have already referred above (and in chapter 7) to Alan Hunt's *The Sociological Movement in Law*, which provides a useful sketch of the relationship between this movement and American realism. Two collections of essays worth looking at are C. Campbell and P. Wiles (eds), *Law and Society* and Kahei Rokumoto (ed.), *Sociological Theories of Law* in the Dartmouth Series. As a fairly general work, there is much of value in W. Chambliss and R. Seidman, *Law, Order and Power*. There are also, as we shall see, some eminently readable accounts of the works of the leading sociologists of law. Keep an eye on the *Journal of Law and Society* for articles which adopt an explicitly 'sociological perspective' on law.

WHAT IS A SOCIOLOGICAL PERSPECTIVE?

Beware of catch-phrases. It is, however, possible to identify certain essential features of a 'sociological perspective' in general, and of its application to law, in particular. Sociologists tend to employ three important concepts which, to most legal theorists, are alien. They are the ideas of social structure, social stratification and social function. The first suggests that in any society there are a number of institutions (legal, cultural, political, economic etc.) which form the *social structure* and which interact in a variety of complex ways: thus one institution or group may exert greater political or economic influence than another, hence the idea of *social stratification* (which includes problems of class conflict, sex and race discrimination). These institutions and groups may be analysed in terms of their particular *social function* (e.g., sociologists may seek to explore the function of the church in contemporary Uganda).

Sociologists, using these central ideas, who have sought to explain the nature and operation of law in society, regard law as merely one (albeit an important and ubiquitous) feature of that society. They generally reject the idea (most closely associated with legal positivism) that there can be a value-free explanation of law. I say 'generally' because there are certain sociologists (notably Donald Black in *The Behavior of Law*) who purport to give a value-free sociology of law. (For an attack on Black, see A. Hunt, 'Dichotomy and contradiction in the sociology of law' (1981) 8 Br J Law & Soc 47, an extract from which may be found in *Lloyd's Introduction to Jurisprudence*, pp. 594–602. The question of a 'value-free' sociology is, however, a difficult and controversial one: some might argue that we can never escape our own values when we describe anything. The best we can hope for is that we should *recognise* this fact and make *explicit* our own moral or ideological values.)

The sociologist of law, therefore, is concerned to analyse and interpret the part played by law and legal administration in effecting certain observable forms of conduct or behaviour. He will attempt to present certain 'types' of society in which the role or function of law may be examined. Thus, as will be shown in a moment, Durkheim, in seeking to explain the problem of 'social cohesion', postulates two 'types' of society in which law performs significantly different purposes. Or, to take a few more modern examples, an influential dichotomy is drawn by Ferdinand Tönnies (in *Community and Association*) between societies which conform to the *Gemeinschaft* type (community) and the *Gesellschaft* type (association). The former is based on shared, common interests in which the public and private are indistinguishable. The latter, on the other hand, assumes a society of atomic individuals with private interests. To these types, Kamenka and Tay have added a third, the 'bureaucratic-administrative' type (see, e.g., 'Beyond bourgeois individualism: the contemporary crisis in law and legal ideology', in E. Kamenka and R. S. Neale (eds), *Feudalism, Capitalism and Beyond*, p. 48). Yet another tripartite typology is proposed by Nonet and Selznick (in their book *Law and Society in Transition: Toward Responsive Law*). They suggest a threefold classification based on the models of 'repressive law', 'autonomous law' and 'responsive law' as phases through which law passes.

POUND

Roscoe Pound (1870–1964), the leading exponent of 'sociological jurisprudence', lived a long and productive life. His prolific output, with its propensity for 'classification' (Pound was, in his early years, a botanist) is, to a large extent, consolidated in his five-volume work, *Jurisprudence*, which was published in 1959. It constitutes a powerful reaction against English analytical legal theory, and demonstrates a knowledge of and sympathy for Continental juristic thought. But as Hunt (*The Sociological Movement in Law*, p. 14) points out, Pound's assault on traditionalism was part of a wider movement in the social sciences which laid seige on what Jhering (1818–92) called the 'jurisprudence of conceptions'. Pound emphasises the importance of the distinction between 'law in books' and 'law in action'. His purpose was not, however, confined to identifying the tension between the two, but he wanted to show how they could be *harmonised*. He sought, in other words, to make the latter conform to the former. As he puts it, 'In a conflict between the 'law in books' and the national will, there can be but one result, let us not be legal monks' ('Law in books and law in action' (1910) 44 Amer Law Rev 12).

Social Interests and 'Jural Postulates'

For Pound the task of lawyers and legislators is 'social engineering'. By identifying and protecting certain 'interests', the law ensures social cohesion. An 'interest' is defined as a 'demand or desire which human beings, either individually or through groups or associations or in relations, seek to satisfy'. It is legally protected by attributing to it the status of a legal right. The purpose of social engineering is to construct as efficient a society as possible, one which ensures the satisfaction of the maximum of interests with minimal friction and waste of resources. Pound elaborates his theory of interests in the following detailed classification:

(a) *Individual interests*. These consist of the following interests:

(i) *Personality*. This category includes interests in:

(1) the physical person;
(2) freedom of will;
(3) honour and reputation;
(4) privacy; and
(5) belief and opinion.

(ii) *Domestic relations*. This category includes the interests of individuals in domestic relationships and of society in institutions such as family and marriage.

(iii) *Interests of substance*. This category includes interests of:

(1) property;
(2) freedom of industry and contract;
(3) promised advantages;
(4) advantageous relations with others;
(5) freedom of association; and
(6) continuity of employment.

(b) *Public interests.* These consist of:

(i)   *Interests of the State as juristic person.* This category includes:

(1) the integrity and freedom of action and honour of the State's
personality; and
(2) claims of the politically organised society, as a corporation, to
property acquired and held for corporate purposes.

(ii)   *Interests of the State as guardian of social interests.*

(c) *Social interests.* They include:

(i)   *Social interests in the general security.* This covers those branches of
the law which deal with:

(1) general safety;
(2) general health;
(3) peace and order;
(4) security of acquisitions; and
(5) security of transactions.

(ii)   *Social interests in the security of social institutions.* This category consists
of:

(1) domestic institutions;
(2) religious institutions;
(3) political institutions; and
(4) economic institutions.

(iii) *Social interests in general morals.*
(iv)   *Social interests in the conservation of social resources.* This category
includes:

    (1)   conservation of natural resources; and
    (2)   protection and training of dependants and defectives.

  (v)   *Social interests in general progress.* This category covers:

    (1)   economic progress, which covers:

       I   freedom of use and sale of property;
       II   free trade;
       III   free industry; and
       IV   encouragement of invention by the grant of patents;

    (2)   political progress, which covers:

       I   free speech; and
       II   free association;

    (3)   cultural progress, which covers:

       I   free science;
       II   free letters;
       III   free arts;
       IV   promotion of education and learning, and
       V   aesthetics.

  (vi)   *Social interests in individual life.* This category relates to:

    (1)   self-assertion;
    (2)   opportunity; and
    (3)   conditions of life.

You can perhaps now see how Pound as botanist may have influenced Pound as jurist! But this is not the end of his complex taxonomy, for in the next phase of the argument, having categorised these interests recognised by the law, Pound proceeds to examine the various legal means (including the concepts of rights and duties) by which they are secured. He then argues that when interests conflict, they may be 'weighed' or 'balanced' only against other interests 'on the same plane'. Thus, an *individual* interest must not be weighed against a *public* interest, and so on. He also presents a classification of the institutions of law: he distinguishes between: rules, principles, conceptions, doctrines and standards.

The business of the law, in Pound's view, therefore consists in satisfying as many interests as possible. But, how are we to know whether *new* interests qualify for recognition? He suggests that they might be tested by reference to certain 'jural postulates of civilisation'. These consist of those (changing) assumptions which exist in 'civilised society': no intentional aggression; beneficial control over what people acquire under the existing social and economic order; good faith in dealings; due care not to injure; control over dangerous activities and so on.

If you find this attempt at precise categorisation too formalistic or even artificial, that is the least of the criticisms that it has attracted.

Critique of Pound

Eleven main sorts of criticism may be identified. First, Pound's 'objective' classification of interests and accompanying jural postulates 'reads like a political manifesto in favour of a liberal and capitalist society' (*Lloyd's Introduction to Jurisprudence*, p. 527). It also rests on a *consensus* model of society in which there is a considerable degree of shared values. Many sociologists regard a *conflict* model as a more accurate description of reality: see chapter 9. Secondly, his model of competing interests 'pressing for recognition and security' overlooks the extent to which the law recognises *vested* rights. Thirdly, he assumes that it is a simple matter to know the *real* interests of people, but we are all manipulated, to a greater or lesser extent, by advertising and other forms of persuasion. Fourthly, how do we actually set about *establishing* people's interests: is it a matter of psychology or market research? Fifthly, should we, in any event, seek to satisfy people's wants? There may be good reason to protect certain interests regardless of whether people want them (e.g., paternalistic legislation relating to pornography or drugs). Sixthly, his inventory seems almost irretrievably vague and nebulous. What, for instance, is to be accommodated by the social interest in 'peace and order' or 'self-assertion'.

Seventhly, even if we regard the list as helpful, it raises a plethora of difficulties: is there really any fundamental distinction between public and social interests? Is the difference between individual and social interests not one between different *types* of interest as much as one between interests that exist on different *levels*? Are the three types of interest equal in status? Eighthly, the idea of 'balancing' notwithstanding, when it comes to a judge selecting between competing interests, 'each situation has a pattern of its own, and the different types of interest and activities that might be involved are infinitely various. It is for the judge to translate the activity involved in the case before him in terms of an interest and to select the ideal with reference to which the competing interests are measured' (Dias, *Jurisprudence*, p. 435). In other words, the listing of interests is less important than the judicial attitudes towards particular activities. Ninthly, Pound assumes that claims pre-exist law, but certain claims actually result from law (e.g., welfare legislation). Tenthly, what does it mean to 'recognise' an interest? There is a grey area in which an activity may be permitted without being 'recognised' by the law. Finally, Pound establishes his jural postulates by generalising a value which is *already legally protected*; but if new claims are, as he proposes, to be judged by reference to jural postulates, they will be recognised only if similar claims already receive legal protection. This hardly suggests a particularly dynamic process of law reform.

There are many more criticisms in the literature. Two important commentaries on Pound's jurisprudence are J. Stone, *Human Law and Human Justice*, ch. 9, and E. W. Patterson, *Jurisprudence: Men and Ideas of the Law*, p. 518 ff. You will want, in addition to reading these critiques and adding your own evaluation, to compare Pound with others who adopted a sociological standpoint as well as with those jurists who have considered the role of interests and rights: see chapters 6 and 10.

Critics are hard on Pound. Even if, as Hunt puts it, he 'used sociology when he saw fit; he cannot be regarded as having developed a sociological theory of law' (*The Sociological Movement in Law*, p. 34), he undoubtedly exerted a considerable influence on sociological jurisprudence. More than that, he laid the foundation for an approach to law that looked beyond traditionalism to an alternative perspective rooted in 'law in action'.

EHRLICH

It is sometimes said that Pound's theory has much in common with the views of Eugen Ehrlich (1862–1922). In particular, it is suggested that there is a strong resemblance between Pound's 'law in action' and Ehrlich's idea of 'living law'. The limitations of the equation are examined in D. Nelken, 'Law in action or living law? Back to the beginning in sociology of law' (1984) 4 LS 157. This question is returned to below.

Ehrlich, like Pound, recognised that the formal sources of law provide an incomplete picture of what law is really like — the 'living law'. This is to be distinguished from what he called 'norms of decision' (rules found in the civil codes, judicial decisions and statutes) which are the norms to be enforced by the courts when parties resort to litigation. 'Living law' is 'the law which dominates life itself even though it has not been posited in legal propositions' (*Fundamental Principles of the Sociology of Law*, p. 493). As he puts it (op. cit., p. 488):

To attempt to imprison the law of a time or of a people within the sections of a code is about as reasonable as to attempt to confine a stream within a pond. The water that is put in the pond is no longer a living stream but a stagnant pool.

So, for example, the law of contract is better understood by empirical studies than by reading textbooks and judicial decisions. This might be illustrated by the well-known research conducted by Stewart Macauley into commercial practices in Wisconsin. He showed that, instead of concerning themselves with the rules of offer and acceptance, consideration etc., hardened business-men were frequently not only ignorant of those rules, but found ways of avoiding the law and lawyers whenever possible. As one respondent put it, 'One doesn't run to lawyers if he wants to stay in business because one must behave decently' ('Non-contractual relations in business', *Am. Sociol Rev*, vol. 28 (1963), p. 55 at p. 61). For business people the law of contract is far less important than the actual operation of commercial practice. A British survey reached similar conclusions: H. Beale and T. Dugdale, 'Contracts between businessmen' (1975) 2 Br J Law & Soc 45. In brief terms, therefore, if we wish to obtain a reliable insight into the actual practice of law, we need to penetrate the social context in which it is played out.

Ehrlich's work has not assumed a major place in the sociology of law (though he coined the phrase), and critics have found a number of flaws in his theory of the 'living law'. In particular, he fails to provide a coherent theory of the relationship between the 'living' law and the State (which plays a significant part in the development of the 'living law'). Nelken (1984) 4 LS 157, 173, raises several difficulties with the very concept of the 'living law': what, if anything, do the various norms of the 'living law' (relating to families, organisations and business activity) actually have *in common*? To what extent do these organisations and associations reproduce within themselves Eh-rlich's two types of law, having *both* 'norms for decision' and 'living law'? Can groups and associations be defined *apart* from the norms that constitute them? How do the norms of 'living law' *arise*? What are the relationships of opposition, incorporation and symbiosis between *State* 'norms for decision' and the 'living law' of groups? How do the norms of some groups affect the norms held dear in other associations? Nelken says that the answers to these questions depend on the development of a 'sociology of norms' rather than a sociology of law. If so, perhaps Ehrlich may be forgiven for failing to provide the answers, though it does render his theory narrower than it might otherwise have been. Still, his influence has not been inconsiderable (especially in anthropology), and his ideas are described by Cotterrell (*The Sociology of Law*, p. 31) as 'a powerful challenge to lawyers' typical assumptions about the nature and scope of law and of its importance'.

DURKHEIM

Among the leading figures of sociology, Émile Durkheim (1858–1917) stands tall. You will be expected to have a fairly detailed knowledge of his contribution to the sociology of law and, to this end, you will find ch. 4 of

Alan Hunt's book, *The Sociological Movement in Law*, admirably clear. Durkheim's various writings on law have been (for the first time) collected and edited in a very useful book (with a good introduction) by S. Lukes and A. Scull, *Durkheim and the Law*.

Durkheim's general concern may be simply stated: what is it that holds society together? Throughout his major works (especially *The Division of Labour in Society*, first published in French in 1893) he is preoccupied with 'social solidarity' — and law plays a central role in the transition from mechanical to organic solidarity; it is an 'external' index which 'symbolises' the nature of social solidarity (see below). Though his analysis of law is complex, there are essentially two major claims that he makes (and it is unlikely that you will be expected to know a great deal more about his *sociologie du droit*). First, he argues that as society develops from religion to secularism, from collectivism to individualism, law becomes less penal and more 'restitutive' in character. Secondly, he claims that the function of punishment is an expression of collective sentiments by which social cohesion is maintained. Each claim is briefly looked at.

Law and Social Solidarity

For Durkheim, society produces two distinct forms of social solidarity: 'mechanical' solidarity and 'organic' solidarity. The former is to be found in simple, homogeneous societies which have a uniformity of values and lack any significant division of labour. 'Collectivism' is highly developed while 'individualism' is barely present. The latter, on the other hand, is to be found in societies which have a developed division of labour and, hence, exhibit a strong degree of 'interdependence'. Instead of homogeneity there is considerable differentiation; 'individualism' replaces 'collectivism'.

The law reflects 'all the essential varieties of social solidarity.' As he puts it (in *The Division of Labour in Society*, p. 68) in an oft-quoted statement:

Since law reproduces the principal forms of social solidarity, we have only to classify the different types of law to find therefrom the different types of social solidarity which correspond to it.

Durkheim identifies also an important relationship between *mechanical* solidarity and *repressive* law; and between *organic* solidarity and *restitutive* law. This is explained by reference to the features of these two forms of cohesion described above. Law in the former is essentially penal, but, with increasing differentiation, disputes tend to be resolved by recourse to restitutive law (which includes all civil law, procedural law and major parts of constitutional and administrative law).

In this analysis, Durkheim treats law and morality as virtually synonymous. Law is derived from and is an expression of society's morality. In the
absence of moral commitment to support it, law ceases being a part of society.

The Function of Punishment

For Durkheim crime is closely connected to the social values expressed in the
'collective conscience': an act is criminal:

> ... when it offends strong and defined states of the collective conscience.
> ... we must not say that an action shocks the common conscience because
> it is criminal, but rather than it is criminal because it shocks the common
> conscience. (*The Division of Labour in Society*, pp. 80–1.)

Crime is an inevitable feature of social life; indeed, it is a factor in public health,
an integral part of all healthy societies. And *punishment* is a crucial element in his
notion of crime: the State acts to reinforce the 'collective conscience' by
punishing those who offend against the State itself. Punishment is defined as 'a
passionate reaction of graduated intensity that society exercises through the
medium of a body acting upon those of its members who have violated certain
rules of conduct' (op. cit., p. 96). He is in no doubt that the function of
punishment is vengeance and that it is a necessary 'act of defence' (op. cit., p. 87).

In his essay 'Two laws of penal evolution' (translated by T. Anthony Jones
and Andrew Scull, in Lukes and Scull, *Durkheim and the Law*, p. 102), he
propounds the following two 'laws':

(a) 'The intensity of punishment is the greater the more closely societies
approximate to a less developed type — and the more the central power
assumes an absolute character.'

(b) 'Deprivations of liberty, and of liberty alone, varying in time according to the seriousness of the crime, tend to become more and more the normal
means of social control.'

The former is qualitative, the latter quantitative. His argument, in relation to
the first, is that in primitive societies the death penalty is 'augmented' by a
variety of gruesomely imaginative 'torments': 'death by ashes' (suffocation
under a pile of ashes), crucifixion, burning alive, being cooked alive, being
crushed under an elephant and other similarly grisly methods. Durkheim's
point is that as societies progress, the form of punishment becomes less
violent and less harsh. But since punishment results from *crime*, he identifies
a correlation between the evolution of crime and the forms of social solidarity.
He distinguishes between two types of crime: 'religious criminality' (acts
'which are directed against collective things') and 'human criminality' (acts
'which only injure the individual'). Each type will attract its own form of

punishment, and it will therefore change according to the type of crime. He concludes:

> Seeing as, in the course of time, crime is reduced more and more to offences against persons alone, while religious forms of criminality decline, it is inevitable that punishment on the average should become weaker. (*Durkheim and the Law*, p. 126.)

Critique of Durkheim

You will (again) want to attach almost as much importance to the criticism that Durkheim's theory has attracted as to the theory itself. Here — for starters — is a very brief sketch of 10 criticisms. You may expand on each of them. First, it is too narrow: his treatment of law as 'a completely moral phenomenon' neglects the extent to which law and morality often conflict. Secondly, his views of primitive societies are a priori, and there is empirical evidence that tends to refute his assumption that, for example, they lack a division of labour (see Hunt, *The Sociological Movement in Law*, pp. 70–1). Thirdly, his theory of how law becomes increasingly restitutive does not, in the view of several critics, provide a coherent account of this development. Fourthly, in his explanation of the transition from mechanical to organic solidarity, he gives no description of the *intermediate* stages between primitive and modern societies. Fifthly, it has been argued by modern social scientists that, contrary to Durkheim's thesis, repressive law was actually *less* important in simple or primitive societies. Sixthly, his concept of the State has been attacked: he regards the State as the expression of the collectivity; it is treated merely as an instrumental organ — as a means by which offenders are punished. Seventhly, Durkheim's insistence on reducing punishment to its retributive features has not met with critical acclaim; it is generally considered to ignore the deterrent, rehabilitative, reformist aspects of punishment. On the other hand, eighthly, he neglects the punitive dimension of *civil* law and, at the same time, fails to account for the growing intrusiveness of the criminal law into, e.g., labour relations. Ninthly, his suggestion that crime 'is a factor in public health' has been denied by several writers who, in general, find it unconvincing on a number of grounds (see Hart's essay 'Social solidarity and the enforcement of morality' in his *Essays in Jurisprudence and Philosophy*, p. 248, for the connections between this thesis and Lord Devlin's 'disintegration thesis'). Finally, Durkheim's 'two laws of penal evolution' have been attacked on several counts. In particular, the basis of the distinction between 'religious' and 'human' crimes has been questioned: on what ground for instance, are some acts treated as attacks upon the collective, while others (simply because they cause injury to persons) are not?

Despite these (and many other) misgivings, few deny Durkheim's influence on the sociology of law. As Hunt says, 'the persistent sociologism of Durkheim ensures that his work will remain a significant point of reference' (*The Sociological Movement in Law*, p. 92). Like the curate's egg, Durkheim's theory seems to be regarded as good in parts. Lukes and Scull (*Durkheim and the Law*, p. 27) put it as follows:

> Current research may continue to endorse the value of Durkheim's insistence on studying law in its social and historical context, and on the need to tease out the connections between law and the forms of social relations. Such research may also reiterate his emphasis on the central importance of law to the understanding of social life in general. ... It does so, however, only while rejecting the larger theoretical system within which these propositions were once embedded.

You ought to be able to answer a question with a quotation such as this as its aperitif.

WEBER

A trained lawyer, Max Weber (1864–1920) accords law a rigorous and systematic social and historical analysis which occupies a focal place in his general sociological theory. He is unquestionably the most prominent and influential social theorist, and it is not uncommon to find him revered by his contemporary successors. Your lecturer will hope, but not expect, that you read Weber's great works, especially *Economy and Society: An Outline of Interpretive Sociology* and *Max Weber on Law in Economy and Society*. And I harbour similar hopes. I will say only that his writings are rich in their intellectual and social investigation of law and legal history, and you will be richer in knowledge and understanding through studying them. But, if this is to dwell in the realm of the fantastic, you will find an excellent guide in A. T. Kronman's *Max Weber*, and Hunt's *The Sociological Movement in Law* contains a lucid account in ch. 5. Frank Parkin's little book, *Max Weber*, is also a useful general introduction. See, too, Cotterrell, *The Sociology of Law*, pp. 148–61. You will find extracts from Weber in Lloyd's *Introduction to Jurisprudence*, pp. 552–62.

Essentially, Weber's project was to explain the development of capitalism in Western societies. And a key element in his explanation is the existence of a 'rational' legal order. He employs certain 'ideal types' along with the development of particular concepts of rationality to demonstrate the movement toward capitalism. His starting-point is the *individual*: social action can be understood only by reference to its meaning, purpose and intention for the individual. This method he calls *Verstehen*. His sociology of law may be considered under three heads.

Weber's Typology of Law

Weber's definition of law (from *Max Weber on Law in Economy and Society*, p. 5) resembles the traditional positivist, formal conception:

> An order will be called *law* if it is externally guaranteed by the probability that coercion (physical or psychological), to bring about conformity or avenge violation, will be applied by a *staff* of people holding themselves specially ready for that purpose.

His typology of law is based on the various types of legal thought, and 'rationality' is the key. Thus he distinguishes between 'formal' systems and 'substantive' systems. It is important to note that the crux of this distinction is the extent to which the system is 'internally self-sufficient', i.e., the rules and procedures required for decision-making are available within the system. The second distinction is between 'rational' and 'irrational': these terms describe the manner in which the materials (rules, procedures) are applied in the system. Thus the highest stage of rationality is reached where there is an 'integration of all analytically derived legal propositions in such a way that they constitute a logically clear, internally consistent, and, at least in theory, gapless system of rules, under which, it is implied, all conceivable fact situations must be capable of being logically subsumed' (*Max Weber on Law in Economy and Society*, p. 62) — shades of Dworkin: see chapter 6.

Taken together, these two distinctions yield a fourfold scheme of law-making and adjudication which may be illustrated as in table 8.1.

Table 8.1   Weber's internal typology of law

	RATIONAL	IRRATIONAL
SUBSTANTIVE	Substantively rational	Substantively irrational
FORMAL	Formally rational	Formally irrational

Examples of each type of legal thought are given by Weber, as follows:

(a)   *Substantively irrational law.* Weber calls this 'Khadi justice' (after the procedure used in Islamic law) where decisions are made *ad hoc*, based on ethical, emotional and political considerations; cases are decided on their own merits without reference to general principles.

(b) *Substantively rational law*. This is exemplified by certain theocratic legal systems and 'the patriarchal system of justice' which recognises no separation between law and morals. There is some attempt to construct a doctrinal system of rules and principles.

(c) *Formally rational law*. This is exemplified by the codes of civil law countries which are derived from Roman law. It is a gapless legal system which contains answers to all legal problems.

(d) *Formally irrational law*. Examples are to be found in primitive systems which employ trial by ordeal or oracle. Decisions are made on the basis of tests beyond the control of human intellect.

Weber then proposes a second typology based on:

(a)   the mode of law-creation;
(b)   the formal qualities of the law so created; and
(c)   the type of justice attained.

He argues that law passes through the following four phases:

(a)   charismatic legal revelation through 'law prophets';
(b)   empirical creation and finding of law by legal *honoratiores* (those who have a specialised expert knowledge and occupy a position of social prestige by virtue of their economic situation, and who receive little or no remuneration for this);
(c)   imposition of law by secular or theocratic powers; and
(d)   systematised elaboration of law and professionalised administration of justice.

The relationship between the two typologies may be illustrated as in table 8.2.

Table 8.2 Weber's typologies of legal development

MODE OF CREATION	FORMAL QUALITIES	TYPES OF JUSTICE
Charismatic	Magical, irrational	Charismatic
Empirical	Reliance on *honoratiores*	Khadi justice
Secular, theocratic	Theocratic substantive rationality	Empirical
Professionalised	'Sublimation of concepts'	Rational

This representation (adapted from Hunt, *The Sociological Movement in Law*, p. 107) squeezes a long and complicated analysis into a very small space. It therefore calls for further elaboration — *from you*! For instance, the idea of the 'sublimation of concepts' occurs in Weber's account of legal thought (in the important chapter in *Max Weber on Law in Economy and Society*, 'The legal *honoratiores* and the types of legal thought'). Describing the development of the legal profession in Roman and English law, he remarks that the 'sublimation of juristic thinking' (by which he seems to mean systematisation or rationalisation) requires a bureaucratic frame-work. Thus, in Rome:

> ... the necessity of systematic juristic studies was greatly increased by the imperial system of legal administration through appointed officials and its rationalisation and bureaucratisation, especially in the provincial service.... The systematic rationalisation of the law in England, for example, was retarded because no bureaucratisation occurred there. As long as the jurisconsults dominated the Roman legal administration of justice as the legal *honoratiores*, the striving for systematisation was feeble, and no codifying and systematising intervention by the political authority occurred (p. 222).

Weber's general thesis is that the formal rationalisation of law in Western societies is a result of 'capitalism ... interested in strictly formal law and legal procedure' and 'the rationalism of officialdom in absolutist States [which] led to the interest in codified systems and in homogeneous law' (*The Religion of China*, p. 149). This is *not*, however, an economic explanation (he is therefore sometimes called 'the bourgeois Marx'). There are, in his view, a number of factors that account for this development, including, in particular, the growth of *bureaucracy* which established, as we saw above, the basis for the administration of a rational law conceptually systematised. Other causal factors are the legal profession and legal education (which stressed the conceptual and rational elements of law) and 'natural law' (which results from the tension between formal law and substantive justice).

Weber's Theory of Legitimate Domination

Weber's attempt to explain why people believe they are obliged to obey the law leads him to draw his well-known distinction between three types of legitimate domination: *traditional* (where 'legitimacy is claimed for it and believed in by sanctity of age-old rules and powers'), *charismatic* (based on 'devotion to the exceptional sanctity, heroism or exemplary character of an individual person') and *legal-rational* domination (which rests on 'a belief in the legality of enacted rules and the right of those elevated to authority under such rules to issue commands'). It is, of course, this third type that is a central feature of Weber's account of law. And, though the concept of legal-rational authority is bound up with Weber's theory of value (which argues for the sociologist of law adopting a detached view of his subject), the important correlation is between this form of domination and the modern bureaucratic State. Under the other forms of domination, authority resides in *persons*; under bureaucracy it is vested in *rules*. The hallmark of legal-rational authority is its so-called *impartiality*. But it depends upon what Weber calls the principle of 'formalistic impersonality': officials exercise their responsibilities 'without hatred or passion, and hence without affection or enthusiasm. The dominant norms are concepts of straightforward duty without regard to personal considerations' (*Economy and Society*, p. 225). I shall resist the temptation to examine this fascinating subject in any detail — but you should not! (Make sure you read Kronman, *Max Weber*, ch. 3. An interesting essay is R. Cotterrell, 'Legality and political legitimacy in the sociology of Max Weber', in D. Sugarman (ed.), *Legality, Ideology and the State*, p. 69.) Essentially, Weber argues, as I have said, that while the legitimacy of the first two types depends on a specific relationship between ruler and subject, the source of the legitimacy of legal-rational domination is *impersonal*: obedience is therefore owed to the *legal order*. The importance of Weber's sociology of law — at least for students of jurisprudence — is the correlation between the various typologies: see table 8.3.

Table 8.3 Weber's analysis of law and legitimacy

DOMINATION	LEGITIMATION	LEGAL THOUGHT	JUSTICE	JUDICIAL PROCESS	OBEDIENCE	ADMINISTRATION
Traditional	Traditional	Formal irrationality substantive rationality	Secular or theocratic empirical	Empirical and/or substantive and/or personal (Khadi-justice)	Traditional (personal) duty to e.g., king	Patrimonial (hereditary)
Charismatic	Charismatic	Formal irrationality substantive irrationality	Charismatic	Revelation: empirical	Response to charisma of leader	None in pure ideal type
Legal-rational	Legal-rational	Logical formal rationality	Rational	Rational	Owed to legal order	Bureaucratic-professional

But there are a host of important claims that Weber makes in pursuit of the basis of legitimate domination. The detail with which you explore this important (and extremely influential) aspect of Weber's sociology of law will, of course, depend on the approach adopted by your lecturer. Nevertheless, as I cannot repeat too often (or can I?), devoting your time to the careful study of *any* of the theorists accommodated within jurisprudence's large mansion, will serve you well. Except in the most 'traditional', compartmentalised course (which, happily, seems to be a thing of the past) your knowledge of the works of writers who are dealt with only cursorily, or even omitted altogether, by your teacher, can only advance and illuminate your study of legal theory. I would therefore advise you to give Weber's sociology of law your close attention. In particular, note that for Weber political domination draws its legitimacy from the existence of a system of rationally made laws which stipulate the circumstances under which power may be exercised. This form of legitimacy is, in Weber's view, the core of all stable authority in modern societies. Thus, legal rational rules determine the scope of power and provide its legitimacy. This means, as Cotterrell (in Sugarman, *Legality, Ideology and the State*, p. 71) puts it:

> In Weber's view, in order to understand political legitimacy under conditions of legal domination it is not necessary to evaluate the *content* of the law. The existence of law — in particular conditions and in a particular form — provides *its own ideological basis whatever its substantive content*. And the action of the State, in accordance with law, derives legitimacy from law. Emphasis added.)

In other words, legal domination is not dependent upon the extent to which the law reflects the *values* to which people who accept its legitimacy subscribe.

Capitalism and Law

Weber is commonly associated with the view that economic forces do not affect the law. But, while this does not misrepresent his argument, it is a crude oversimplification. What Weber actually seeks to show is that law is affected only *indirectly* by economic circumstances. He conceives of law as being 'relatively autonomous'; or, in his words, 'generally it appears ... that the development of the legal structure has by no means been predominantly determined by economic factors' (*Max Weber on Law in Economy and Society*, p. 131). It is more accurate, therefore, to say that for Weber, law is *fundamentally related to*, but not *determined by* economic factors.

His argument (which is further considered below in the context of an examination question) may be summarised as follows: rational economic conduct ('profit-making activity' and 'budgetary management') is at the heart of the capitalist system; this rationalism is facilitated by the certainty and predictability of logically formal rational law. Hence, the presence of this type of law *assists* but does not *cause* the advance of capitalism. He uses the example of England to prove (or, in the view of some critics, to disprove) his thesis that only where the law is systematised so as to ensure the predictability of economic relations, can capitalism develop. By his own admission, however, the emergence of capitalism in England occurred *without* a formally rational legal system. Weber shows how, in many respects, the English common law was, during the development of the capitalist economy, highly *irrational*. In particular, unlike the logical, systematic codification and procedure of the *Corpus Juris* of Justinian, English law was a hit-and-miss affair, with a reliance on legal fictions and an archaic procedure based on writs, oaths and irrational modes of proof. He is therefore forced to conclude that 'England achieved capitalistic supremacy among the nations not because but rather in spite of its judicial system' (*Max Weber on Law in Economy and Society*, p. 231). How are we to interpret Weber's apparent ambiguity? You should read Professor Summers's spirited defence of Weber in *Max Weber*, ch. 6, and the discussion below.

Critique of Weber

It is impossible here to do justice to the vast sweep of Weber's sociology of law. He has a great deal of insight into the law of contract, 'natural law', religion, leadership, beliefs and social action. It is easy to see why he remains so important a sociologist — despite (or is it because of?) the appearance of so many 'new' and more exotic social theories. As far as his 'jurisprudence' is concerned, it would not be difficult to devise an entire course based upon the richness of his writings about law. This is not to say, of course, that Weber lacks his detractors. His work has been subjected to close and sustained scrutiny by generations of sociologists. Eight main kinds of criticism may be mentioned, though many other general and particular critiques have been made.

At the most general level, Hunt (*The Sociological Movement in Law*, pp. 130–3) identifies three central 'problematics' which Weber poses for the sociology of law. Each points up certain limitations of his theory. First, his treatment of the relationship between law and domination is restricted and even distorted by his reduction of domination to the personal relationship between ruler and ruled. It leads him to treat 'the ideological form of the legal order ... as the real form of legal or political relations' (op. cit., p. 131). This is a profound point which I take to mean that the process of domination is more complex than its formal, legal manifestation. Secondly, Weber's analysis of the relation between law and the bureaucratic State is distorted by his concern with legitimacy: this accords unwarranted primacy to this aspect of the political structure. Thirdly, in his discussion of the relationship between law and the economic order, Weber adopts an excessively empiricist view. Fourthly, his sociology is sometimes considered to be incapable of answering many of the questions of modern law; thus Lloyd (*Introduction to Jurisprudence*, p. 518) asks how the problems of the contemporary welfare State can be solved by reference to a theory 'irreversibly committed to a model of capitalism tied to *laissez-faire* economics'. Fifthly, his concept of legal domination exhibits an unduly positivist view of law: '... the highly complex ideological elements of law must be analysed in ways that cannot utilise the ideal type method, if conditions of legitimacy are to be understood in relation to social change' (Cotterrell in Sugarman, (ed.), *Legality, Ideology and the State*, p. 88).

A sixth criticism is aimed at another feature of Weber's theory of domination: why should 'bureaucracy' qualify as a type of 'domination'? In the case of traditional or charismatic leaders it is clear that they are 'dominating', since no one has the authority to tell them what to do. But bureaucrats, almost by definition, are told by someone what to do. The conundrum is well expressed by Parkin (*Max Weber*, p. 89):

> If bureaucracy does attempt to exercise domination it usurps the authority of a nominally superior body. In other words it uses its power illegitimately. Thus, in the light of Weber's own account, bureaucracy can hardly be an example of 'legitimate domination'. If it acts legitimately it is not dominant; if it exercises domination it ceases to be legitimate.

Seventhly, the 'England problem' has, as we shall see, attracted its share of criticism. In addition to the difficulties of its (apparent, though misunderstood) causal claim, it posits a model in which law remains fairly static. If (as Weber suggests) law provides a common-sense context in which rational purposive action is taken, this implies that should the law change it would cease having this function. And the nature of law *is* constantly changing; for persuasive evidence of such change in relation to the 'rule of law' and 'discretionary regulation', see Cotterrell, *The Sociology of Law*, pp. 168–87. Eighthly, contemporary critics doubt the applicability today of Weber's claim that in the late 19th century the *Rechtsstaat* (the State whose legitimacy is based on the 'rule of law') formal rationality triumphed over substantive rationality. He argues that this lent modern law a neutrality which made the basis of authority independent of acceptance by citizens of particular moral or political values. Critics suggest that modern law exhibits a fundamental reversal towards *substantive* rationality. This takes the form of the growing acceptance of discretionary regulation which is influenced by substantive questions of policy.

AUTOPOIESIS

The question of legal 'closure' is a recurring theme in critical theory (see chapter 10). The concept describes the way in which the law operates autonomously from other disciplines or practices, and the fact that the law often reproduces and validates itself. Professor Cotterrell provides a good summary:

> To adopt an idea of legal closure is to claim that law is self-standing and irreducible or has an independent integrity which is normally unproblematic, natural or self-generated, not dependent on contingent links with an extralegal environment of knowledge or practice. ('Sociological perspectives on legal closure' in Alan Norrie (ed.), *Closure or Critique*, p. 175.)

The law is a law unto itself. This self-referential notion has recently been developed to offer a full-blown sociological account of the legal system by the German theorists Niklas Luhmann and Gunther Teubner who, employing a biological metaphor, have called their theory 'autopoiesis'. Its importance may perhaps be gauged by the fact that *Lloyd's Introduction to Jurisprudence* devotes some 27 pages to extracts from the works of the two writers. Read them.

In this vision of the law (as some sort of physiological process), extralegal information (economics, science etc.) is received, but the law somehow ingests it and, as if by some biological process, transforms it into a form that is legal. In this way the law is constantly reproducing its own normative form. Thus the law's self-absorbed autonomy does not rule out the receipt of data cognitively. This, more or less, enables law to acquire an autonomous sovereignty over all its views. More than that, the law develops an ability to *think* independently, thereby achieving almost complete closure, at least normatively.

This complex (and, at times, slightly obscure) sociological theory seeks to deny the possibility of authentic normative change in the law. It is explained instead by Luhmann as 'the structural coupling of system and environment'. In other words, there is no direct causative link between the extralegal world and the law itself; there is no noisy 'input', merely the gentle hum of the legal system reproducing itself. But if the law is, as Teubner puts it, 'an autonomous epistemic subject that constructs a social reality of its own' are we not in danger of reifying it, treating the law as an object? Do we not risk abandoning the power of human beings to control and change legal norms? Moreover, as Freeman asks, if legal systems are autopoietic, how are they born? Where do they come from, and why did they appear? 'Unless the first legal system was not autopoietic or not a legal system (by what test?), it seems it must have had its source in the extralegal environment, whether this was religion, morality, or power' (*Lloyd's Introduction to Jurisprudence* p. 550). Is the theory the sociological equivalent of Kelsen's pure theory of law? Discuss.

WHITHER THE SOCIOLOGY OF LAW?

While the sociology of law is generally acknowledged to have come of age, a number of doubts have been expressed about its future. Generally regarded as the 'second phase' (after the emergence of sociological jurisprudence) in the development of the sociological movement in law, it is frequently doubted whether the sociology of law has an adequate 'theoretical' ground-ing. By this is meant that, though there has been a considerable growth in *socio-legal studies* (you will find full accounts in Cotterrell, *The Sociology of Law*, of the numerous empirical studies of the courts, the jury, the police, the legal profession etc.), not enough attention has been paid to the difficulties inherent in the concept of 'law' and the 'legal system'. They are, in the course of these projects, treated as 'unproblematic' when (as I hope is by now clear!) they are anything but. On the other hand, it is sometimes argued that sociologists of law are, in some instances, narrowly 'positivistic' in their preoccupation with legal 'definition'. You will form your own conclusions. Certainly, in the work of Roberto Unger (especially *Law in Modern Society*) and Jürgen Habermas (especially in *Legitimation Crisis*; see K. Raes, 'Legalisation, communication and strategy: a critique of Habermas' approach to law' (1986) 13 J Law & Soc 183), there is a wealth of sociological and political 'theory'.

Alan Hunt (*The Sociological Movement in Law*, p. 137) complains that:

> ... at root the contemporary status of sociology of law is marked precisely by a lack of clarity as to its nature, purpose and direction; it is a hot-house plant, the forced offspring of the deficiencies of sociological jurisprudence and the jurisprudential tradition in general.

For further and better particulars read Hunt's ch. 6; it contains a penetrating diagnosis of — and prognosis for — the sociological movement in legal theory.

THE EXAMINATION

This is a large subject. It would clearly be sensible to devote most of your energies to the big four: Pound's theory of interests, Ehrlich's 'living law', and the typologies of Weber and Durkheim are obviously of major importance. But you should be ready — as always — to draw comparisons between them, and not merely to know what they say and what others have said of them. Thus, you may be asked to compare, say, the sociologies of Pound and Ehrlich. I have already referred to Nelken's interesting article on this subject. You would also attempt to draw your own distinctions. Thus, yet again, I recommend, as an excellent aid to understanding and (hence?) memory, that you draw a line down a page and head one side Pound, the other Ehrlich (see table 8.4). Do not, however, neglect the *similarities* between the theories or theorists you are comparing.

Table 8.4 Pound and Ehrlich compared

POUND	EHRLICH
He conceives of society as groups of individuals united in their pursuit of the interest in diminishing resources.	He adopts a less individualistic approach: individual behaviour is channelled by norms of social groups.
His principal concern is to harmonise the 'law in books' and the 'law in action'.	He does not regard 'norms for decision' and 'living law' as in competition: they are applied under different conditions: the former in disputes, the latter in normal circumstances.
His conception of law is largely rule-based.	His distinction between 'norms for decision' and 'living law' reveals a more complex conception of law.
His distinction between 'law in books' and 'law in action' is confined to actions by citizens.	His distinction between 'norms for decision' and 'living law' extends to decision-making by judges, law-makers and other officials.
He regards law as a method of 'social control', a tool for social engineering.	He sees law as a development from social forces rather than a tool for social engineering.
Norms are the claims made by competing groups in society.	His theory of norms is more complex: they reflect shared feelings, behaviour and identity.

A subject, referred to in the outline of Weber's theory above, that sometimes attracts the interest of examiners, is the relationship between law and capitalism in Weber's sociology. It is important, not only because of the so-called 'England problem' encountered by Weber, but because of the growing recognition in legal theory of the connection between law and economics, an issue which is prominent both in Marxist theory and the 'economic analysis of law' propounded, in particular, by Richard Posner: see chapter 9. You should not therefore be surprised to find that you are asked to contrast the views of Weber and Marx in respect of their approaches to the relationship between law and capitalism. For Weber, of course, formally rational law is considered one of the preconditions of capitalism because it provides the necessary certainty and predictability that is an essential if entrepreneurs are to pursue profit-making enterprises. The achievement of this formal rationality required, in Weber's view, the systematisation of the legal order, a systematisation which he found singularly absent in the English law. How, then, does he explain the emergence of capitalism in England?

This question has exercised many sociologists who offer a variety of explanations for this apparent contradiction in Weber's work. First, it is clear that although English law lacked the systematic order of the Roman law (especially after Justinian), it was, as Weber himself recognised, a highly *formalistic* legal order. Indeed, Weber characterised such formalism (exhibited, for instance, in proceedings under the writ system) as irrational. And this formalism, says Weber, effected a stabilising influence on the legal system which produced a greater degree of security and predictability in the economic market-place. A second feature of the English legal system to which Weber ascribes considerable significance in the advancement of capitalism is the legal profession. He shows how lawyers in England traditionally served as advisers to businessmen and corporations. This enabled and encouraged them to modify the law to suit the interests of their commercial clients. Coupled with the centralisation of the Bar in London, close to the City, and the monopolisation of legal education by the Inns of Court, this ensured that lawyers were a group which was 'active in the service of propertied, and particularly capitalistic, private interests and which has to gain its livelihood from them' (*Max Weber on Law in Economy and Society*, p. 318).

Another factor was that, unlike Continental practice, lawyers in England approximated to 'craft guilds' in their education, training and specialisation which 'naturally produced a formalistic treatment of the law, bound by precedent' (op. cit., p. 201). This led to what Weber calls, following Roman law, 'cautelary jurisprudence': emphasis is laid on drafting instruments and devising new clauses to prevent future litigation. This phenomenon resulted in a close relationship between lawyers and their (mostly commercial) clients. In other words, this feature of legal practice compensated for the lack of systematisation in the law itself.

You may therefore want to argue that what Weber is really saying is that England developed a capitalist economic system despite the absence of legal systematisation, because other important components of the legal system engendered it, but that it may have developed even more rapidly and more efficiently if the common law had been less irrational and unsystematic. Yet (as Kronman, *Max Weber*, p. 123, shows) it sometimes seems as if Weber suggests that capitalism flourished in England precisely *because* the common law was never rationally systematised! Such a view has a certain ring of logic for it is arguable that rational consistency of the law may actually impede the economic pragmatism that suits the economic needs of capitalism. But this does not seem to be an accurate representation of Weber's thesis, and a number of difficulties remain in respect of the extent to which he actually makes *causal* connections between economic and legal factors. Kronman (*Max Weber*, p. 125) describes as 'causal agnosticism' Weber's refusal to assign causal primacy to either economic or legal conditions. This seems to me to be an important (and neglected) aspect of the question. Kronman (*Max Weber*, pp. 125–30) goes on to show that Weber identifies three ways in which the law influences economic factors. First, it provides a relatively stable set of rules for the protection of contractual expectations. Secondly, certain legal concepts (e.g., agency and negotiability) are crucial to economic development. Thirdly, specific economic legislation may encourage certain forms of enterprise or economic organisation. On the other hand, economic factors may influence law; a good example is the manner in which lawyers in England placed themselves at the disposal of commercial clients.

In his analysis of this reciprocal relationship, Weber frequently points to exceptions, limitations or even contradictions of this connection. In Kronman's words (*Max Weber*, p. 129):

Every strong claim that he makes regarding the influence of one or the other is qualified, somewhere in the text, by an assertion that the influence has only been partial or indirect and has in any case been exerted in the opposite direction as well. To some extent, this agnostic conclusion is unilluminating.

And, he might have added, frustrating! But perhaps this is the mark of a genuine scientist: he is not merely seeking to prove his hypothesis, but, in the seach for truth, he pays equal attention to those phenomena that may refute it. Real life is acknowledged to be too complex to admit of simple or comforting causative links.

FURTHER READING

Black, Donald, *The Behavior of Law* (New York; London: Academic Press, 1976).
Campbell, C. M., and Wiles, Paul (eds), *Law and Society* (London: Martin Robertson, 1979).

Chambliss, William, and Seidman, Robert, *Law, Order, and Power*, 2nd ed. (Reading, Mass; London: Addison-Wesley, 1982).

Cotterrell, Roger, *Law's Community: Legal Theory in Sociological Perspective* (Oxford: Clarendon Press, 1995).

Cotterrell, Roger, *The Sociology of Law: An Introduction* (London: Butterworths, 1984).

Durkheim, Émile, *The Division of Labor in Society*, transl. George Simpson (London: Collier-Macmillan, 1964).

Ehrlich, Eugen, *Fundamental Principles of the Sociology of Law*, transl. W. L. Moss (Cambridge, Mass: Harvard University Press, 1936) (Harvard Studies in Jurisprudence, vol. 5).

Hunt, Alan, *The Sociological Movement in Law* (London: Macmillan, 1978).

Kronman, Anthony R., *Max Weber* (London: Edward Arnold, 1983).

Lukes, Steven, and Scull, Andrew (eds), *Durkheim and the Law* (Oxford: Martin Robertson, 1983).

Nonet, Philippe, and Selznick, Philip, *Law and Society in Transition: Toward Responsive Law* (New York: Octagon Books, 1978).

Parkin, Frank, *Max Weber* (Chichester: Ellis Horwood, 1982).

Pound, Roscoe, *Jurisprudence* (St Paul, Minn: West Publishing Co., 1959).

Rokumoto, Kahei (ed.), *Sociological Theories of Law* (Aldershot: Dartmouth, 1994).

Schubert, Glendon A. (ed.), *Judicial Behavior: A Reader in Theory and Research* (Chicago, Ill: Rand McNally, 1964).

Teubner, Gunther (ed.), *Autopoietic Law: A New Approach to Law and Society* (Berlin: Walter de Gruyter, 1987).

Tönnies, Ferdinand, *Community and Association*, transl. and supplemented Charles P. Loomis (London: Routledge & Kegan Paul, 1974).

Turner, Stephen P., and Factor, Regis A., *Max Weber: The Lawyer as Social Thinker* (London: Routledge, 1994).

Weber, Max, *Economy and Society: An Outline of Interpretive Sociology*, ed. Guenther Roth and Claus Wittich (New York: Bedminister Press, 1968).

Weber, Max, *Max Weber on Law in Economy and Society*, ed. Max Rheinstein, transl. Edward Shils and Max Rheinstein (Cambridge, Mass: Harvard University Press, 1954) (20th Century Legal Philosophy Series, vol. 6).

Weber, Max, *The Religion of China: Confucianism and Taoism*, transl. and ed. Hans H. Gerth (Glencoe, Ill: The Free Press, 1951).

9 JUSTICE: LEFT, RIGHT AND CENTRE

What is justice? How is it to be secured? Is there a necessary connection between law and justice? Questions like these have exercised the minds of thinkers since Plato and Aristotle. Theories of justice are a significant, and abiding, concern of moral, political and legal theory. You will be told of the contributions of these great Greek philosophers to the problem of justice and, after studying their modern counterparts (Bentham, Rawls, Nozick), you may be inclined to wonder whether we have got any closer to defining this elusive ideal. There is, as you might expect, a large body of literature on the general question of justice. Useful collections of essays may be found in T. Morawetz (ed.), *Justice* and E. Kamenka and A. Tay (eds), *Justice*. A careful discussion of various theories of justice is to be found in C. Perelman, *The Idea of Justice and the Problem of Argument* and J. R. Lucas, *On Justice*.

Before embarking on a consideration of the different approaches to justice (as promised by the title of this chapter) it is worth briefly mentioning Aristotle's analysis of the subject in bk. 5 of his *Nicomachean Ethics* which still forms the starting-point for most discussions of justice. For him justice consists in treating equals equally and unequals unequally, in proportion to their inequality. He recognised that the equality implied in justice could be arithmetical — based on the identity of the persons concerned, or geometrical — based on maintaining the same proportion. This is Aristotle's famous distinction between *corrective* or *commutative* justice, on the one hand, and *distributive* justice, on the other. The former was, in his view, the justice of the courts which was applied in the redress of crimes or civil wrongs. It required that all men were to be treated equally. Distributive justice is concerned with giving each according to his desert or merit. This, in Aristotle's view, was principally the concern of the legislator.

In *The Concept of Law*, Professor Hart argues (p. 156) that the idea of justice:

> consists of two parts: a uniform or constant feature, summarised in the precept 'Treat like cases alike' and a shifting or varying criterion used in determining when, for any given purpose, cases are alike or different.

He suggests that today the principle that, prima facie, human beings are entitled to be treated alike has become so widely accepted that racial discrimination is usually defended on the ground that those discriminated against are not 'fully human'.

The subject of justice is, needless to say, a very large one. It is normally beyond the scope of most jurisprudence courses to pursue the complex philosophical debates that have raged for so long. This chapter is therefore devoted to three central theories of justice. I shall first consider utilitarianism and its modern alternative, the economic analysis of law (including Robert Nozick's radical approach to the problem). Next I shall sketch the main features of John Rawls's important theory of 'justice as fairness'. Finally (and somewhat uncomfortably in a chapter on justice) I shall consider Marxist theories of law and state.

UTILITARIANISM

On one level, utilitarianism represents an assault on the metaphysics that characterised a good deal of 18th-century political philosophy. Indeed, as we saw in chapter 3, Bentham spends much of his energy fulminating against natural rights (which he called 'nonsense on stilts') and, in particular, Blackstone. But it is much more. It has a profound moral basis which takes as its premise the proposition that the fundamental objective of morality and justice is that happiness should be maximised. Though there are a number of classical utilitarian theories (including those of John Stuart Mill and Henry Sidgwick) it is Jeremy Bentham's formulation that tends to be the one that is most familiar to students of jurisprudence. This sometimes leads to an equation of Bentham and utilitarianism which is to overlook the fact that his form of utilitarianism is what J. J. C. Smart calls 'hedonistic' and may be contrasted with G. E. Moore's 'non-hedonistic' utilitarianism, and Mill's intermediate position. You should therefore be careful, when discussing utilitarianism, to indicate that you, at least, recognise its different forms. In practice, however, most jurisprudence courses tend to confine their study to classical utilitarianism as represented by Jeremy Bentham. His general view is well captured in this famous passage from *An Introduction to the Principles of Morals and Legislation*, ch. 1, para. 1:

Nature has placed mankind under the governance of two sovereign masters, *pain* and *pleasure*. It is for them alone to point out what we ought to do, as well as to determine what we shall do. On the one hand the standard of right and wrong, on the other the chain of causes and effects, are fastened to their throne.... The *principle of utility* recognises this subjection, and assumes it for the foundation of that system, the object of which is to rear the fabric of felicity by the hands of reason and of law. Systems which attempt to question it, deal in sounds instead of sense, in caprice instead of reason, in darkness instead of light.

To this end Bentham devised his 'felicific calculus' by which we might test the 'happiness factor' of any action. This much is reasonably straightforward. But too many students are so impressed (or amused) by Bentham's classification of 12 pains and 14 pleasures and its attractive (or crude) simplicity that they barely progress beyond generalities about the defects of the theory. Serious students will want to read J. J. C. Smart and Bernard Williams's *Utilitarianism: For and Against* in which these two distinguished philosophers present both sides of the argument in a sustained analysis of the theory's merits and demerits. A helpful discussion of the subject may also be found in ch. 1 of N. E. Simmonds, *Central Issues in Jurisprudence*.

The essence of utilitarianism is its *consequentialism*. It is important therefore to distinguish consequentialist from *deontological* systems of ethics. The former is self-explanatory, the latter is its opposite: it holds that the rightness or wrongness of an action is logically independent of its consequences — 'Let justice be done though the heavens fall' is one of its proud slogans. Utilitarianism therefore looks to the future; it is concerned to maximise happiness or welfare or some other 'good'. Philosophers distinguish two forms of utilitarianism: 'act utilitarianism' and 'rule utilitarianism'. The former adopts the position that the rightness or wrongness of an action is to be judged by the consequences, good or bad, of the *action itself*. The latter argues that the rightness or wrongness of an action is to be judged by the goodness or badness of *the consequences of a rule that everyone should perform the action in like circumstances* (Smart and Williams, *Utilitarianism: For and Against*, p. 9).

Most discussions of utilitarianism (including this one) concern themselves with act utilitarianism, though in the context of legal theory it is not uncommon to find appeals made to 'ideal rule utilitarianism' which provides that the rightness or wrongness of an action is to be judged by the goodness or badness of a rule which, *if observed*, would have better consequences than any other rule governing the same action. This version of rule utilitarianism has obvious advantages in the context of a judge who is called upon to decide whether the plaintiff should be awarded damages against the defendant: clearly he should ignore the effect of his judgment on the *particular* indigent defendant. It may be contrasted with 'actual rule utilitarianism' which holds that the rightness of an action is to be judged by reference to a rule which is *actually observed* and whose acceptance would maximise utility.

Consequences

What does it mean to say that a utilitarian is concerned to evaluate the *consequences* of our actions? Consider the following illustration (adapted from Simmonds, *Central Issues in Jurisprudence*, pp. 17–18): I am stranded on a desert island with no one but a dying man who, in his final hours, entrusts me with £10,000 which he asks me to give to his daughter, Rita, if I ever manage to return to England. I promise to do so, and, after my rescue, I find Rita living in a mansion; she has married a millionaire. The £10,000 will now make little difference to her financial situation. Should I not instead donate the money to charity? As a utilitarian, I consider the possible *consequences* of my action. But what *are* the consequences? I must weigh the result of my broken promise against the benefit of giving the £10,000 to the RSPCA. Would keeping my promise have better consequences than breaking it? If I break my promise, I may be less likely to keep other promises I have made, and others may be encouraged to take their own promise-keeping less seriously. I must, in other words, attempt to calculate *all* the likely consequences of my choice. But a non-consequentialist Kantian might argue that the reason why I should give the money to Rita is that I have *promised* to do so. My action ought to be guided not by some uncertain *future* consequence, but by an unequivocal *past* fact: my promise. My reply might be that I *do* consider the past fact of my promise — but only to the extent that it affects the *total consequences* of my action of giving the money to the RSPCA instead of to Rita. I might also say that it is absurd to argue that I am obliged to keep *every* promise I make. Suppose, I argue, I promise to meet you at the pub at 8 p.m. On the way I am run over by a bus and end up in hospital. You would (I hope!) not regard me as immoral because I fail to keep my promise to you. It is surely *implied* that my promise is subject to certain (unspecified) exceptions. We begin to see the complexity of the utilitarian/deontological debate.

Preferences

Bentham's version of hedonistic act utilitarianism is generally considered too quaint for modern tastes, while the 'ideal' act utilitarianism of Moore (who, broadly speaking, thought that certain states of mind, such as those of acquiring knowledge, had an *intrinsic* value independent of their pleasant-ness) and J. S. Mill (who argued that there are higher and lower pleasures — implying that pleasure is a necessary condition for goodness, but that goodness depends on qualities of experience other than pleasantness and unpleasantness) are regarded as somewhat £)££litist. This is largely because these writers tend to substitute their own preferences for the preferences they thought people *ought* to have. Modern utilitarians therefore talk of maximising the extent to which people may achieve what they *want*; we should seek to satisfy people's *preferences*. This has the merit of not imposing any conception of 'the good' which leaves out of account individual choice: you may prefer backgammon to Bach or billiards to Beethoven. But it raises certain difficulties of its own; see chapter 10.

Critique of utilitarianism

Moral philosophers have spilled a good deal of ink disputing the value of consequentialism in general and utilitarianism in particular. It is unlikely that there will be time in your jurisprudence course to treat the subject in detail, but you will need to know its essence, if only to understand its modern outgrowth, the economic analysis of law, and also to appreciate theories, especially Rawls's, which seek to avoid the drawbacks of utilitarianism. The attacks on utilitarianism are many and varied. I shall identify eight such criticisms. A fundamental assault on utilitarianism is made by those — who include Bernard Williams (in Smart and Williams, *Utilitarianism: For and Against*) and Rawls himself (see page 194 ff) — who argue that it fails to recognise the 'separateness of persons'. It suggests that utilitarianism, at least in its pure form, treats human beings as means rather than ends in themselves. This important attack consists, in Professor Hart's view (expressed in his essay, 'Between utility and rights', in his *Essays in Jurisprudence and Philosophy*, p. 198 at pp. 200–2), of four main points which may be summarised as follows:

(a)   Separate individuals are important to utilitarians only in so far as they are 'the channels or locations where what is of value is to be found'.

(b)   Utilitarianism treats individual persons equally, but only by effectively treating them as having *no* worth, for their value is not *as persons*, but as 'experiencers' of pleasure or happiness.

(c)   Why should we regard as a valuable moral goal the mere increase in totals of pleasure or happiness abstracted from all questions of *distribution* of happiness, welfare etc?

(d)   The analogy used by utilitarians, of a rational single individual prudently sacrificing present happiness for later satisfaction, is false for it treats my pleasure as replaceable by the greater pleasure of others.

These four criticisms contain most of the issues that lie at the heart of many of the other attacks, of which the following may be mentioned. Why *should* we seek to satisfy people's desires? Certain desires are unworthy of satisfaction (e.g., the sadist who wants to torture children). Note that Bentham's catalogue includes 'the pleasure of malevolence'.

A third attack is one made by Rawls: he argues that utilitarianism defines what is right in terms of what is 'good'; but this means, he says, that it begins with a conception of what is 'good' (e.g., happiness) and then concludes that an action is *right* in so far as it maximises that 'good'. See his alternative, page 169. Fourthly, utilitarianism is concerned only with maximising welfare; many regard the more important question as the just *distribution* of welfare. Fifthly, many critics point to the impracticability of *calculating* the consequences of one's actions: how can we know in advance what results will follow from what we propose to do. Sixthly, are our wants and desires not manipulated by persuasion, advertising and the like? If so, can we separate our 'real' preferences from our 'conditioned' ones? Should we, as utilitarians, then set about trying to suggest to people that they *should* prefer reading Kelsen to sunbathing? If so, how do we justify doing this? If we answer that the principle of utility requires us to do this, we are saying that the 'felicific calculus' includes not only what we *want*, but also what we may one day *decide* to want as a result of persuasion or 're-education'!

Seventhly, is it possible (or, if it is, is it desirable?) to balance my pleasure against your pain? On a larger scale, can judges or legislators, when faced with a choice between two or more courses of action, realistically (or even sensibly) weigh the majority's happiness against a minority's misery? Eighthly, how far into the future do (or can) we extend the consequences of our actions? Or to put it slightly differently, as Williams does (in Smart and Williams, *Utilitarianism: For and Against*, p. 82): 'No one can hold that everything, of whatever category, that has value, has it in virtue of its consequences. If that were so, one would just go on for ever, and there would be an obviously hopeless regress.'

There are many other arguments and counter-arguments. Note, too, that utilitarianism may be treated as a system of *personal* morality or as one of *social or political* decision. As far as legal theory is concerned it is usually the latter. Bentham, of course, sought to show that, on the basis of the former, we could generalise outwards to the latter. And many of the important law reforms of the 19th century are attributable to its influence as a political theory. But, it has few supporters today. Instead, it appears in the nether garments of the so-called 'economic analysis of law'.

THE ECONOMIC ANALYSIS OF LAW

This modern form of utilitarianism has, as its launching-pad, the proposition that the rational man or woman always chooses to do what will maximise his or her satisfactions. And if they want something badly enough they will be prepared to *pay* for it. The guru of this latter-day economic hedonism, Richard

Posner, though he denies that he adopts a utilitarian position, argues (especially in his *The Economic Analysis of Law* and *The Economics of Justice*) that much of the common law can be explained by this simple fact of life. Judges frequently decide hard cases by choosing an outcome which will maximise the wealth of society. By 'wealth maximisation' Posner means a situation in which goods and other resources are in the hands of those people who *value them most*; that is to say, those people who are willing (and able) to *pay* more to have them. So, for example, if I buy your copy of *The Concept of Law* for £5 when the most I was *willing* to pay for it was £6, my wealth has been increased by £1. In the same way, society maximises its wealth when all its resources are distributed in such a way that the sum of everyone's transactions is as high as possible. And this, argues Posner, is as it *should* be; his analysis is thus both descriptive and normative. Moreover, in a series of essays, he and other members of the so-called Chicago school, attempt to demonstrate how common law judges have (mostly unconsciously) been guided by these economic considerations. Thus, in the development of the law of negligence, Posner argues, the imposition of liability normally depends on what is most efficient economically. In his words (*The Economic Analysis of Law*, p. 179):

> The common law method is to allocate responsibilities between people engaged in interacting activities in such a way as to maximise the joint value, or, what amounts to the same thing, minimise the joint cost of the activities.

And how does it do this?

> It may do this by redefining a property right, by devising a new rule of liability, or by recognising a contract right, but nothing fundamental turns on which device is used (loc. cit.).

Much of this provocative post-utilitarian revisionism is dressed up in the jargon of economics; the innocent jurisprudence student is therefore expected to understand (and employ) terms such as 'optimality', 'transaction costs', 'damage costs', 'precaution costs'. But don't panic; most of these intimidating concepts actually stand for fairly straightforward ideas. Thus, 'optimality' is simply what is best for the parties to a transaction. Indeed, even the test of Pareto optimality (named after the Italian economist Vilfredo Pareto) describes a situation which cannot be altered without making at least one person think he is worse off than he was prior to the change. Nor should you find the so-called Kaldor-Hicks test beyond comprehension: it is satisfied when the alteration in the allocation of resources produces enough money to compensate those who are losers. The concept of 'diminishing marginal utility' refers to the fact that £1 given to an impoverished beggar would have a major effect on his wealth, whereas to a millionaire £1 would make almost no difference at all.

And the widely used Coase theorem (after the economist Ronald Coase) postulates a situation in which one outcome is the most 'efficient'. For example, a factory emits smoke which causes damage to laundry hung outdoors by five nearby residents. In the absence of any corrective measures, each resident would suffer £75 in damages, a total of £375. The smoke damage may be prevented in one of two ways: either a smoke-screen could be installed on the factory's chimney, at a cost of £150, or each resident could be provided with an electric tumble-drier at a cost of £50 per resident. The *efficient* solution is obviously to install the smoke-screen since it eliminates total damage of £375 for an outlay of only £150, and it is cheaper than purchasing five electric driers for £250. But the question raised by Coase is whether the efficient outcome would result if the right to clean air were assigned to the residents or if the right to pollute is given to the factory. In the case of the former, the factory has three choices: pollute and pay £375 in damages, install a smoke-screen for £150, or buy five tumble-driers for the residents at a total cost of £250. The factory would, naturally, install the smoke-screen: the efficient solution. If there is a right to pollute, the residents have three choices: suffer their collective damages of £375, buy five driers for £250, or buy a smoke-screen for the factory for £150. They, too, would choose to buy the smoke-screen. The efficient outcome would therefore be achieved *regardless of the assignment of the legal right*. This simple hypothesis assumes that the residents would incur no costs in coming together in order to negotiate with the factory. Coase calls this 'zero transaction costs'. But real life is more complex: certain costs would be incurred in this process. The simple version of the Coase theorem may therefore be stated as follows: where there are zero transaction costs, the efficient outcome will occur regardless of the choice of legal rule. You can see why, for 'economists of law', the Coase theorem (which has a more complex version where there are 'positive transaction costs') is so important. A useful, untechnical introduction to the subject (from which I have borrowed the above example) is A. M. Polinsky, *An Introduction to Law and Economics*.

I cannot here explore these interesting questions (which have become an integral part of many jurisprudence courses) further. But there is much in the economic analysis to stimulate lawyers into thinking about just solutions — at least where it is possible to place an economic value on costs and benefits. It has therefore been applied, with some success, to the problem of measuring the efficiency of our systems of accident compensation. A powerful attack on the foundation of the theory has been launched by Ronald Dworkin. Two of his essays, in particular, may be consulted with benefit: 'Is wealth a value?' and 'Why efficiency?', both of which are reproduced in *A Matter of Principle*, at p. 237 and p. 267 respectively. Judge Posner has attempted to defend his economic analysis (and is further attacked by Dworkin) in Marshall Cohen (ed.), *Ronald Dworkin and Contemporary Jurisprudence*, pp. 238 and 295. See, too, *Lloyd's Introduction to Jurisprudence*, pp. 454–63 for extracts from this Dworkin-Posner debate. Note the ambitious claim Posner makes for his theory:

> I have tried to develop a moral theory that goes beyond classical utilitarianism and holds that the criterion for judging whether acts and institutions are just or good is whether they maximise the wealth of society. This approach allows a reconciliation among utility, liberty, and even equality as competing ethical principles. (*The Economics of Justice*, p. 115. See *Lloyd's Introduction to Jurisprudence*, p. 463.)

And it is, of course, Posner's view that judges have proceeded on this assumption in the development of the common law, a thesis which Dworkin dismisses: 'It has not achieved the beginning of a beginning' (*A Matter of Principle*, p. 265). It would be impossible to do justice to this debate here, but four major criticisms of the economic analysis of law may be briefly identified. Each, of course, stands in need of elaboration. First, the theory rests on the assumption that wealth maximisation is a value (in itself or instrumentally) that a society would regard as worth trading off against justice, but as Dworkin puts it, '... increasing social wealth does not in itself make the community better' (*Law's Empire*, p. 288). Secondly, the theory oversimplifies what is a complex matter; in the words of one critic, "What people want' is presented in such a way that while in form it is empirical it is almost wholly non-falsifiable by anything so crude as fact' (A. A. Leff, 'Economic analysis of law: some realism about nominalism' (1974) 60 Va LRev 451, 456). Thirdly, the theory merely reflects a particular ideological preference: it reinforces and advances the capitalist, free-market system. Fourthly, what does the theory have to do with *justice*? It presupposes an *initial* distribution of wealth — which may be wholly unjust. 'Efficiency' therefore becomes a means of rationalising, and sustaining, existing inequalities.

NOZICK

The political philosophy of Robert Nozick (*Anarchy, State, and Utopia*), along with the writings of certain other theorists (notably F. A. Hayek in a number of works, particularly *The Road to Serfdom* and *The Constitution of Liberty*), represents another challenge to the very idea of wealth distribution as postulated, in particular, by John Rawls (see page 168). This attack comes from the right, though, in the case of Nozick at least, in a number of respects, the orthodox right finds his theory uncongenial. For example, his emphasis (some might prefer to say obsession) with the *individual* is inhospitable to the nationalism that is the hallmark of much of the philosophy of the so-called 'new right'. Secondly, Nozick's profound individualism leads him to reject any form of paternalism; he therefore argues that since individuals own their bodies, they should be free to use them for whatever purpose they choose. This sounds a death knell for the legislation proscribing homosexuality or the possession of drugs which the right generally support. But while there is always a danger in ideological labelling, Nozick's version of liberal capitalism hardly belongs on the left or even the centre of the political spectrum.

For Nozick liberty and equality are irreconcilable: we cannot, he argues, interfere with the distribution of resources in society without interfering with the liberty of individuals. Any attempt at 'patterned' distribution (like the one advocated by Rawls; see page 193) presupposes a State with excessive powers. The State, in Nozick's view, is 'intrinsically immoral' (*Anarchy, State, and Utopia*, p. 51); therefore, following Spencer and Locke (see chapter 5), he proposes a 'minimal State' whose functions are limited to the 'night-watchman' protection against force, theft and fraud, the enforcement of contracts and a few other essentials. A State that goes beyond this narrow model is an infringement of individual freedom which is based on the 'separateness of persons'. We should be concerned not with redistributing resources, but with protecting individuals' rights to *what they already have*. In other words, the question of whether a particular distribution of goods is just should be answered by reference to whether the *initial acquisition* was just. So, where I acquired my property by freely entering into a contract, I am entitled to keep it, hence Nozick's 'entitlement theory' of justice.

The theory is based on the following three sets of principles:

(a) *Principles of acquisition*: they determine the circumstances under which persons are able to acquire ownership of previously unowned resources.

(b) *Principles of transfer*: they determine the methods by which the ownership of resources may be transferred between persons.

(c) *Principles of rectification*: they determine how an *unjust* acquisition or transfer of property should be rectified (e.g., where property has been acquired fraudulently).

An immediate question arises about this comforting historical entitlement theory: what if the distribution of goods in society at large is manifestly unjust? Nozick's reply is that 'If each person's holdings are just, then the total set (distribution) of holdings is just' (*Anarchy, State, and Utopia*, p. 153). This cavalier hostility toward a fairer redistribution of social goods sticks in the throats of many who value social justice. But, however abhorrent you may find Nozick's theory, be sure to attack it on stronger grounds than the student who, in an examination, asserted that 'Nozick is a crypto-fascist'. The publication of *Anarchy, State, and Utopia* excited a fair amount of controversy (partly because its author is a relatively young Harvard professor who was taught by John Rawls) and the book has been subjected to a good deal of (often indignant) criticism. Depending on how much time is spent on Nozick in your course, you will want to read some of this criticism: you will find a useful collection of essays in J. Paul (ed.), *Reading Nozick*. Here I shall mention only six criticisms of Nozick's views (the merest outline of which has been sketched above). First, his account rests on an oversimplified conception of the individual who is isolated from society; moreover his

> ... world not only excludes the ever-growing role of the State within contemporary capitalism; it is also radically pre-sociological, without social structure, or social or cultural determinants of, and constraints upon, the voluntary acts and exchanges of its component individuals'. (S. Lukes, 'State of nature', in *Essays in Social Theory*, p. 194.)

Secondly, Nozick's assault on utilitarianism is, as Hart shows, ('Between utility and rights', in *Essays in Jurisprudence and Philosophy*, p. 205) paradoxical:

> ... it yields a result identical with one of the least acceptable conclusions of an unqualified maximising utilitarianism, namely that given certain conditions there is nothing to choose between a society where few enjoy great happiness and very many very little, and a society where happiness is more equally spread.

A utilitarian would regard the aggregate or average welfare in both societies as the same. Nozick, of course, treats the condition as a historical one. But neither, Hart seems to be suggesting, is willing to disturb the existing pattern of distribution, however unequal. A third sort of criticism concerns the Nozickian model of the minimal 'night-watchman' State. How does this State *emerge* from a state of nature, as Nozick argues it does, without infringing individual rights? And, as Lloyd (*Introduction to Jurisprudence*, p. 373) asks:

> How is the minimal State to be controlled? How is it to be kept minimal? How are the economically advantaged to be stopped acquiring political power? The minimal State and an alert citizenry [are] supposed to stop this happening. How is destitution to be prevented and relieved? Nozick's answer, naïve in the extreme, points to the free operation of the market, voluntary uniting and private philanthropy.

Fourthly, Nozick's oft-quoted comparison of income tax to forced labour has been attacked by a number of critics (including Hart, *Essays in Jurisprudence and Philosophy*, p. 206) who question the legitimacy of treating the two as remotely equivalent. In Hart's words:

> Is taxing a man's earnings or income, which leaves him free to choose whether to work and to choose what work to do, not altogether different in terms of the burden it imposes from forcing him to labour? Does it really sacrifice him or make him or his body just a resource for others?

Fifthly, why should we accept Nozick's limitation of rights to those of property and the negative right to liberty? What of rights to welfare? Nozick would, of course, reply that to recognise such rights implies that individuals have a right to the assistance *of others*; this would undermine his whole premise which is based on the 'separateness' of persons. But we are surely entitled to object that this entirely neglects the interests of the weaker members of society.

Sixthly, Nozick's reliance on Locke's theory of individual property seems misguided. We saw in chapter 5 that Locke argues that we acquire ownership over a thing by mixing our labour with it. But, as N. E. Simmonds, *Central Issues in Jurisprudence*, pp. 56–7, asks, can this apply to *natural resources*? If I apply my labours to extracting oil from beneath the ocean, the Lockean theory would presumably permit me to claim ownership of the oil I have extracted. But, unlike a table I build, I did not bring the oil into being: on what ground should I be able to assert an exclusive right over the full value of the oil? Note that, though Nozick mounts a frontal attack on Rawls's theory of justice, both share a hostility to utilitarianism. It would be a useful exercise to compare how and why each comes to reject utility as a basis for a just society.

RAWLS

John Rawls's massive book, *A Theory of Justice* is, by the admission of one of its most vehement critics, Robert Nozick:

> ... a powerful, deep, subtle, wide-ranging, systematic work in political and moral philosophy which has not seen its like since the writings of John Stuart Mill, if then. It is a fountain of illuminating ideas, integrated together into a lovely whole. Political philosophers now must either work within Rawls' theory or explain why not. (*Anarchy, State, and Utopia*, p. 183.)

You will be well advised to pay close attention to this important revival of social contractarianism (see chapter 5). In an ideal world, you should read the book itself. This is not, however, an ideal world and even the most conscientious student will find neither the time nor the patience to plough through its 600 (often difficult) pages. There are several admirable commentaries on *A Theory of Justice* to which you will doubtless be referred. My own preference — from a student's point of view — is *Reading Rawls*, edited by N. Daniels, which contains a helpful introduction and a number of illuminating essays (especially those by T. Nagel, R. Dworkin, T. M. Scanlon, R. Miller and H. L. A. Hart). Many of the criticisms made of the book are answered in Rawls's book *Political Liberalism* published in 1993, where he develops his theory of justice into a comprehensive political and institutional theory of democracy. I shall here provide a sketch of the four most important general aspects of the original theory, followed by a brief critique.

The Rejection of Utilitarianism

Like Nozick and Dworkin (see chapters 6 and 9), Rawls regards utilitarianism as an unsatisfactory means by which to measure justice. His attack on utility is, however, different from both of theirs (and I shall devote more attention to it in the section on the examination, pages 204–7). Suffice it to say here that Rawls's hostility toward utilitarianism is based largely on two features of the theory. First, that it fails to recognise the separateness or distinctness of individual persons; this is an aspect that many anti-utilitarians (including Dworkin and Nozick) find unacceptable. Secondly, Rawls argues that quesions of justice are *prior to* questions of happiness. In other words, it is only when we regard a particular pleasure as just that we can say whether it has any value. How do we know whether John's enjoyment of torture should be counted as having any value *before* we know whether the practice of torture is itself *just*? (See the discussion of utilitarianism, pages 180–4.) Thus, whereas utilitarianism defines what is right in terms of what is good, Rawls regards what is right as prior to what is good.

Social Contractarianism

Rawls's theory of justice as fairness is rooted in the idea of the social contract (see chapter 5). In *A Theory of Justice*, p. 11, he expresses the objective of his project as follows (emphasis added):

My aim is to present a conception of justice which generalises and carries to a higher level of abstraction the familiar theory of the social contract as found, say, in Locke, Rousseau, and Kant. In order to do this we are not to think of the original contract as one to enter a particular society or to set up a particular form of government. Rather, the guiding idea is that the principles of justice for the basic structure of society are the object of *the original agreement*. They are the principles that *free and rational persons* concerned to further *their own interests* would accept in an *initial position of equality* as defining the fundamental terms of their association. These principles are to regulate all further agreements; they specify the kinds of social cooperation that can be entered into and the forms of government that can be established. This way of regarding the principles of justice I shall call *justice as fairness.*

Read this passage twice. It captures, I think, the essence of Rawls's theory of justice. The phrases I have italicised are key elements in his social contractarian argument, the attraction of which is the objectivity it seeks to present. We must, Rawls argues, distinguish between people's genuine judgments about justice and their subjective, self-interested views. In doing so, it is plain that the position adopted by a hypothetical neutral outsider concerning what is just is likely to be fairer than that which we hold as parties who have a vested interest in the outcome. Once we have arrived at those objective principles, we should measure them against our own judgments. The inevitable distinction between the two must be corrected by our modifying our own judgments in such a way that we eventually reach a situation in which the two are similar: this is the position of 'reflective equilibrium' (*A Theory of Justice*, pp. 20 and 48–51).

The Original Position

Most students enjoy Rawls's imaginary picture of the POP (people in the 'original position') sitting ('under a tree' according to at least one!), each shrouded in a 'veil of ignorance', debating the principles of justice. This ignorance prevents them from knowing to which sex, class, religion or social position they belong. Each person represents a social class, but they do not know whether they are clever or stupid, strong or weak. Nor do they know in which country or in what period they are living. They possess only certain elementary knowledge about the laws of science and psychology. In this state of blissful ignorance they must unanimously decide upon the general principles that will define the terms under which they will live as a society. And, in doing so, they are moved by rational self-interest: each seeks those principles which will give him or her (but they do not know their sex!) the best chance of attaining his or her chosen conception of the good life (whatever that happens to be). So stripped of their individuality, the POP will opt, says Rawls, for a 'maximin' principle. This strategy may be explained by Rawls's own gain and loss table (*A Theory of Justice*, p. 153) (slightly adapted):

	Circumstances		
Decisions	C1	C2	C3
D1	−£700	£800	£1,200
D2	−£800	£700	£1,400
D3	£500	£600	£800

I must choose from among several possible circumstances. So, if I choose D1, and C1 occurs, I will lose £700, but if C2 occurs I will gain £800 and, if I am really lucky and C3 should occur, I will gain £1,200. And similarly in respect of decisions D2 and D3. Gain g therefore depends on the individual's decision d and the circumstances c. Thus g is a function of d and c. Or, to express it mathematically $g = f(d, c)$. Which decision would I choose? The maximin principle dictates that I opt for D3 because in this case the *worst* that can happen to me is that I gain £500 — which is better than the worst for the other actions (in which I stand to lose either £800 or £700).

Similarly, the POP, as rational individuals, would choose principles which guarantee that the worst condition one might find oneself in, when the veil of ignorance is lifted, is the least undesirable of the available alternatives. In other words, I will select those principles which, *should I turn out to be at the bottom of the social pile*, will be in my best interests. So, argues, Rawls, the POP will choose the following two principles.

The Two Principles of Justice

First principle. 'Each person is to have an equal right to the most extensive total system of equal basic liberties compatible with a similar system of liberty for all.'

Second principle. 'Social and economic inequalities are to be arranged so that they are both:

(a)   to the greatest benefit of the least advantaged, consistent with the just savings principle, and
(b)   attached to offices and positions open to all under conditions of fair equality of opportunity.'

You should know these two principles intimately, but a most important feature is that the first has 'lexical priority' over the second. Or, to put it simply, the POP put *liberty above equality* — because of the 'maximin' strategy described above: no one would wish to risk his or her liberty when the veil of ignorance is removed and it is revealed they are among the least well-off members of society. By the same token of maximin reasoning, they will opt for clause (a) of the second principle — the so-called 'difference principle'. This ensures that the worst anyone could be is 'least advantaged' and, if they do belong to this group, they will benefit from this clause. It would be rational for them to choose this principle rather than either total equality or some form of greater inequality, because of the respective risks of being worse off or reducing the prospects of improving their lot. And, they will be better able to 'improve their lot' in a society which places liberty above equality; this is because various 'social primary goods' (which Rawls defines to include rights, liberties, powers, opportunities, income, wealth and especially self-respect) are more likely to be attained in a free society.

Another reason why Rawls argues that the difference principle will appeal to the POP is that it is preferable to its two chief competitors: the 'system of natural liberty' and the idea of 'fair equality of opportunity'. The former consists in an untrammelled market economy which makes no attempt to redistribute wealth. The POP would reject this principle, he argues, because it 'permits distributive shares to be improperly influenced by ... factors so arbitrary from a moral point of view'. Thus the accident of being born into a wealthy family would be relevant, whereas, morally speaking, it ought not to be. The latter bases people's prospects on their natural talent and the energies they expend in applying them effectively. This is clearly preferable to the system of natural liberty, but it is, in Rawls's view open to a similar objection: why should an individual's talents be any more morally relevant than the fact that he is the son of a millionaire? In neither case do these accidents have anything to do with *desert*. Choosing the difference principle, however, means that individuals who have natural talents may increase their wealth only if, in the process, they also increase the wealth of the *least advantaged*.

The second principle contains two important limitations that ensure that the least advantaged benefit from the social arrangements selected. First, the 'just savings principle': this refers to the need for the POP (who do not, of course, know which stage of civilisation their society has reached: are they in the First World or the Third?) to ask themselves how much they would be willing to save at each stage of advance, on the assumption that all other generations will save at the same rates. The principle therefore:

> ... assigns an appropriate rate of accumulation to each level of advance. Presumably this rate changes depending upon the state of society. When people are poor and saving is difficult, a lower rate of saving should be required; whereas in a wealthier society greater savings may reasonably be expected since the real burden is less. Eventually once just institutions are firmly established, the net accumulation required falls to zero. (*A Theory of Justice*, p. 287.)

The POP will therefore save some of their resources for future generations.

The second limitation refers to the fact that all offices should be open to all (and not, as one examination candidate suggested that 'offices should be open at all hours'!). Rawls is here referring to job opportunities.

Political Liberalism

In the decades since the publication of *A Theory of Justice* in 1972, Rawls has revised, refined and modified his ideas in a number of essays, culminating in

1993 in the publication of his book *Political Liberalism*. He takes into account the plethora of criticism (and misunderstanding) that his earlier work (itself the outcome of a similar process) provoked. While there are numerous amendments and explanations, I shall mention only those that strike me as the most significant.

First, it is clear that, although many critics regarded his principles of justice as a sort of Archimedean point in ethics which would provide a universal standard of social justice, Rawls intended no such thing. His theory is meant to apply to modern constitutional democracies. Secondly, he demonstrates another feature of the modesty of his thesis: the idea of 'justice as fairness' is a *political* rather than an epistemological or metaphysical task. It is, in other words, a conception of justice that is fundamentally practical. It is supposed to be philosophically neutral, to transcend philosophical controversy.

Thirdly, in pursuit of an elusive 'overlapping consensus', Rawls posits his principles of justice as the terms under which members of a pluralistic, democratic community with competing interests and values might achieve political accord. His conception of political liberalism acknowledges that this consensus may be challenged by the establishment by the State of a shared moral or religious doctrine. But the community's sense of justice would prevail over the State's interpretation of the public good. See his article, 'The idea of an overlapping consensus' (1987) 7 Oxford J Legal Stud 1.

Fourthly, the first principle of justice which originally requires that each person have an equal right to 'the most extensive total system of equal basic liberties' now consists in an equal right to 'a fully adequate scheme of equal basic liberties'. Fifthly, Rawls demonstrates how the two principles of justice might, following the 'original position', be adopted constitutionally (the first principle is enshrined in the constitution), legislatively (the second principle may be accepted by democratic decision), and, judicially (the courts ensure that the supreme law of the constitution is defended against the vagaries of legislative activity).

This may seem a slightly romantic, Utopian vision of social and political harmony. Rawls denies this:

> ... an initial acquiescence in a liberal conception of justice as a mere *modus vivendi* could change over time first into a constitutional consensus and then into an overlapping consensus. In this process I have supposed that the comprehensive doctrines of most people are not fully comprehensive, and this allows scope for the development of an independent allegiance to the political conception that helps to bring about a consensus ... [which] leads people to act ... in accordance with constitutional arrangements, since they have reasonable assurance (based on past experience) that others will also comply. Gradually, as the success of political cooperation continues, citizens gain increasing trust and confidence in one another.

This is all we need to say in reply to the objection that the idea of overlapping consensus is Utopian. (*Political Liberalism*, p. 168, *Lloyd's Introduction to Jurisprudence*, p. 485; see the extract on pp. 477–85.)

Persuaded? Professor Freeman is not. He argues that the new emphasis on 'real people' and 'overlapping consensus' actually makes the difference principle harder to accept. Is it possible to apply the principle without some normative judgment about what 'equality' is? What, he asks, is 'equal pay'? Is it to be related to need, production, effort, or value of the work?' ... can we believe that consensus could actually be achieved once people were aware of the normative ambiguities within equality?' (*Lloyd's Introduction to Jurisprudence*, pp. 365–6.) A nice question for an essay.

Critique of Rawls

Some of the earlier doubts persist. As I have already said, his book has generated a prodigious body of critical literature. And the criticism relates both, in the most general sense, to Rawls's project as a whole (his social contractarianism, his 'deep theory') and to specific attacks upon detailed aspects of the conceptual tools he employs (the 'original position', the 'difference principle', 'reflective equilibrium', the 'maximin rule' and so on). I shall mention only seven main sorts of criticisms that have been made. Each requires detailed elaboration. First, as we have seen, some (notably Nozick) attack the very notion of any patterned distribution of social goods. Secondly, the 'original position' has been criticised both as a hypothetical device (it is highly artificial; can people *really* be stripped of their values?) and, more importantly, as necessarily supplying the outcome that Rawls postulates. Thus Ronald Dworkin ('The original position' in Daniels (ed.), *Reading Rawls*, p. 16) argues that at the core of Rawls's 'deep theory' is the right of each individual to equal concern and respect. But, says Dworkin, this right is a consequence not of the social contract but a presupposition of Rawls's *use* of the contract. Similarly, several critics have doubted whether the POP would *necessarily* opt for Rawls's two principles and, even if they did, why should they prefer liberty to equality? (See, in particular, Professor Hart's essay, 'Rawls on liberty and its priority', in both his *Essays in Jurisprudence and Philosophy*, p. 223 and Daniels (ed.), *Reading Rawls*, p. 230.) What about the winner-takes-all philosophy that many have? Why should the POP not prefer this more adventurous alternative? Critics have also argued that it is unclear how conflicts between basic liberties are to be resolved. Some have even detected a conflict between Rawls's first and second principle themselves: 'Is it not the case that inequalities in wealth and power always produce inequalities in basic liberty?' (*Lloyd's Introduction to Jurisprudence*, p. 364).

Fourthly, an important criticism relates to the alleged 'bias' that is exhibited by the theory. This ranges from the presupposed 'deep theory' identified by Dworkin (above) to the ideological bias implicit in Rawls's assumptions about the POP. Thus, from a Marxist point of view, it has been argued by several writers (see M. Fisk, 'History and reason in Rawls' moral theory', in Daniels (ed.), *Reading Rawls*, p. 53; R. Miller, 'Rawls and Marxism', ibid., p. 206; W. Lang, 'Marxism, liberalism and justice', in E. Kamenka and A. Tay (eds), *Justice*, p. 116) that Rawls makes several traditional, bourgeois, liberal assumptions. For instance, he regards people as naturally 'free'; but they are largely a product of their class interests. Similarly, his conception of the State is a consensus rather than a conflict model (see chapter 8). As Richard Miller (op. cit.) shows, in a class-divided society (in which no institutional arrangement acceptable to the best-off class is acceptable to the worst-off) the difference principle is unlikely to be chosen by the representatives of the best-off class. Rawls's theory therefore assumes a non-egalitarian structure of society. As H. A. Bedau puts it, it 'provides the nearest thing we have to a rational assessment of why the poor should allow the wealthy to keep most of that wealth and not, as in Marxist ideology, seek to expropriate it without so much as a thank you' ('Inequality, how much and why?', (1975) 6 J Soc Philos, p. 25).

Fifthly, the difference principle has itself been subjected to criticism from a variety of standpoints. It assumes that natural talents are a 'collective asset'; is this acceptable? If they are, Nozick argues, the same could be said for bodily organs; is this acceptable? Does the difference principle really promote equality or simply make everyone worse off? Sixthly, Rawls's conception of 'social primary goods' is attacked: would the POP necessarily choose these things (rights, power, money etc.) in preference to, say, a caring society in which all are treated as equals? Does it not assume that people are acquisitive, greedy and selfish? Finally, some have doubted whether Rawls has provided a theory of justice at all! According to certain critics, justice is about *deserts*: it is just that we should get what we *deserve*. Thus, if you work hard at studying jurisprudence you deserve the reward of doing well. But, in Rawls's theorem, hard work need be rewarded in order only to secure that the worst-off do as well as possible.

MARX

The theories of Karl Marx (1818–83) and Friedrich Engels (1820–95) continue, of course, to exert a declining influence on political theory and practice. Marxist interpretations of history, art and literature are now commonplace. And there has, in recent years, been a considerable interest (and literature) in Marxist jurisprudence. Although neither Marx nor Engels provide a compre-hensive or systematic account of law, there are, scattered throughout their numerous writings, several observations about the relationship between law and economics (or material conditions). These have been hunted down and edited in a useful collection, M. Cain and A. Hunt (eds), *Marx and Engels on Law*. (See too P. Phillips, *Marx and Engels on Law and Laws*.) For an admirably lucid and concise introduction to the subject consult Hugh Collins's *Marxism and Law*. As general accounts of Marx's general political theory, it is hard to find a better text than S. Avineri, *The Social and Political Thoughts of Karl Marx*. I also recommend R. Miliband's *Marxism and Politics*. An accessible general collection is D. McLellan (ed.), *Karl Marx: Selected Writings*. And there are several important essays in C. Varga (ed.), *Marxian Legal Theory*. You will also find a helpful discussion of the principal features of Marxist theories of law in ch. 11 of *Lloyd's Introduction to Jurisprudence*, including several well-chosen extracts from Marx, Engels and leading Marxist theorists. That should keep you reasonably busy! The usual problem arises of doing justice to a large and expanding subject within a crowded jurisprudence course. Thus, though you will be expected to have a knowledge of the essentials of Marxist political philosophy, you may (and should) legitimately concentrate on its application to the law and the State.

Marxism, as such, offers an explicit theory of justice only in the sense that both Marx and Engels argue that there is no *absolute* concept of justice; justice is what is acceptable in and necessary for a given mode of production. On this question, see S. Lukes, *Marxism and Morality*. In his analysis of capitalism, Marx eschews moral judgments; he claims that his account is a scientific one. Yet his writings bristle with moral condemnations of the exploitation and alienation that are endemic to the capitalist system: he refers, for instance, to it 'stultifying human life into a material force'. At the same time, however, both he and Engels reject the view that there is any objective standard of justice which transcends the economic relations of a society. Thus, for one leading political philosopher, Marx is saying that 'justice' does 'not provide a set of independent rational standards by which to measure social relations, but must itself always in turn be explained as arising from and controlling those relations' (S. Lukes, 'Marxism, morality and justice', in G. H. R. Parkinson (ed.), *Marx and Marxisms*, p. 177 at p. 197). It seems, then, that Marxism conceives of 'justice' and morality as fundamentally related to the dominant relations of production (see below).

Historicism

A central feature of Marxist theory developed in his great work *Capital* is its historicism: social evolution is explained in terms of inexorable historical forces. Replacing Hegel's dialectical theory of history, Marx adopted his well-known theory of 'dialectical materialism'. Hegel explained the unfolding of history in terms of the development of a thesis, its opposite (or antithesis) and, out of the ensuing conflict, its resolution in a synthesis which absorbs and transcends, negates and preserves both thesis and antithesis. Marx argues that each period of economic development has a corresponding *class* system. Thus during the period of hand-mill production, the feudal system of classes existed. When steam-mill production developed, capitalism replaced feudalism. Under a capitalist system, three principal social classes exist: the landowners, capitalists and wage labourers. But he foresaw the crystallisation of just two classes: the 'bourgeoisie' (those who own the means of production) and the 'proletariat' or 'working class' (who are forced to sell their labour). Classes are determined by the means of production, and therefore an individual's class is dependent on his relation to the means of production. Marx's 'historical materialism' is based on the fact that the means of production are materially determined; it is dialectical, in part, because he sees an inevitable (i.e., necessary, logically determined) conflict between those two hostile classes. A revolution would eventually occur because the bourgeois mode of production, based on individual ownership and unplanned competition, stands in contradiction to the increasingly non-individualistic, social character of labour production in the factory. The proletariat would seize the means of production and establish a 'dictatorship of the proletariat' which would, in time, be replaced by a classless, communist society in which law would eventually 'wither away'.

Note the meaning of these two (often misused) terms:

(a) 'Relations of production': men enter into these relations in order to exploit natural resources by whatever technology is available at a given time in history.

(b) 'Productive forces': the combination of the 'relations of production' (which depend on the nature of the available natural resources) and the knowledge of technologies for their exploitation.

Base and Superstructure

This metaphor has generated lively debate. In his preface to *A Contribution to the Critique of Political Economy*, Marx draws an important distinction between the economic or material 'base' or 'infrastructure' of a society and its social 'superstructure'. The material base, Marx argues, determines the form and content of the superstructure. Three major problems have arisen in respect of this crucial aspect of Marx's historical materialism. First, is the material base confined to economic factors or does it include *the law*? One modern answer is (following J. Plamenatz in, e.g., *Man and Society*, vol. 2, p. 280 ff.) that economic relations cannot be described without reference to legal rules. In other words, capitalism, or any other mode of production, depends on the law and legal system for the establishment of economic relations. But this view is opposed: G. A. Cohen (in *Karl Marx's Theory of History: A Defence*) has argued that we should regard the base as consisting exclusively of material factors. This is because we should read any reference in the base to legal 'rights' and 'duties' to refer to 'powers', which are not 'legal'. The debate simmers; for a summary see Collins, *Marxism and Law*, pp. 77–85. Secondly what is meant by the 'superstructure'? It seems to have a number of uses in Marx's writing, including the legal and political institutions which express the relations of production and the forms of consciousness which reflect a particular class view of the world.

However, as far as the law is concerned, there is no doubt that Marx conceived it (along with various political and cultural phenomena) as belonging to the superstructure of any society. Thirdly (and most important-ly), what is the relationship between base and superstructure? This subject has occupied a central place in Marxist theory. It is, of course, linked to the first question above concerning the extent to which law constitutes a part of the material base, but, whatever view is taken on that matter, it is essential to know precisely *how* the base affects the superstructure. You will not be expected to have a detailed grasp of this intriguing problem but you should have some view regarding the position of law. There are broadly two views of the nature of the relationship between base and superstructure and the position of law. The first has been labelled 'crude materialism' for it argues that the law simply 'reflects' the economic base: the form and content of legal rules correspond to the dominant mode of production. This is generally regarded as providing a simplistic and incoherent explanation of *how* law does so. The second view is known as 'class instrumentalism' for it argues that the law is a direct expression of the will of the dominant class. Its implausibility resides in the claim that the dominant class actually has a united or corporate 'will' of which it is conscious. These, and other, difficulties have led certain Marxist theorists (including Collins, *Marxism and Law*, p. 81) to recommend the abandonment of the base-superstructure model. An alternative explanation for the crucial relationship between economic conditions and the law may lie with Marx's theory of ideology.

Ideology

The argument shifts to the manner in which individuals develop a 'conscious-ness' of their predicament. In an equally famous passage of the preface to *A Contribution to the Critique of Political Economy* Marx declared: 'It is not the consciousness of men that determines their being, but, on the contrary, their social being that determines their consciousness'. That is to say that our ideas are not arbitrary or fortuitous, they are a result of economic conditions. We absorb our knowledge from our social experience of productive relations. This provides, in part, an explanation of the way in which *law* comes to maintain the social order that (as a matter of the 'natural order of things' rather than as a corporately willed desire) represents the interests of the dominant class.

How does this 'dominant ideology' come to be tacitly accepted by members of society as the 'natural order of things'? One answer is that through a variety of social institutions an 'ideological hegemony' is established, which ensures that (educationally, culturally, politically — and legally) this dominant set of values prevails. This explanation first appears in the prison writings of the Italian Marxist, Antonio Gramsci (*Selections from the Prison Notebooks*, pp. 195–6 and 246–7), and is developed (to a high level of sophistication) in the writings of Louis Althusser ('Ideology and ideological State apparatuses', in *Lenin and Philosophy*, pp. 121–73). If you wish to pursue this fascinating question further there are two books which devote a fair amount of space to the relationship between law and ideology: P. Hirst, *On Law and Ideology*, chs. 2 and 3; and C. Sumner, *Reading Ideologies*, chs. 1, 2 and 6. The law's role in this process is subtle and complex. It is a sort of 'symbolic framework' within which individuals and groups interpret their rights, interests and conflicts. Collins (*Marxism and Law*, p. 50) puts it well:

> The legal system plays a vital role.... In particular the legal framework of rules and doctrines provides a comprehensive interpretation and evaluation of social relationships and events which is in tune with the main themes in the dominant ideology. Because the legal system is encountered frequently in daily life, its systematic articulation and dissemination of a dominant ideology are some of the chief mechanisms for the establishment of ideological hegemony.

As Cotterrell explains: 'Legal ideology can be thought of ... not as legal doctrine itself but as the 'forms of social consciousness' reflected in and expressed through legal doctrine' (*The Sociology of Law*, p. 122).

Marxism's materialist account of law is often met with the claim that it appears to be refuted by reformist legislation which advances the interests of the working class. How, it is asked, can such laws represent the dominant ideology or interests? One popular answer (associated with Nicos Poulantzas, *Political Power and Social Classes*) is to describe the State as 'relatively autonomous'. It argues that the capitalist State is not entirely free to act as it pleases (in the interests of the ruling class), but is constrained by certain social forces. Nevertheless it will not allow any fundamental challenge to the capitalist mode of production; it is, at bottom, 'a committee for managing the common affairs of the whole bourgeoisie' (Marx and Engels, *Manifesto of the Communist Party*).

Goodbye to Law?

Law is a vehicle of class oppression. In a classless society there is therefore no need for law. This is the essence of the argument first implied by Marx in his early writings (especially *The Critique of the Gotha Programme*), popularised by Engels in *Anti-Düring* and restated by Lenin in *The State and Revolution*. In its more refined version the thesis claims that, following the proletarian revolution, the *bourgeois* State would be swept aside and replaced by the dictatorship of the proletariat. Society, after reactionary resistance has been defeated, would have no further need for law or State: they would 'wither away'. A major difficulty with this prognosis is its bland equation of law with the coercive suppression of the proletariat. It neglects the fact not only that a considerable body of law serves other functions, but that, even (or especially) a communist society requires laws to plan and regulate the economy. To assert that these are not 'law' is to invite scepticism.

A more sophisticated version of this theory is to be found in the work of the Soviet jurist Evgeny Pashukanis (1891–1937). His so-called commodity-exchange theory of law regards law as protecting the rights of individuals in a *contractual relationship*. All law, he argued, could be explained as reflections of this contractual commodity exchange — even criminal law (with its 'contract' between State and citizen under which a tariff of punishments is provided if the individual should offend the law). In a communist society there could be no law: law would eventually disappear to be replaced by administration. A lucid exposition of his theory may be found in R. Warrington, 'Pashukanis and the commodity form theory', in D. Sugarman (ed.), *Legality, Ideology and the State*, p. 43. Some of the limitations of what Lloyd, somewhat harshly, describes as Pashukanis's 'crude materialism' are mentioned in *Lloyd's Introduction to Jurisprudence*, pp. 867–70. To Stalin in 1936 these limitations were so grave as to result in Pashukanis's liquidation: see E. Kamenka and A. Tay, 'The life and afterlife of a Bolshevik jurist', Probl. Communism, vol. 19, No. 1 (January-February 1970), p. 72. Pashukanis's argument that law would disappear became, under Stalin, an embarrassment. So Pashukanis did.

Legal Fetishism

Neglect at your peril one important conclusion of Marxist legal theory: there is nothing special about law. The root of historical materialism is the proposition that law is (to paraphrase I. D. Balbus) 'the result of one particular kind of society' rather than that society is the result of the law ('Commodity form and legal form: an essay on the 'relative autonomy of the law' ' (1977) 11 Law & Soc Rev 571, 582). 'Legal fetishism' is the condition, in Balbus's words, where 'individuals affirm that they owe their existence to the Law, rather than the reverse'. Just as there is a form of commodity fetishism, there is a form of legal fetishism which obscures from legal subjects the origins of the legal system's powers and creates the impression that the legal system has a life of its own. As Balbus puts it ((1977) 11 Law & Soc Rev 571, 584):

> Commodity fetishism and legal fetishism are ... two inseparably related aspects of an inverted, 'topsy-turvy' existence under a capitalist mode of production in which *humans are first reduced to abstractions, and then dominated by their own creations.*

The best defence against this affliction is the vulgar model which consigns law (along with literature and politics) to 'part of the superstructure'. But if (as was suggested above) this model is to be rejected and law is regarded as part of the material base, how is Marxist theory to resist the malady? Collins (*Marxism and Law*, p. 98) provides the following answer:

> Marxists need not follow legal fetishism into the wider excesses of that ideology. Marxists can accept that other social rules as well as laws serve to constitute the foundation for a social formation and to preserve social order.... it is wrong for Marxists to ridicule political philosophies which assume the necessity for law, though they need not concur with them in their entirety.

There thus seems to be a limited degree of legal fetishism intrinsic in the more sophisticated version of the base-superstructure model.

But many Marxists *do* unequivocally reject the legal fetishism which regards law as a distinct, special or identifiable phenomenon which has a unique and autonomous form of reasoning and thought. It has to be said, however, that developments in contemporary Soviet and especially Chinese Marxism (at least at the time of writing!) raise considerable doubts about the continued application of this approach to law in these societies.

Conflict or Consensus?

Classical Marxist theory rejects, in particular, the idea that the law can be a neutral body of rules which guarantees liberty and legality. It spurns, in short, the idea of the rule of law. Indeed, in the opening words of Collins's book: 'The principal aim of Marxist jurisprudence is to criticise the centrepiece of liberal political philosophy, the ideal called the rule of law' (p. 1). Equally, the concept of 'justice' is largely contingent upon material conditions. To espouse the idea of the rule of law would be to accept the image of law as a neutral arbiter which is above political conflict and remote from the control of particular groups or classes. But Marxists reject this 'consensus' model of society. Of course, the choice between a 'consensus' and 'conflict' model of society is at the core of our understanding of society. Implicit in almost all theories of law is a consensus view. It perceives society as essentially unitary: the legislature represents the common will, the executive acts in the common interest, the law is a neutral referee that is administered 'without fear or favour' for the common good. There are no fundamental conflicts of values or interests. Any conflicts that arise do so at the *personal* level: A sues B for damages for breach of contract etc. Structural conflicts between *groups* (if they exist at all) are transposed into questions about the enforcement of *individual* obligations.

At the other end of the spectrum is the 'conflict' model which conceives of society as divided between two opposing camps: those who have property and power, and those who do not. Conflict lies at the heart of society so that individuals or smaller groups have their position defined by the very *structure* of the society: they exist as components of one or other of the two sides. Law in this image, far from being a neutral referee, is actually *the means* by which the dominant group maintains its domination. Closely related to this problem is the subject of individual rights and Marxism which is considered in an examination question below.

THE EXAMINATION

You must expect specific questions on particular theories of justice (especially Rawls's), as well as those which seek to elicit a comparative analysis of, say, the relative merits of Marxist and liberal theories of justice. A growing number of examiners, however, more sensibly (and perhaps more imaginatively) prefer to limit their questions to a narrower aspect of a particular theory of justice (e.g., the socialist conception of rights) or a comparison between a single concept as employed by various theorists (e.g., 'wealth distribution' in Marx, Rawls and Nozick). I shall consider two questions of this sort.

Recent jurisprudential debate has focused on the question: Can a socialist accept rights? Much of the discussion has been generated by a few pages in the book, *Whigs and Hunters*, by the well-known Marxist historian, E. P. Thompson. A more detailed analysis of the question appears in *The Left and Rights: A Conceptual Analysis of the Idea of Socialist Rights* by Tom Campbell. The matter has been further developed by N. E. Simmonds in a recent article, 'Rights, socialism and liberalism' (1985) 5 Legal Studies 1, to which Professor Campbell has responded (1985) 5 Legal Studies 14. You should also try to read essays by I. Markovits ('Socialist vs bourgeois rights' (1978) 45 U Chi L Rev 612), C. Sypnowich (*The Concept of Socialist Law* and 'Law as a vehicle of altruism' (1985) 5 Oxford J Legal Stud 276) and A. Merritt ('The nature and function of law: a criticism of E. P. Thompson's *Whigs and Hunters*' (1980) 7 Br

J Law & Soc 194). Though these works are, in the light of recent political events in East Europe and the former Soviet Union, a little dated, there is much of value in them. On the question of the theoretical approaches to rights in China, see Albert H. Y. Chen, 'Developing theories of rights and human rights in China' in Raymond Wacks (ed.), *Hong Kong, China and 1997: Essays in Legal Theory.*

It is often argued that the very notion of individual rights is *incompatible* with socialism. In very broad (and perhaps rather crude) terms, this argument generally rests on the irreconcilable conflict between the egoism of liberal theory and the communitarianism of socialism. Some Marxists therefore explicitly reject the concept and language of rights (except perhaps for advancing short-term tactical objectives). They argue that social change does not occur as a consequence of our moralising about rights. Neither Marx nor Engels addressed themselves *explicitly* to the nature of rights in a socialist society; they were more concerned to uncover the deception of bourgeois ideas and institutions. There are, however, a number of (sometimes ambiguous) statements in their work which may be read to suggest that in a socialist society individual rights *will not be necessary.*

It is very important to grasp the fact that for Marx (at least in his early writing) the achievement of political revolution would be to end the separation between 'civil society' and the State. As he declares in *On the Jewish Question:*

> ... the citizen is proclaimed the servant of egoistic man ... the sphere in which man behaves as a communal being is degraded to a level below the sphere in which he behaves as a partial being.
> ... man as a member of civil society counts for true man, for man as distinct from the citizen, because he is man in his sensuous, individual, immediate existence, while political man is only the abstract fictional man, man as an allegorical or moral person.
> ... the actual individual man must take the abstract citizen back into himself and, as an individual man in his empirical life, in his individual work and individual relationships become a species-being; man must recognise his own forces as social forces, organise them, and thus no longer separate social forces from himself in the form of political forces. Only when this has been achieved will human emancipation be completed.

Marx argues that democratic participation is the only way of ending the alienation of the people from the State. His own view of socialist rights (or rights under socialism) therefore seems to rest upon his rejection of the essential characteristics of a capitalist society: the exploitation and alienation it causes. He contrasts the 'rights of citizens' with the 'rights of man'. The former are *political* rights exercised *in common* with others and involve *participation* in the community. The latter, on the other hand, are *private* rights exercised *in isolation* from others and involve *withdrawal* from the community. In the same essay he says, 'Not one of the so-called rights of man goes beyond egoistic man ... an individual withdrawn into himself, his private interests and his private desires'. And, most importantly, from the point of view of Marx's central argument concerning private property: 'The practical application of the right of man to freedom is the right of man to private property'. Some commentators have argued that Marx should not be taken to mean here that these 'rights of man' (equality before the law, security, property, liberty) are *not important*; but rather that the very *concept* of such rights is endemic to a society based on *capitalist* relations of production. This is a difficult argument to sustain for in much of his writing Marx sought to show that these rights had no independent significance.

You should also note the Marxist claim that capitalism is destructive of *real* individual liberty. According to Marx, private property represents the dominance of the material world over the 'human element', while communism represents the triumph of the human element over the material world. Marx used the concept of 'reification' to describe the process under which social relations assume the form of relations between *things*. In a capitalist society, he saw this 'reification' as the result of the 'alienation' of workers from the product of their work: the 'general social form of labour appears as the property of a thing'; it is 'reified' through the 'fetishism of commodities''. Capitalist relations *seem* to protect individual freedom (e.g., 'freedom of contract') but the reality is very different: equality before the law is merely a *formal* property of exchange relations between private property owners: 'This equal right ... is ... a right of inequality in its content, like every right' (*Critique of the Gotha Programme*). Your understanding of socialist rights will clearly be aided by your understanding of 'rights' in general: see chapter 10.

Revolutionary Marxists have little truck with rights (largely because they are an expression of a capitalist economy and will not be required in a classless, socialist society). This rejection appears to be based on four objections to rights (identified by Campbell in *The Left and Rights*). They may be very briefly stated as follows:

(a)   *Their legalism.* Rights subject human behaviour to the governance of *rules.*

(b)   *Their coerciveness.* Law is a coercive device. Rights are tainted for they protect the interests of capital.

(c)   *Their individualism.* They protect self-interested atomised individuals.

(d)   *Their moralism.* They are essentially moral and Utopian, and hence irrelevant to the economic base.

Professor Campbell, however, suggests that by adopting an *interest-based* theory of rights (as opposed to power or contract-based theories) socialist rights become an important element in ensuring democracy. He argues (*The Left and Rights*, p. 123) that any form of socialism will require *authoritative rules* — if only to facilitate cooperative and educational activities. Some of these rules will be directed toward the protection of the *individual* — i.e., rights are constituted. The *interests* (and therefore the rights) of the individual are distinguishable from the acceptance of society as an 'aggregate of competitive and egoistic individuals'. This permits an accommodation of human rights in a socialist society.

Drawing on the writing of Campbell and the interesting comparison by Markovits (1978) 45 U Chi L Rev 612 between East and West Germany, table 9.1 may be used as a summary of the major differences between 'socialist rights' and 'bourgeois rights'.

Table 9.1 Bourgeois and socialist rights compared

BOURGEOIS RIGHTS	SOCIALIST RIGHTS
They are entitlements.	They are policy pronouncements.
They are ends.	They are a means to some end.
They are political.	They are more organisational.
They are less so.	They are positive.
They depend on the activation of the right-holder.	They are less so.
They protect individuals against the attacks of others.	They advance harmonious communal life.
They are conditional on the right-holders fulfilling their own obligations.	They are dependent on others fulfilling their correlative obligations.
They relate to a supporting set of sanctions.	They relate to mandatory rules but not to supporting sanctions.
They are (or seek to be) clearly defined.	They are intentionally vague.
Their exercise and violation are private affairs.	These are public affairs.
They are not so.	They are largely economic.
They are 'legalistic' and individualistic.	They are not.

The view that rights are necessarily 'individualistic' in the sense intended by Campbell has been attacked from a number of perspectives. Simmonds (1985) 5 LS 1 contends that his description of liberal theory as implying a society of 'competitive and egoistic individuals' is too crude (see Campbell's reply (1985) 5 LS 14). Sypnowich (1985) 5 Oxford J Legal Stud 276 attacks (at p. 284), *inter alia*, Campbell's equation of individual rights and alienated society:

In the search for a vehicle which mediates the relations of individuals with the community, socialists should look to law, which upon its restructuring

in the transformation of economic and political relations, will better fulfil
the bourgeois promises of liberty and equality.

This sort of critique is strongly reminiscent of E. P. Thompson's view of the
rule of law expressed in *Whigs and Hunters*, pp. 258–69. After a detailed
investigation of the effects of the so-called Black Act in the 18th century in
England, Thompson considers some of the threats to civil liberties and
democratic rights emanating from the modern State. He argues that Marxists
tend to dismiss *all* law as merely an instrument of class rule and to treat civil
liberties as no more than an illusion which obscures the realities of class rule.
But law, he says, is not merely an instrument of class domination, but also a
'form of mediation' between and within the classes. Its *function* is not only to
serve power and wealth, but also to impose 'effective inhibitions upon power'
and to subject 'the ruling class to its own rules'. He rejects the Marxist
isolation of law as a distinctive part of the superstructure separate from its
base; in his study of the Black Act he says (*Whigs and Hunters*, p. 261) he
discovered that law 'was deeply imbricated within the very basis of
productive relations.... we cannot ... simply separate off all law as ideology,
and assimilate this also to the State apparatus of a ruling class.' (versus
Althusser). And, with a resounding, rhetorical flourish, he concludes (p. 266):

> ... the rule of law itself, the imposing of effective inhibitions upon power
> and the defence of the citizen from power's all-intrusive claims, seems to
> me to be an unqualified human good. To deny or belittle this good is, in this
> dangerous century when the resources and pretensions of power continue
> to enlarge, a desperate error of intellectual abstraction. More than this, it is
> a self-fulfilling error, which encourages us to give up the struggle against
> bad laws and class-bound procedures, and to disarm ourselves before
> power. It is to throw away a whole inheritance of struggle *about* law, and
> within the forms of law, whose continuity can never be fractured without
> bringing men and women into immediate danger.

How is it possible for a distinguished, self-confessed Marxist historian to
embrace the rule of law as an 'unqualified human good'? We have already
seen that the 'principal aim of Marxist jurisprudence is to criticise the
centrepiece of liberal political philosophy, the ideal called the rule of law'
(Collins, *Marxism and Law*, p. 1). And Collins adds (p. 145) that 'Marxists are
... inconsistent when they both uphold the virtues of legality and liberty and
at the same time criticise the rule of law'. Has something gone badly wrong
here? One answer is that 'Thompson is not a Marxist historian' (Merritt (1980)
7 Br J Law & Soc 194, 210). But at least seven other responses may briefly be
made. First, to argue for restraints on authoritarian rule does not commit
Marxists to a wholesale adulation of the rule of law. Secondly, some critics

have argued that Thompson commits the very offences which he lays at the door of those whom he describes as 'modern Marxists', namely reductionism and functionalism; yet he is himself both reductionist (for he reduces all law to a restraint on power) and functionalist (for he describes law as a means of mediating between and within the classes). But law is not the only method of inhibiting State power; what of political institutions, the press, trade unions etc? Thirdly, to define law as an inhibition of power presupposes the existence of a power alienated from the people which *needs* to be inhibited. But this is to accept the bourgeois state as given and unchangeable when, to paraphrase Balbus, law is a result of one particular kind of society, rather than society being the result of law.

Fourthly, Thompson appears to accept (*Whigs and Hunters*, p. 268) that there is an 'essential' notion (or core meaning) of law which is *outside* the base-superstructure model and which is unrelated to class-bound instrumentalism; yet he seeks to eradicate 'essentialism' from his own work. Sixthly, one is never entirely clear what he means by the 'rule of law'; his definition oscillates between a formal and substantive notion. Constitutional lawyers may find this ambiguity about so important a concept a little hard to swallow! Seventhly, it is sometimes alleged that Thompson's own historical account of the Black Act contradicts his conclusion about the rule of law (see Merritt (1980) 7 Br J Law & Soc 194, 211–14). To some critics, Thompson's embrace of the rule of law constitutes part of his attack on the 'new' theoretical Marxism (associated especially with the works of Althusser and Poulantzas), an attack which he continues in his important book, *The Poverty of Theory*. It is unlikely that you will be expected to enter this perilous territory, but if you are you will find a useful map in Perry Anderson's *Arguments Within English Marxism*.

An example of the second type of question is now considered. The following question is from a recent LLB examination paper.

To what extent does Rawls's theory of justice avoid the pitfalls of utilitarianism?

Two difficulties immediately present themselves. First, the question does not specify which *version* of utilitarianism, the pitfalls of which Rawls is supposed to have avoided, is in issue. Secondly, how much detail of Rawls's theory of justice is called for? To the first question there is a relatively simple answer supplied by Rawls himself (*A Theory of Justice*, p. 22):

There are many forms of utilitarianism. . . . I shall not survey these forms here, nor take account of the numerous refinements found in contemporary discussions. My aim is to work out a theory of justice that represents an alternative to utilitarian thought generally and so to all of these different versions of it ... the kind of utilitarianism I shall describe here is the strict classical doctrine.

The second question is slightly more problematic. It is obviously difficult to show whether Rawls has succeeded in his enterprise without examining in some detail his alternative to utilitarianism. You would, I think, need to consider:

   (a)   *The pitfalls of utilitarianism*: its failure to recognise the separateness of persons, difficulties of measuring welfare etc. (see above and chapter 10).
   (b)   *How Rawls seeks to replace utility as a satisfactory theory of justice*: a brief discussion of his social contractarianism: the 'original position', the choice of the two principles of justice, a more detailed discussion of the 'difference principle'.
   (c)   *How Rawls's theory differs from utilitarianism*. He refuses to accept inequalities even if they secure maximum welfare; his conception of welfare is not concerned with benefits, but 'primary social goods' which includes self-respect; he regards the liberty contained in the first principle as non-negotiable — even in order to maximise welfare. You will want to note that some critics argue that there are fewer differences than Rawls appears to realise (see F. Michelman in Daniels (ed.), *Reading Rawls*, p. 319).
   (d)   *Does his theory avoid these pitfalls?* This is an invitation to consider whether, in your view, Rawls's theory of justice obviates some of the difficulties of utilitarianism (see above). You might examine in particular, each of the eight criticisms mentioned in the discussion of utilitarianism (see pp. 183–9) and question whether Rawls manages to avoid similar problems. You might also briefly examine the extent to which Rawls's theory (including his later refinements) encounters *other* difficulties.

FURTHER READING

Althusser, Louis, *Lenin and Philosophy, and Other Essays*, transl. Ben Brewster (London: NLB, 1971).

Anderson, Perry, *Arguments within English Marxism* (London: Verso Editions, 1980).

Avineri, Shlomo, *The Social and Political Thought of Karl Marx* (London: Cambridge University Press, 1968).

Cain, Maureen, and Hunt, Alan, *Marx and Engels on Law* (London: Academic Press, 1979).

Campbell, Tom, *The Left and Rights: A Conceptual Analysis of the Idea of Socialist Rights* (London: Routledge & Kegan Paul, 1983).

Cohen, G. A., *Karl Marx's Theory of History: A Defence* (Oxford: Clarendon Press, 1978).

Collins, Hugh, *Marxism and Law* (Oxford: Clarendon Press, 1982).

Daniels, Norman (ed.), *Reading Rawls: Critical Studies on Rawls'* A Theory of Justice (Oxford: Basil Blackwell, 1975).

Engels, Friedrich, *Anti-Dühring* (Moscow: Foreign Languages Publishing House, 1954).

Hayek, F. A., *The Constitution of Liberty* (London: Routledge & Kegan Paul, 1960).

Hayek, F. A., *The Road to Serfdom* (London: Routledge & Kegan Paul, 1976).

Hirst, Paul, *On Law and Ideology* (London: Macmillan, 1979).

Kamenka, E., and Neale, R. S. (eds), *Feudalism, Capitalism and Beyond* (London: Edward Arnold, 1973).

Kamenka, E., and Tay, A. (eds), *Justice* (London: Edward Arnold, 1979).

Lucas, J. R., *On Justice* (Oxford: Clarendon Press, 1980).

Lukes, Steven, *Essays in Social Theory* (London: Macmillan, 1977).

Lukes, Steven, *Marxism and Morality* (Oxford: Clarendon Press, 1985).

Marx, K., *Capital*, transl. B. Fowkes and D. Fembach (Harmondsworth: Penguin Books Ltd and Random House Inc., 1976).

Marx, K., 'Preface to a Contribution to the Critique of Political Economy' in *Early Writings*, ed., L. Colletti (Harmondsworth: Penguin Books Ltd and NLR, 1975).

Marx, K., 'Critique of the Gotha Programme' in D. McLellan, *The Thought of Marx* (London and Basingstoke: Macmillan, 1971).

Marx, K., 'On the Jewish Question' in D. McLellan (ed.), *Karl Marx: Selected Writings* (Oxford: Oxford University Press, 1977).

Marx, K., and Engels, F., *Manifesto of the Communist Party*, transl. S. Moore, in *Collected Works*, vol. 6. (London: Lawrence and Wishart, 1976).

McLellan, David (ed.), *Karl Marx: Selected Writings* (Oxford: Oxford University Press, 1977).

Miliband, Ralph, *Marxism and Politics* (Oxford: Oxford University Press, 1977).

Morawetz, Thomas (ed.), *Justice* (Aldershot: Dartmouth, 1991).

Nozick, Robert, *Anarchy, State, and Utopia* (Oxford: Basil Blackwell, 1974).

Parkinson, G. H. R., *Marx and Marxisms* (Cambridge: Cambridge University Press, 1982) (Royal Institute of Philosophy Lecture Series, No. 14).

Paul, Jeffrey (ed.), *Reading Nozick: Essays on Anarchy, State, and Utopia* (Oxford: Basil Blackwell, 1982).

Perelman, C., *The Idea of Justice and the Problem of Argument* (London: Routledge & Kegan Paul, 1963).

Phillips, Paul, *Marx and Engels on Law and Laws* (Oxford: Robertson, 1980).

Plamenatz, J. P., *Man and Society: A Critical Examination of Some Important Social and Political Theories from Machiavelli to Marx* (London: Longman, 1963).

Polinsky, A. M., *An Introduction to Law and Economics* (Boston, Mass: Little, Brown & Co., 1983).

Posner, Richard A., *The Economic Analysis of Law*, 2nd ed. (Boston, Mass: Little, Brown & Co., 1977).

Posner, Richard A., *The Economics of Justice* (Cambridge, Mass; London: Harvard University Press, 1981).

Poulantzas, Nicos, *Political Power and Social Classes*, transl. ed. Timothy O'Hagan (London: Verso Editions, 1978).

Rawls, John, *Political Liberalism* (New York: Columbia University Press, 1993).

Rawls, John, *A Theory of Justice* (London: Oxford University Press, 1973).

Raz, Joseph, *The Authority of Law: Essays on Law and Morality* (Oxford: Clarendon Press, 1979).

Rodopi, Wojciech (ed.), *Ethical Dimensions of Legal Theory* (Amsterdam; Atlanta, Ga: Radopi, 1991) (Poznan Studies in the Philosophy of the Sciences and the Humanities).

Rousseau, Jean-Jacques, *The Social Contract and Discourses*, transl. G. D. H. Cole, revised J. H. Brumfitt and J. C. Hall (London: Dent, 1973).

Sartorius, Rolf E., *Individual Conduct and Social Norms: A Utilitarian Account of Social Union and the Rule of Law* (Encino, Calif: Dickenson, 1975).

Smart, J. J. C., and Williams, Bernard, *Utilitarianism: For and Against* (London: Cambridge University Press, 1973).

Sugarman, David (ed.), *Legality, Ideology and the State* (London: Academic Press, 1983).

Sumner, Colin, *Reading Ideologies: An Investigation into the Marxist Theory of Ideology and Law* (London: Academic Press, 1979).

Sypnowich, Christine, *The Concept of Socialist Law* (Oxford: Clarendon Press, 1990).

Thompson, E. P., *The Poverty of Theory, and Other Essays* (London: Merlin Press, 1978).

Thompson, E. P., *Whigs and Hunters: The Origin of the Black Act* (London: Allen Lane, 1975).

Varga, Csaba (ed.), *Marxian Legal Theory* (Aldershot: Dartmouth, 1992).

10   CRITICAL LEGAL THEORY

Although they share certain common features, the important recent developments in legal theory considered in this chapter are probably better analysed
in their own right. Indeed adherents of one 'school' may regard themselves
as at war with members of another! Treating them in single chapter lays me
open to censure. Oh dear. But there is undoubtedly a core set of concerns and
methods. Indeed, the existence of postmodern feminists, the explicitly
postmodernist stance of critical race theory, and the fact that so-called 'second
wave crits' are virtually synonymous with postmodernists may suggest that,
to modify the adage we encountered in chapter 7 about realism, it may be the
case that 'we are all postmodernists now'. After you have studied their
theories, it might be instructive to consider the extent to which the present
approach is justifiable, and even whether *within* each of the approaches, the
theorists do in fact swear allegiance to similar flags. You will find helpful
prologues and readings in separate chapters of *Lloyd's Introduction to
Jurisprudence*. I shall mention other sources for you to consult (there is, alas,
no shortage) below.

   To begin at the beginning, the most significant feature of critical legal theory
is its rejection of what is taken to be the natural order of things, be it the free
market (in the case of Critical Legal Studies), patriarchy (in the case of
feminist jurisprudence), 'metanarratives' (postmodernism) or racism (critical
race theory). These theorists share a profound scepticism about the very
enterprise that has long been assumed to be at the heart of jurisprudence. This
requires, in each case, a little closer inspection.

CRITICAL LEGAL STUDIES

The Critical Legal Studies (CLS) movement is a post-realist coalition of legal theorists that appeared in the 1970s and continues to exert a declining influence on ideas about the politics of rights, which sometimes borders on the nihilistic. If American realism was 'jazz jurisprudence', critical legal studies is its 'rock' successor. CLS is, in many ways, an outgrowth of the American realist movement, though even some of its critics concede that, in important respects, it extends beyond the scepticism of its alleged progenitor. Professor Dworkin puts the matter succinctly (but without much evidence of the constructive interpretation he normally advocates) when he declares that in most of its programme:

> ... save in its self-conscious leftist posture and its particular choice of other disciplines to celebrate, critical legal studies resembles the older movement of American legal realism, and it is too early to decide whether it is more than an anachronistic attempt to make that dated movement reflower. Much of its rhetoric, like that of legal realism, is borrowed from external scepticism: its members are fond of short denunciations of 'objectivism' or 'natural law metaphysics' or of the idea of values 'out there' in the universe. (*Law's Empire*, p. 272.)

This movement of the seventies and eighties has been greeted by many scholars as a breath of fresh air in the sometimes stultifying atmosphere of legal theory. It has certainly excited controversy and rancour (Harvard Law School, where CLS has a significant following, still reels from its impact — though perhaps it has merely brought into the open the inevitable ideological differences that exist between teachers of law in most law schools). It has certainly generated a prodigous literature which, at best, is both challenging and stimulating, but which, at worst, is banal and inane. But see for yourself. A useful starting-point is the book, *The Politics of Law*, edited by D. Kairys. It is very much a 'manifesto' of the movement's creed, and contains several short essays — all written from a 'critical' standpoint — on a variety of branches of substantive law. So, for example, in their essay 'Contract law as ideology', Peter Gabel and Jay M. Feinman argue (p. 183) that:

> ... contract law today constitutes an elaborate attempt to conceal what is going on in the world.... Contract law, like the other images constituted by capitalism, is a denial of [the] painful feelings [of isolation, passivity, unconnectedness and impotence] and an apology for the system that produces them.

You will at once realise that this is no half-hearted criticalness; CLS is a direct attack on the orthodoxy of legal theory, scholarship and education. More than that, it is an important intellectual assault on the very organisation of modern society itself. You will find a number of important essays collected together (with a lively and lucid introduction) by James Boyle, *Critical Legal Studies* in the *International Library of Essays in Law and Legal Theory*, published in 1992. See also M. Kelman, *A Guide to Critical Legal Studies*, and ch. 12 of *Lloyd's Introduction to Jurisprudence*. A helpful symposium is to be found in (1984) 36 Stan LRev (I particularly recommend the essays by Trubek and by Hutchinson and Monahan) and Alan Hunt has produced a bibliography of CLS (1984) 47 MLR 369 and has attempted to assess the importance of the movement in 'The theory of critical legal studies' (1986) 6 Oxford J Legal Stud 1). And see Peter Goodrich's article 'Critical legal studies in England: prospective histories' (1992) 12 Oxford J Legal Stud 195. But this is merely the tip of a vast, expanding iceberg. *Lloyd's Introduction to Jurisprudence*, pp. 936–50, has a concise account of the principal claims of CLS and there is a good set of texts and commentary in Davies and Holdcroft's book, *Jurisprudence*. Most students enjoy Duncan Kennedy's piece on 'Legal education as training for hierarchy' (from Kairys (ed.), *The Politics of Law*, and extracted in *Lloyd's Introduction to Jurisprudence*, pp. 1019–24). Unger's huge, and, at times, impenetrable essay 'The critical legal studies movement' (1983) 96 Harv LRev 561 is not for beginners! On the nihilist strand in CLS, a stimulating essay is J. W. Singer, 'The player and the cards: nihilism and legal theory' (1984) 94 Yale LJ 1. See, too, J. Stick, 'Can nihilism be pragmatic?' (1986) 100 Harv LRev 332. For a useful comment on the Singer/Stick exchange, see S. Fuller, 'Playing without a full deck: scientific realism and the cognitive limits of legal theory' (1988) 97 Yale LJ 549.

There would appear (following Trubek) to be three important ideas that inform CLS: 'hegemonic consciousness' (a concept derived from the writings of the Italian Marxist, Antonio Gramsci); 'reification' (a concept used by Marx and developed in the writings of the Hungarian Marxist, György Lukács); and 'denial' (a concept used in Freudian psychology). By 'hegemonic consciousness' Gramsci meant that social order is maintained by a system of beliefs; in a capitalist society these beliefs are accepted as 'common sense' and part of the natural order by those who are actually subordinated to it. In other words, these ideas are treated as eternal and necessary whereas they really reflect only the transitory, arbitrary interests of the dominant elite. This system of ideas is then 'reified' (a term used by Marx, see chapter 9), i.e., becomes a material thing: it is presented as essential, necessary and objective when, in fact, it is contingent, arbitrary and subjective. Legal thought is also a form of 'denial': it is a means of coping with perceived contradictions that are too painful for us to hold in our conscious mind. It therefore *denies* the contradiction between the promise, on the one hand of, say, equality and freedom, and the reality of oppression and hierarchy, on the other.

Drawing on the work of Roberto Unger (especially his important book *Law in Modern Society* roundly criticised by W. Ewald, 'Unger's philosophy: a critical legal study' (1988) 5 Yale LJ 665.) CLS generally subscribes to the view that the following four ideas prevail in society:

(a) *Law is a 'system'*. This body of 'doctrine', properly interpreted, supplies the answer to all questions about social behaviour.
(b) A *form of reasoning* exists that may be used by specialists to find answers from 'doctrine'.
(c) This 'doctrine' reflects *a coherent view* about the relations between persons and the nature of society.
(d) *Social action reflects norms generated by the legal system* (either because people *internalise* these norms or actual *coercion* compels them to do so).

Each of these four ideas is challenged by CLS:

(a) *It denies that law is a system*. 'Doctrine' never provides a determinate answer to questions, nor can it cover all conceivable situations. This is described as the principle of *indeterminacy*.
(b) *It rejects the view that there is an autonomous and neutral mode of legal reasoning*. This is described as the principle of *antiformalism*.
(c) *It disputes the idea that 'doctrine' encapsulates a single, coherent view of human relations*; instead CLS argues that 'doctrine' represents several different, often competing views, none of which is sufficiently coherent or pervasive to be called dominant. This is described as the principle of *contradiction*.
(d) *It doubts that even where there is consensus, there is reason to regard the law as a decisive factor in social behaviour*. This is described as the principle of *marginality*.

If these four principles (indeterminacy, antiformalism, contradiction and marginality) are accepted, then as Trubek puts it (1984) 36 Stan LRev 575, 579: 'The law, in whose shadow we bargain, is itself a shadow'. If law is indeterminate, all legal scholarship on what the law is becomes merely a form of advocacy; if there is no distinct form of legal reasoning, such scholarship becomes a political debate; if legal 'doctrine' is essentially contradictory, legal argument cannot rely on legal materials if it is not to result in a tie; and if law is marginal, social life must be ordered by norms outside of the law.

As Boyle (*Critical Legal Studies*) demonstrates, there are five major aspects of critical legal theory:

(a) *Legal rules and legal reasoning*. This has two principal strands. The first is largely inspired by Unger, especially his book *Knowledge and Politics*, in which he shows that the liberal theory of the State is based on the view that all values are relative; the market economy and democracy therefore become the natural institutions in a liberal society.

The second proceeds from a sceptical realism which rejects the conventional view, for example, that courts can sensibly interpret language, the division between private and public law, the neutrality of rules, and the centrality of rights. The writings of Kennedy and Gabel have been particularly influential here. Try to read Kennedy's penetrating essay, 'Freedom and Constraint in Adjudication' (reprinted in Boyle (ed.), *Critical Legal Studies*).

(b) *Legal history*. There are a number of important CLS writings on the history of legal concepts and institutions and their relationship with ideological factors. In 'Critical Legal Histories', for instance, Robert Gordon shows how the traditional evolutionary approach neglects the extent to which we have control over our lives:

> We invent shorthand labels like 'modernisation' as a way of summarising what has happened in and trying to generalise about particular societies. Then, by trick of the mind, we suddenly reify our label into a process that *had* to happen the way it did. The next thing you know, we start explaining the whole contingent miscellany of contemporary social practices (especially the nasty ones) as the *natural* outcomes of the 'modernisation process'. But if there is no such single process, there can't be any set of functional responses to it either. (Quoted in Boyle (ed.), *Critical Legal Studies*, p. xxiii.)

(c) *Substantive law*. As already pointed out, CLS does not merely traverse the lofty peaks of abstract theory, but seeks to apply its insights to actual 'black letter' legal issues. There are numerous examples of such work. Boyle (*Critical Legal Studies*, p. 1, n. 57) provides a substantial list which indicates the broad sweep of the analysis.

(d) *Legal practice*. A major line of attack concentrates on the manner in which law consists of symbols (e.g., 'contracting parties') reified to represent the social order. This, in turn, produces an alienated world of repression by rules and authority.

Later CLS has moved towards a full-blown epistemological onslaught on legal thought and the manner in which 'text' stands in need of deconstruction. As Boyle puts it:

> ... in common with deconstructive literary philosophy, post-Wittgensteinian linguistics and the contemporary philosophy of science, [CLS shares] a concern with the 'politics of reason', the connection between epistemology and social power. (Boyle, *Critical Legal Studies*, p. xxxvii.)

These are all large claims and deserve close attention (though I suspect that for most examiners in jurisprudence the subject is a little too obscure to find its way into an examination question; but it would be impressive if you displayed your knowledge of this important movement in legal theory — in the appropriate place).

The CLS movement, though it has its roots in realism, is not, as suggested above, to be regarded merely as a 'new realism'. Both movements are antiformalist and sceptical; both seek to demystify the law: to reveal the law 'in action'. But in at least four important respects CLS differs from realism. First, it is largely uninterested in the pragmatic or empirical concerns (what courts, lawyers, legislators actually 'do') that preoccupied the realists. For CLS the law is regarded as 'problematic' in the sense that it reproduces the oppressive character of society. Secondly, unlike the realists who accepted the distinction between legal reasoning and politics, CLS views it as axiomatic that *law is politics*: there is nothing special about legal reasoning to distinguish it from other forms of reasoning. Thirdly, CLS exhibits a much deeper concern with *theory* than was ever the case with the realists. There is a fairly strong tie with the critical theory of the so-called Frankfurt school and its leading contemporary figure, Jürgen Habermas, as well as writers like Foucault, Unger, and, more recently, deconstructionists such as Jacques Derrida (see below). Fourthly, though the realists were determined to differentiate between legal rules and their actual operation in society, they generally embraced the neutrality of law and the ideology of liberalism. CLS, of course, rejects both.

Trashing the Crits?

The movement, though it now shares a good deal with postmodernist legal theory, to be discussed in a moment, seems to have been eclipsed by it. Fashion is like that. After a perceptive evaluation of CLS, David Jabbari concludes that the American theorists have failed 'to move beyond criticism to the construction of new conceptions of law which show law to be capable of both effecting and regulating social change ... [D]espite its reconstructive aims, the existing components of US critical theory do not overcome a nihilistic attitude to law as a means of changing society ('From criticism to construction in modern critical legal theory' (1992) 12 Oxford J Legal Stud 508, 542). This is contrasted with what the writer calls the European critical theory of law which 'seeks to transcend nihilism by encouraging a greater degree of participation in the processes by which legal and other decision-making is carried on'. (ibid.).

There is no question, however, that CLS has played a significant role in revealing the yawning gap between rhetoric and reality. This continues to drive many of the debates in critical legal theory in general. No mean achievment. In the words of Robert Gordon ('Law and ideology' (1988) 3 Tikkun, extracted in *Lloyd's Introduction to Jurisprudence*, pp. 950–9, 959):

> On the scene, one confronts issues of race and gender and class inequality, of democratic procedure, of relations with clients and the communities they affect, that can be the subject of small initiatives involving small risks. And that is finally what may be the most infuriating and subversive message of the Crits — not at all their supposed 'nihilism', but their insistence, to those who have come to equate maturity and realism with a cynical resignation, that there are grounds for hope.

The radically programmatic, often Utopian, vision of CLS moves much of its writing beyond the more practical, reformist concerns of the American realist movement. The transformative possibilities of law often seem to be undercut by the destructive, even nihilistic, tendencies that characterise some of the more dogmatic adherents of CLS. Professor MacCormick captures this unease:

> It is certainly good advice to scholars and practitioners that they should always be ready to turn any question upside down and to see whether underplayed principles cannot be played up to create a seriously arguable counter to the view which one has initially entertained. The danger of mere dogmatism in legal dogmatics comes from a failure to take seriously the possibility that another view might be argued just as well as one's own initial one and insightful CLS writings at the level of concrete doctrine rather than general programmatics demonstrate this. ('Reconstruction after deconstruction: closing in on critique' in A. Norrie (ed.), *Closure or Critique: New Directions in Legal Theory*.)

Moreover, as MacCormick contends (no tongue in cheek), for all its radicalism, several CLS claims about law's indeterminacy and the role of ideology may be found in the work of one of its principal demons, Hans Kelsen! (See the last chapter of *Pure Theory of Law*.)

FEMINIST JURISPRUDENCE

Most conventional legal theory is gender-blind. But, in neglecting or ignoring the position of women, it condemns them and their experience to oblivion. The response of feminist jurisprudence to that silence has been deafening, and this is reflected in the extraordinary impact this branch of legal theory has had on university courses. In a recent survey of British and Australian institutions, almost half of those questioned covered the subject 'in depth'. This compared with zero only 10 years ago! (H. Barnett, 'The province of jurisprudence determined — again!' (1995) 15 LS 88.) This remarkable phenomenon could itself pose an interesting and provocative examination question!

The literature is, needless to say, prodigious. A useful collection of essays is one recently edited by Frances Olsen, *Feminist Legal Theory* in the International Library of Essays in Law and Legal Theory. I recommend also Katharine Bartlett and Roseanne Kennedy (eds), *Feminist Legal Theory: Readings in Law and Gender* (which contains an invaluable guide to further reading), and Patricia Smith, *Feminist Jurisprudence*. Try, at the very least, to read ch. 13 of *Lloyd's Introduction to Jurisprudence*.

Feminist writing is often unashamedly polemical, sometimes anecdotal, mostly passionate. Since the subject is that of injustice, this is hardly surprising. Just as it is foolhardy to suppose that the fairly discrete standpoints may be accommodated within the rubric of critical jurisprudence, so too one must approach the subject of feminist jurisprudence with caution. Feminists do not, as I have said, speak with a single voice. Why should they? At least four schools of feminist thought may be identified. They are (following Patricia Cain, 'Feminism and the limits of equality (1990) 24 Ga L Rev 803 who concedes that the categories are far from airtight) liberal, radical, cultural and postmodern feminism.

Liberal Feminism

In liberal feminism all persons are regarded as autonomous, rights-bearing agents, and the values of equality, rationality and autonomy are emphasised. Its central claim is that since women and men are equally rational they ought to have the same opportunities to exercise rational choices. This focus on equality is stigmatised by radical feminists (see below) as misguided for 'to argue on the basis of women's similarity to men merely assimilates women into an unchanged male sphere. In a sense, the result is to make women into men' (Cain, p. 804).

But most liberal feminists, while acknowledging that the legal and political system is patriarchal, resist the wholesale onslaught that is a central, though not universal, feature of the radical agenda. They prefer to wage war within the existing institutional framework of discrimination, especially in the field of employment. This is well expressed by one of the leading liberal feminists, Wendy Williams, who prefers equal to differential treatment of women on the ground that the latter inevitably results in more inequality. In her essay, 'The equality crisis: some reflections on culture, courts and feminism' (reproduced in the collection by Bartlett and Kennedy, pp. 15–34), after analysing the law relating to statutory rape, the male-only draft, and pregnancy, she concludes that there are two choices available to women: to claim equality on the ground of similarity to men, or to seek special treatment on the basis of their essential differences:

My own feeling is that, for all its problems, the equality approach is the better one. The special treatment model has great costs. First ... is the reality that conceptualising pregnancy as a special case permits unfavourable as well as favourable treatment of pregnancy.... Second, treating pregnancy as a special case divides us in ways that I believe are destructive in a particular political sense as well as a more general sense.... Third ... what appear to be special 'protections' for women often turn out to be, at best a double-edged sword.... Fourth, ... our freedom of choice about the direction of our lives is more limited than that of men in significant ways. (p. 26.)

Put crudely, therefore, liberal feminism emphasises *equality*, while radical feminism is concerned with *difference*.

Radical Feminism

The preoccupation with difference, expressed most coherently by the leading radical feminist, Catharine MacKinnon in her books, *Feminism Unmodified* and *Towards a Feminist Theory of the State*, challenges the view that, since men have defined women as different, women can ever achieve equality. And since men dominate women, the issue is ultimately one of power. Or to put it less delicately (but perhaps more arrestingly) '... the important difference between men and women is that women get fucked and men fuck' Robin West, 'Jurisprudence and gender' (1988) 55 U Chi L Rev 1).

For Professor MacKinnon (an extract from whose work may be found in *Lloyd's Introduction to Jurisprudence*, pp. 1081–90) and Christine Littleton (pp. 1091–1106) the question seems to be one of redefining 'woman', and seeking to explain and understand the world from her perspective. A good deal of this world is manufactured by males. It is 'phallocentric' and oppressive, especially in the manner in which it encourages or allows violence against women. This leads her, controversially, to advocate a ban on pornography for its depiction of women as sex objects:

The mass production of pornography universalises the violation of women in it, spreading it to all women, who are then exploited, used and abused and reduced as a result of men's consumption of it. In societies pervaded by pornography, all women are defined by it: this is what a woman wants, this is what a woman is. (C. MacKinnon, *Towards a Feminist Theory of the State*, p. 247.)

Yet, despite her attack on the untrammelled free speech that facilitates the debasement of women, and her criticism of the existing patriarchal legal system, and scepticism about debates concerning equality and difference (on the ground that they fail to dislodge the fundamental dominance of men and male values), MacKinnon does not repudiate the law as a vehicle of radical change. This may be contrasted with the view of radical feminists who, like Carol Smart in *Feminism and the Power of Law*, deny that the law can effect genuine equality. And the role and function of the law are, not surprisingly, key questions in feminist legal theory. Nor is the analysis confined to the purely academic. Feminist writers examine the inequalities to be found in the criminal law (especially rape and domestic violence, see N. Lacey, C. Wells and D. Meure, *Reconstructing Criminal Law: Critical Perspectives on Crime and the Criminal Process*; Ngaire Naffine, 'Possession: erotic love in the law of rape' (1994) 57 MLR 10), family law (see Katherine O'Donovan, *Family Law Matters*), contract (see Mary Joe Frug, 'Rescuing impossibility doctrine: a postmodern feminist analysis of contract law' (1992) 140 U Pa L Rev 1029, reproduced in *Lloyd's Introduction to Jurisprudence*, pp. 1214–22), tort, property and other branches of the substantive law, including aspects of public law (see Catharine MacKinnon, *Towards a Feminist Theory of the State*; Deborah Rhode, 'Feminism and the State' (1994) 107 Harv L Rev 1181).

Resisting the charms of the law is a recurring theme in radical feminism. The extent to which reforming the law can satisfy the demands of women at work, in the home, or simply as human beings, is regarded as moot. Thus, Christine Littleton, in challenging the conventional concept of equality, proposes instead 'equality as acceptance' which stresses the consequences rather than the sources of difference. This has obvious legal implications in respect of equal pay and conditions of work. Ann Scales is eloquent in her dismissal of change through the form of law:

We should be especially wary when we hear lawyers, addicted to cognitive objectivity as they are, assert that women's voices have a place in the existing system.... The injustice of sexism is not irrationality; it is domination. Law must focus on the latter, and that focus cannot be achieved through a formal lens. ('The emergence of feminist jurisprudence: an essay' (1986) 95 Yale LJ 1373, p. 1385, reproduced in *Lloyd's Introduction to Jurisprudence*, pp. 1048–62.)

These, and other, disagreements are, as you will see, subtle, complex, and wide-ranging. They frequently take us to the heart of some of the significant concerns of jurisprudence in general.

Cultural Feminism

The cultural strand of feminist writing is largely preoccupied with the problem of women's difference from men, well captured by the title of Carol Gilligan's seminal study, *In a Different Voice: Psychological Theory and Women's*

Development. In this influential work, Gilligan, a psychologist, seeks to show how women's moral values tend to stress responsibility, whereas men emphasise rights. Women look to context, where men appeal to neutral, abstract notions of justice. In particular, she argues, women endorse an 'ethic of care' which proclaims that no one should be hurt. This morality of caring and nurturing identifies and defines the essential difference between the sexes. But it has been criticised, for instance, for its essentialism, and for treating these characteritics as natural when they are a *consequence* of male domination. For lively discussions of these and other difficulties with the difference approach, see C. MacKinnon, *Towards a Feminist Theory of the State*, Ann Scales, 'The emergence of feminist jurisprudence: an essay' (1986) 95 Yale LJ 1773 (reproduced in *Lloyd's Introduction to Jurisprudence*, pp. 1048–62), J. Williams, 'Dissolving the sameness/difference debate: a post-modern path beyond essentialism in feminist and critical race theory' (1991) Duke LJ 296, and A. Harris, 'Race and essentialism in feminist legal theory' (1990) 42 Stan L Rev 581.

According to Patricia Cain, cultural and radical feminists differ in that the former focus upon a positive aspect of women's 'special bond' to others, while the latter concentrate on a negative dimension: the sexual objectification of women. Moreover, certain cultural feminists (she mentions Robin West, see the reading from her important essay, 'Jurisprudence and gender' 1988) 55 U Chi L Rev 1, in *Lloyd's Introduction to Jurisprudence*, pp. 1062–81) embrace the idea that 'woman' has a 'discoverable natural essence'. West contends that the maleness of the law derives from an assumption of separateness. But, unlike men, women are more 'connected' — through the biology of pregnancy, breastfeeding and even sex. This has powerful moral consequences. In the words of Carol Gilligan (*In A Different Voice*, pp. 159–60):

> The moral imperative ... [for] women is an injunction to care, a responsibility to discern and alleviate the 'real and recognisable trouble' of this world. For men, the moral imperative appears rather as an injunction to respect the rights of others and thus to protect from interference the rights to life and self-fulfilment.

Postmodern Feminism

Postmodernism (as mentioned above) generally rejects the idea of the 'subject'. This question will be returned to below. But for present purposes it is necessary to understand the unacceptability to postmodernists of any objective truths. Concepts such as 'equality', 'gender', and even 'woman' are treated with profound scepticism. Indeed, the very idea that things have properties which they must possess if they are to be that particular thing (i.e., that they have 'essences') is repudiated by many postmodernists. This so-called 'essentialism' is detected by postmodern feminists in the work of radical feminists such as MacKinnon who argues that beneath the surface of women lies 'precultural woman'. Similarly, essentialist concepts like 'the law' or 'patriarchy' are suspect.

The critical feminist project is well put by Deborah Rhode in her article, 'Feminist critical theories' (1990) 42 Stanf L Rev 617 (which you will find extracted in *Lloyd's Introduction to Jurisprudence*, pp. 1036–48):

> What distinguishes feminist critical theories from other analysis is both the focus on gender equality and the conviction that it cannot be obtained under existing ideological institutional structures. This theoretical approach partly overlaps, and frequently draws upon other critical approaches, including CLS and critical race scholarship. At the most general level, these traditions share a common goal: to challenge existing distributions of power.

Leading postmodernist feminists, such as Drucilla Cornell and Frances Olsen, draw on the work of psychoanalysts such as Jacques Derrida and Julia Kristeva to create what Cornell calls an 'imaginative universal' which transcends the essentialism of real experience and enters the realm of mythology. Try to read her argument in 'The doubly-prized world: myth, allegory and the feminine' (1990) 75 Cornell L Rev 644.

The maleness of law, the 'phallocentrism' of society, are important themes in postmodern feminist writing. In an influential essay, Katherine Bartlett attempts to show that in analysing the practice of law by courts and lawyers, at least three 'feminist legal methods' are used: 'asking the women question', 'feminist practical reasoning', and 'consciousness-raising' ('Feminist legal method' (1990) 103 Harv L Rev 829). The first seeks to uncover 'the gender implications of rules and practices which might otherwise appear to be neutral or objective'. Discriminatory rules and practices are thereby revealed and attacked. Feminist practical reasoning 'challenges the legitimacy of the norms of those who claim to speak, through rules, for the community'. In particular, it emphasises the women's perspective in, say, rape and domestic violence cases. Finally, consciousness-raising is 'an interactive and collaborative process of articulating one's experiences and making meaning of them with others who also articulate their experiences'. In other (simpler) words, it attempts to understand and reveal their oppression.

In seeking an appropriate feminist epistemology Bartlett argues for what she calls 'positionality' which recognises the contingency of values and knowledge. Even the political commitment of feminists is provisional and requires critical evaluation and revision:

> Like the postmodernist position ... positionality rejects the perfectibility, externality of truth. Instead the positional knower conceives of truth as

situated and partial. Truth is situated in that it emerges from particular involvements and relationships. These relationships, not some essential or innate characteristic of the individual, define the individual's perspective and provide the location for meaning, identity, and political commitment.

This would seem to be the case with most human experience, but it serves to drive feminist method away from essentialism and, perhaps, relativism, though I am less sure about the latter (see below).

Other Feminisms

Though the above taxonomy accounts for the major strands in contemporary feminist jurisprudence, the richness of feminist legal thought extends beyond it to include, among others, Marxist, socialist, existentialist, structuralist, post-structuralist, and deconstructionist and linguistic schools. The involvement of feminism in psychoanalytic theory has already been noted. The oppression of women plainly lends itself to a cornucopia of explanations and this is evident in the range of available theories. But it is more than that. Questions of biology, language, politics, and economics cannot simply be roped off and designated 'male' or 'female'; they provide important tools by which to understand social life. Thus, your study of feminist theory is bound to lead you well beyond the traditional boundaries of jurisprudence (if they still exist).

Critique

One cannot criticise feminism (or anti-sexism), any more than one can attack anti-racism. One can, of course, criticise feminist legal theory, but one difficulty is that it is a moving target. One must be specific. Nor should such criticism be regarded as necessarily unfriendly to the feminist project. Indeed, as we have seen, feminists are often their fiercest opponents (and it would be a good idea to note these attacks and counter-attacks in your reading). So, for example, echoing the unease expressed by a number of writers, Carol Smart, a leading British feminist theorist, declares that the form that the movement has taken in the 1980s 'has been defined by the interests largely of white, North American, feminist legal scholars. . . . Feminist jurisprudence tends to be limited by the very paradigm it seeks to judge. In criticising law for being male, it cannot escape the related criticism of promoting a (classless, white) female point of view as the solution' ('Feminist jurisprudence' in P. Fitzpatrick (ed.), *Dangerous Supplements: Resistance and Renewal in Jurisprudence*, p. 156). Smart, it will be recalled, doubts the power of the law to achieve social change, and disparages 'law's overinflated view of itself' (*Feminism and the Power of Law*, p. 3).

The alleged exclusion of black, lesbian and working-class women from the feminist canvas seems to have been corrected in recent years by a vast literature, especially by and about black women in the United States. Among the more accessible (and less solipsistic) works is Marlee Kline, 'Race, racism, and feminist legal theory' (1989) 12 Harv Women's LJ 115.

But this sort of critique is internal rather than external: radical feminists obviously join issue on several matters with liberal feminists. Psychoanalytic theorists plainly proceed from a different position from Marxist feminists. Carol Gilligan's views on women's values, and Catharine MacKinnon's views on pornography have generated a huge debate among feminists. And there are, of course, disputes about the nature and function of the law in achieving equality (if that is indeed what is sought: another contentious question). There are a number of studies of the efficacy of the legal system in this regard (see, for instance, Deborah Rhode, *Justice and Gender: Sex Discrimination and the Law*; S. Atkins and B. Hoggett, *Women and the Law*).

I find the postmodern tendency towards contextualism (which is hard to distinguish from relativism) a little hard to take for it seems to provide a convenient mask for injustice enacted in the specious name of 'local culture'. Thus Katharine Bartlett's notion of 'positionality' (mentioned above) all too easily slides into ethical relativism: if truth is socially constructed, oppression becomes simpler to justify. (But see her recent essay, 'Tradition, change, and the idea of progress in feminist legal thought' (1995) Wis L Rev 303 in which this standpoint appears not to feature.)

Some would deny the utility or integrity of the feminist legal enterprise as a whole. It has been argued, more or less, that the house of jurisprudence has many rooms, and rather than hiving off the 'special interests' of certain groups, however oppressed, the perennial questions of law and human existence are universal and transcend these differences. The exclusivity of feminist jurisprudence defeats its noble purpose. The Utopianism of some feminist writing has also attracted criticism, as has the occasional confusion between theory and practice, the strategy (e.g., to outlaw sexual harassment) may be more successful than the 'grand' theory upon which it is built.

POSTMODERN JURISPRUDENCE

Postmodernism, originally a movement in art, has come late to legal theory where it continues to exert considerable influence. It is a very broad church that both inspires and accommodates theorists of many kinds and disciplines: language, literature, psychology, history, linguistics, art and so on. Now law. Where should the beleagured student of jurisprudence start? A good place is ch. 14 of *Lloyd's Introduction to Jurisprudence* which contains some useful readings and a helpful (if slightly exasperated) summary of this difficult (perhaps one should say challenging) subject. See too Dennis Patterson (ed.), *Postmodernism and Law*.

Writers in this genre sometimes seem keen to impress readers with the self-conscious sweep of their erudition. Reading their work is often heavy going. There are rich pickings here for 'Pseuds Corner'. The effort to comprehend may produce less pleasure than pain. But first aid is available. A number of collections, such as *Postmodern Jurisprudence* by Douzinas and Warrington will ease some of your suffering. The symposium 'Postmodernism and Law' in (1991) 62 U Colo L Rev is also a useful seam which I have worked in some of what follows. There are also some stimulating, if taxing, essays in Douzinas, Goodrich and Hachamovitch, *Politics, Postmodernity and Critical Legal Studies*.

What Is It?

In his influential book, *The Postmodern Condition: A Report on Knowledge*, Jean-François Lyotard (one of the movement's most important standard-bearers) declares: 'I define *postmodern* as incredulity toward metanarratives' (p. xxxiv). Large concepts, universal values, 'master narratives' are regarded by postmodernist, iconoclastically, as redundant, if not meaningless. The great historical epochs, developments and ideas (especially those associated with the Enlightenment (and the Enlightenment itself)) are treated with deep suspicion. The conventional assumption that human 'progress' is 'evolving' toward 'civilisation' or some other end is repudiated in postmodern thinking. Instead, interpretation and understanding is to be sought in the experience of individuals:

> ... instead of fixing the a priori priority of a historical subject, as orthodox Marxism did, or instead of sweeping the question of the subject under the carpet of social knowledge, as both structuralists and post-structuralists have done, the task ahead consists of analysing, in concrete terms, our historical trajectories as subjects both at the biographical and the macro-level. Modern men and women are configurations or networks of different subjectivities.... contemporary capitalist societies consist of four structural places to which four structural subjectivities correspond: the subjectivity of the family corresponds to the *householdplace*; the subjectivity of the class corresponds to the *workplace*; the subjectivity of the individual corresponds to the *citizenplace*; the subjectivity of the nation corresponds to the *worldplace*. (Boaventura de Sousa Santos, 'The postmodern transition: law and politics' in A. Sarat and T. R. Kearns (eds), *The Fate of Law* (Ann Arbor, Mich: University of Michigan Press, 1991) and in *Lloyd's Introduction to Jurisprudence*, pp. 1206–7.)

A leading postmodernist political theorist, Chantal Mouffe, also stresses the anti-essentialist, anti-foundationalist rejection of 'metanarratives' and the crisis of confidence in reason:

... what one means when one refers to postmodernity in philosophy is to recognise the impossibility of any ultimate foundation or final legitimation that is constitutive of the very advent of the democratic form of society and thus of modernity itself. This recognition comes after the failure of several attempts to replace the traditional foundation that lay within God or nature with an alternative foundation lying in man and his reason. These attempts were doomed to failure from the start because of the radical indeterminacy that is characteristic of modern democracy. Nietzsche had already understood this when he proclaimed that the death of God was inseparable from the crisis of humanism. (C. Mouffe, 'Radical democracy: modern or postmodern' in A. Ross (ed.), *Universal Abandon? The Politics of Postmodernism*, p. 34, quoted by Richard M. Thomas, 'Milton and mass culture: toward a postmodernist theory of tolerance' (1991) 62 U Colo L Rev 525, 527–8.)

Thus, postmodernist accounts of society (and the role of law within it) reveal a disenchantment with formalism, essentialism, statism, Utopianism, and even democracy. But they question a great deal more. Critical theory, whether aesthetic or ethical, seeks to subvert 'foundational' ideas of truth 'whether founded in transcendental conceptions of truth or in an acceptance of the self's unchallenged place at the centre of any analysis' (D. Tallack (ed.), *Critical Theory: A Reader*, p. 358). This attack proceeds from a variety of standpoints and employs several methods. You will probably be expected to dip into works by Michel Foucault, Jacques Derrida, Jacques Lacan, Jürgen Habermas, Richard Rorty, Charles Taylor, Michael Walzer, and Alasdair MacIntyre, to name but a few. You will soon recognise that the breadth of this formidable scholarship extends well beyond the boundaries of any course in jurisprudence.

The Subject

The postmodern preoccupation with the 'subject' generates, especially in the context of the law, some interesting analysis of the individual as moral agent, as rights-bearer, or simply as player in the legal system. Several accounts are explicitly psychological or linguistic (with the structural psychoanalytical theories of Lacan and the poststructuralist ideas of Derrida exerting considerable influence here). Others are more political (the prolific writings of Habermas figure prominently).

While the postmodern subject is sometimes described as dead, it is perhaps more accurate to describe him or her as moribund: '... dispersed, decentered network of libidinal attachments, emptied of ethical substance and psychical inferiority, the ephemeral function of this or that act of consumption, media experience, sexual relationship, trend or fashion' (Terry Eagleton, 'Capitalism, modernism and postmodernism' (1985) 152 New Left Review 71, quoted by William MacNeil, 'Righting and difference' in Raymond Wacks (ed.), *Human Rights in Hong Kong*, p. 117–18.)

It has been suggested by James Boyle ('Is subjectivity possible? The postmodern subject in legal theory' (1991) 62 U Colo L Rev 489), following Foucault, that contemporary political and legal argument 'can best be understood as a debate over the essential characteristics of the subjects whose actions those arguments describe and prescribe':

> The subjects of our economic theories and the legal subjects of corporate law, the subjects behind [Rawls's] veil of ignorance and the subjects of civil society all mingle uneasily, finding little in common, like guests at a bad cocktail party. If postmodernism has anything to offer here, it is by giving us another stylistic prejudice, which might offer a new arrangement of our material ... a riotously clashing collage of subjects.... Bizarre as it may seem, the way we handle the legal subject could offer us a vision of postmodern practice — a practice that could simultaneously use and transform its raw material. (p. 524.)

Seems pretty bizarre to me.

J. M. Balkin attempts to uncover the true nature of the legal subject in 'Understanding legal understanding: the legal subject and the problem of legal coherence' (1993) 103 Yale LJ 105. See too Jennifer Wicke, 'Postmodern identity and the legal subject' (1992) 62 U Colo L Rev 455 (some of which is extracted in *Lloyd's Introduction to Jurisprudence*, p. 1178). The legal subject, according to postmodern accounts like Balkin's, is neglected or even effaced by conventional legal theory. What can this mean? It seems to suggest that when we as individuals attempt to understand the law, its content, nature and objectives, we bring our subjective experience to bear on what we encounter. So? Well, this fundamental process is missing from accounts of the law offered by Hart, Dworkin and other mainstream jurists. Really? Kelsen? Finnis? The Scandinavian realists? This would make a stimulating essay or examination question.

The Object

Postmodernist legal thought has an important political object. Impatience with the modern State's bureaucratic suffocation of the individual, the overarching presence of the State, the increasing globalisation of markets, and universalising of values, has provoked a need to redefine and nurture the individual. It has also (perhaps inevitably) witnessed a new pragmatism:

> Pragmatism attracts postmodernists for several reasons. It rejects foundationalism: knowledge is radically contingent; the test of knowledge is efficacy; thinking is instrumental, functional, problem-solving. Secondly, in its contemporary reinterpretation at least, pragmatism is progressive, emancipatory and democratic. Pragmatists are concerned with the relationship of knowledge and power and the ways in which discourse, whether in science, politics or ethics, is linked to structures of domination. (M. D. A. Freeman (ed.), *Lloyd's Introduction to Jurisprudence*, p. 1152.)

A down-to-earth set of goals (economic, ecological, political) is accompanied by the advocacy of a more inclusive community that emphasises the special predicament of women, minorities, the dispossessed and the poor. A popular expression (to be found also among CLS and feminist theorists) is 'empowerment'. But the radical postmodern political agenda is a complex one which may generate confusion or what has been called a 'multiplication of ideologies'.

Language

Much of what we do is transacted through words, written and spoken. These 'signs' are an essential feature of social intercourse and their meaning and interpretation are inseparable from our understanding of the world. The subject of semiotics is devoted to the study of the uses of language and, in particular, its ideological content and consequences. Umberto Eco has said (somewhere) that 'semiotics is, in principle, the discipline studying everything which can be used in order to lie'.

The inspiration for modern semiotics is the work of Ferdinand de Saussure whose model of language, developed in the early part of this century, was used by a number of structualists (especially Roland Barthes) in the 60s to 'decode' restaurant menus, advertisements, fashion, and several other linguistic expressions of the modern age. The following famous extract from Saussure's work launched a thousand structuralists. It will, I think, help you to grasp the essentials of this strand in critical theory:

> ... in language there are only differences. Even more important: a difference generally implies positive terms between which the difference is set up; but in language there are only differences *without positive terms*. Whether we take the signified or the signifier, language has neither ideas nor sounds that existed before the linguistic system, but only conceptual

and phonic differences that have issued from the system. The idea or phonic substance that a sign contains is of less importance than the other signs that surround it. (*Course in General Linguistics*, transl. W. Baskin, C. Bally and A. Sechehaye with A. Reidlinger.)

Language, according to Saussure, creates the subject (me, you), not the other way around. The possibilities of this fascinating insight have been explored in a variety of ways by several theorists (Barthes, Derrida, Paul de Man, Foucault, Julia Kristeva).

The law is, of course, expressed by and through language. And legal semiotics has much to offer legal theory in its pursuit not only of the interpretation of text, but also in understanding some of the central questions of jurisprudence, as a leading scholar in the field, Bernard Jackson, persuasively argues in 'On scholarly developments in legal semiotics' (1990) 3 Ratio Juris 415, an extract from which may be found in *Lloyd's Introduction to Jurisprudence*, pp. 1246–53. See, too, his book *Semiotics and Legal Theory*. Should your teacher be bold enough to venture down this interesting jurisprudential path, you will almost certainly be referred to Jackson's work as well as that of another distinguished British semiotician, Peter Goodrich, especially his books, *Reading the Law: A Critical Introduction to Legal Method and Techniques*, and *Languages of Law*.

Semiotic analysis proceeds beyond mere interpretation of the law's words and symbols and their meaning. It attempts to uncover ('demystify') the political, psychological and social functions of legal language. The nature of legal discourse, in other words(!), may, in many instances, turn out to be little different from political or moral debate. An important distinction, of course, is that, like Alice, courts or legislatures decide what a word or phrase shall mean. Jackson (in the extract in *Lloyd's Introduction to Jurisprudence*) makes several ambitious claims for the rapidly developing discipline of legal semiotics, including its ability to clarify problems concerning legal validity, truth, the debate between normativism and realism, the concept of the unity of a legal system, the sociology of law, and the 'sensitive' reading of legal texts. The last-mentioned activity is perceptively pursued by Peter Goodrich in his *Reading the Law*.

Critique

'[P]ostmodernists just want to have fun. Postmodernist strategies and styles are often playful, jokey, and ironical. . . . Intellectual and artistic life can be boring, pretentious, and ponderous. Postmodernists help us to lighten up' (D. Jamieson, 'The poverty of postmodernist theory' (1991) 62 U Colo L Rev 577, 579). Are you leaping about with joy? Jargon-ridden theorising that generally takes itself extremely seriously is not my idea of fun. Nor, it seems, Jamieson's.

The expansiveness of postmodernism makes it hard to criticise. Certainly, there are those who at least call themselves (or are described by others as) postmodernists whose writing may be condemned for its apocalyptic or Utopian drift. Also some indulge in the very generalities they are supposed to reject: 'equality', 'democracy', 'empowerment' and so on. These are sitting ducks. The more than occasional collapse into subjectivity should be watched. Also the friendly tolerance of virtually any argument in the name of postmodernism (with proper credentials and citations) is a disturbing (indeed, irritating) feature of an 'anything goes' philosophy that sometimes wallows in self-contradiction and even nihilism. (Nihilism is not, however, an entirely negative philosophy. You will find a good summary of its chief claims by Peter Goodrich in *Reading the Law*, pp. 210–17.)

More frustrating is the tendency to co-opt the opposition. As a result:

> According to postmodernism, because of the 'instability of meaning', the 'surplus of meaning', the 'deferral of the subject', or the 'failure of a metaphysics of presence', there is no distinction between reading or misreading a text.... Other distinctions, such as those between logic and rhetoric, and between argument and entertainment are denied or dissolved as well. (Jamieson (1991) 62 U Colo L Rev 577, pp. 582–3.)

Ouch! This is an intellectual dead-end which, to mix metaphors, paralyses rather than promotes analysis, let alone serious normative enquiry. If the truth is always contingent, contextual and shifting, how are we to decide how to live, what is right or wrong? The death of the subject seems also to undermine the political project that much postmodern thought seeks to advance. If my identity as a person is so unstable or if I am merely the site of conflicting ideas and images, then how can I be held responsible for my actions?

It is not a homogeneous movement. Nor, as with any 'school', is the quality or writing evenly distributed. The best of postmodernist legal theory is, as you will discover, highly sophisticated, provocative, unsettling. Its catholic sweep — literature, psychology, semiotics — generates flashes of genuine insight which illuminate with their originality and perception. Many of the arguments, though their shape and object are necessarily different, have already been contested in other arenas, most conspicuously art and literature. We should not lament this; postmodernist literary theory is rich in ideas and intelligence. Law and legal practice are always in need of rigorous deconstruction. But be wary of imitation and spectacle. Resist cults. As the distinguished South African novelist and scholar, J. M. Coetzee, has said,

'Romanticism was cultish in its day, modernism was cultish: movements that capture the public imagination attract hangers-on, and hangers-on swell out the sideshows, the cults' ('Interview on Kafka' in *Doubling the Point: Essays and Interviews*, David Atwell (ed.), p. 202.) Beware of hangers-on.

Critical Race Theory

Critical race theory (CRT) has been described as 'the heir to both CLS and traditional civil rights scholarship' (Angela P. Harris, 'The jurisprudence of reconstruction' (1994) 82 Calif L Rev 741, p. 743). Harris's essay is a 'foreword' to a symposium in this number of the journal. It is a useful starting-point for an understanding of this new intellectual movement that traces its birth to a conference held in Madison, Wisconsin in 1989. This 'outsider jurisprudence' or 'jurisprudence of construction' (phrases coined by Mari Matsuda, see 'Public response to racist speech: considering the victim's story' (1989) 87 Mich L Rev 2320, p. 2323) is, in Professor Harris's words:

> ... aided by their engagement of what I call the 'politics of difference'. One benefit of this engagement is a long and rich tradition of wrestling at a practical level with the questions of identity that legal postmodernists have raised in the abstract. A second, deeper benefit is a commitment to the tension itself. For people of colour, as well as for other oppressed groups, modernist conceptions of truth, justice, and objectivity have always been both indispensable and inadequate. The history of these groups — the legacy of the politics of difference — is a primer on how to live, and even thrive, in philosophical contradiction. ((1994) 82 Calif L Rev 741, p. 744.)

In one of the leading inaugural CRT essays, Kimberlé Crenshaw argues that the American civil rights movment, despite its important victories against discrimination, left racist ideology intact ('Race, reform, and retrench-ment: transformation and legitimation in antidiscrimination law' (1988) 101 Harv L Rev 1331, see *Lloyd's Introduction to Jurisprudence*, pp. 1222–37.) According to Harris:

> The deeper race-crits dig, the more embedded racism seems to be; the deeper the race-crit critique of Western culture goes, the more useful postmodernist philosophy becomes in demonstrating that nothing should be immune from criticism. By calling everything taken for granted into question, postmodernist critique potentially clears the way for alternative accounts of social reality, including accounts that place racism at the centre of Western culture. ((1994) 82 Calif L Rev 741, p. 749.)

Similar faith in deconstructive methods of exposing racism is expressed by Robert Chang ('Toward an Asian American legal scholarship: critical race theory, poststructuralism, and narrative space' (1993) 81 Calif L Rev 1243) and by Cheryl Harris in her interesting essay, 'Whiteness as property' (1993) 106 Harv L Rev 1707.

But where CRT departs most significantly from full-blown postmodernist accounts is in its acknowledgement of the relevance of conventional 'rights talk' in the quest for equality and freedom (see below). Its critique of contemporary society and law therefore seems to be a partial one. It nevertheless presents a range of concepts for analysis, particularly the concept of 'race' itself. CRT appears to presage a revival of the values and methods trashed by CLS. A return to modernism, a *renaissance* of normative jurisprudence?

THE EXAMINATION

Anything is possible. One subject on which critical theorists, including feminists and postmodernists, like to attack is that of rights. The concept of rights is examined briefly in its more orthodox setting, in ch. 11 and I looked at Ronald Dworkin's rights thesis in ch. 6. The present question (which could well find its way into your examination paper) is the other side, as it were, of the coin: taking rights cynically. It is a matter that has figured fairly prominently in critical legal theory. A wholesale assault on the concept of rights is an important feature of all three accounts of society that we have considered in this chapter. The lowest common denominator resides in a deconstructive critique of both the indeterminacy of rights and their tendency to shore up prevailing social and political hierarchies.

Adherents of *critical legal studies* regard rights as one of the features of liberalism which appear to be objective, neutral and protective of freedom, whereas, in reality, rights perpetuate the individualism that is actually destructive of true freedom. This rights-scepticism engenders either an outright rejection of the concept of rights or the formulation of an alternative vision of rights that extends beyond the communitarian to what the Brazilian social theorist, Roberto Unger, champions as an element in a programme of 'empowered democracy'.

Much *feminist legal theory* eschews rights as formal, hierarchical and patriarchal. Law in general, and rights in particular, reflect a male viewpoint 'characterised by objectivity, distance and abstraction' (E. M. Schneider, 'The dialectic of rights and politics: perspectives from the women's movement' in K. T. Bartlett and R. Kennedy (eds), *Feminist Legal Theory: Readings in Law and Gender*, p. 319). In the words of leading feminist legal theorist, Catharine MacKinnon: 'Abstract rights ... authorise the male experience of the world' (C. MacKinnon, 'Feminism, Marxism, method and the State: toward feminist jurisprudence' (1983) 8 Signs: Journal of Women, Culture & Society, 63). But, although Elizabeth Kingdom recommends 'abandoning the concept of rights as a means of pressing feminist claims in law' (quoted in C. Smart, 'Feminism and the law: some problems of analysis and strategy' (1986) 14 Int J Sociol of Law 109), she restricts that rejection to the appeal to women's right to choose and the right to reproduce, resisting 'any extrapolation from that argument a kind of policy essentialism to the effect that every and any mention of rights must be expunged from the feminist dictionary of legal politics' (E. F. Kingdom, *What's Wrong with Rights? Problems for Feminist Politics of Law*). Her argument is that appeals to rights often conceal inadequate theories of law in respect of women's social position. Such theories tend to be essentialist and therefore unacceptable to many feminist theorists.

The *postmodern* assault on rights lies primarily in its hostility towards the possibility of an autonomous, rational individuated subject. This controlling idea of rights discourse in the liberal tradition is 'trashed' by poststructuralists, and looks instead to 'what is negated and denied in the process of its construction: a postructuralist critique of the totalising narratives of liberal political and legal thought would therefore expose how the latter tend to constitute the domain in which the subject may express itself politically in such a way as to effect a closure around the realm of the political itself' (A. Barron, 'The illusion of the "I": citizenship and the politics of identity' in A. Norrie (ed.), *Closure or Critique: New Directions in Legal Theory*). In other words, the rights-bearing subject has been bled both of meaning and authentic existence. The structural, psychological and linguistic patterns of this offensive constitute, through the analysis of social theorists like Michel Foucault, Louis Althusser, and Jacques Lacan, a serious threat to the idea of the universal subject. The poststructuralist onslaught of, in particular, Jacques Derrida, denies the very idea of the subject having an 'essence', and hence the impossibility (indeed, meaninglessness) of rights discourse.

Critical race theory, on the other hand, despite its postmodernist leanings, is notable for its recognition of the importance of 'rights talk' in the struggle against racism in the United States. This seems to mark something of a retreat from the postmodernist hostility towards rights, and a willingness to embrace modernist normative concerns with liberty, equality and justice. Kimberlé Crenshaw is unequivocal in endorsing the centrality of individual rights in the past and the future: 'Rights have been important. They may have legitimated racial inequality, but they have also been the means by which oppressed groups have secured both entry as formal equals into the dominant order and the survival of their movement in the face of private and State repression' ('Race, reform and retrenchment' (1988) 101 Harv L Rev 1331, p. 1348). For another argument along these lines (of which there are now several) look at Patricia Williams, 'Alchemical notes: reconstructing ideals from deconstructed rights' (1987) 22 Harv CR CL L Rev 401). The Re-Enlightenment?

FURTHER READING

Atkins, S., and Hoggett, B., *Women and the Law* (Oxford: Basil Blackwell, 1984).

Bartlett, Katharine, and Kennedy, Roseanne (eds), *Feminist Legal Theory: Readings in Law and Gender* (Boulder, Colo: Westview Press, 1991).

Boyle, James D. A. (ed.), *Critical Legal Studies* (Aldershot: Dartmouth, 1992).

Cornell, Drucilla, *Beyond Accommodation* (London: Routledge, 1991).

Douzinas, Costas, Goodrich, Peter, and Hachamovitch, Yifat, *Politics, Postmodernity and Critical Legal Studies* (London: Routledge, 1994).

Douzinas, C., and Warrington, R. (with McVeigh, S.), *Postmodern Jurisprudence: The Law of the Text in the Texts of the Law* (London: Routledge, 1991).

Fish, Stanley, *There's No Such Thing as Free Speech* (New York: Oxford University Press, 1994).

Fitzpatrick, P. (ed.), *Dangerous Supplements: Resistance and Renewal in Jurisprudence* (London: Pluto Press, 1991).

Foucault, Michel, *The Order of Things: An Archaeology of Human Sciences* (New York: Pantheon, 1973).

Gilligan, Carol, *In A Different Voice: Psychological Theory and Women's Development* (Cambridge, Mass: Harvard University Press, 1982).

Goodrich, Peter, *Languages of Law* (London: Weidenfeld & Nicholson, 1990).

Goodrich, Peter, *Reading the Law: A Critical Introduction to Legal Method and Techniques* (Oxford: Basil Blackwell, 1986).

Graycar, Regina and Morgan, Jenny, *The Hidden Gender of Law* (Sydney: Federation Press, 1990).

Hirst, Paul, *On Law and Ideology* (London: Macmillan, 1979).

Kairys, David (ed.), *The Politics of Law: A Progressive Critique* (New York: Pantheon Books, 1982).

Kelman, Mark, *A Guide to Critical Legal Studies* (Cambridge, Mass: Harvard University Press, 1987).

Kingdom, Elizabeth F., *What's Wrong with Rights? Problems for Feminist Politics of Law* (Edinburgh: Edinburgh University Press, 1991).

Kramer, Matthew H., *Critical Legal Theory and the Challenge of Feminism* (Lanham, Md: Rowman & Littlefield, 1995).

Lacey, N., Wells, C., and Meure, D., *Reconstructing Criminal Law: Critical Perspectives on Crime and the Criminal Process* (London: Weidenfeld & Nicholson, 1990).

Lyotard, Jean-François, *The Postmodern Condition: A Report on Knowledge* (Manchester: Manchester University Press, 1984).

MacIntyre, Alasdair, *After Virtue: A Study in Moral Theory* (London: Duckworth, 1982).

MacKinnon, Catharine, *Feminism Unmodified: Discourses on Life and Law* (Cambridge, Mass: Harvard University Press, 1987).

MacKinnon, Catharine, *Towards a Feminist Theory of the State* (Cambridge, Mass: Harvard University Press, 1989).

Naffine, Ngaire, *Law and the Sexes: Explorations in Feminist Jurisprudence* (London: Allen & Unwin, 1990).

Norrie, Alan (ed.), *Closure or Critique: New Directions in Legal Theory* (Edinburgh: Edinburgh University Press, 1993).

O'Donovan, Katherine, *Family Law Matters* (London: Pluto Press, 1993).

O'Donovan, Katherine, *Sexual Divisions in Law* (London: Weidenfeld & Nicholson, 1985).

Olsen, Francis E. (ed.), *Feminist Legal Theory* (Aldershot: Dartmouth, 1994).

Patteson, Dennis (ed.), *Postmodernism and Law* (Aldershot: Dartmouth, 1994).

Rhode, Deborah, *Justice and Gender: Sex Discrimination and the Law* (Cambridge, Mass: Harvard University Press, 1989).

Rorty, Richard, *Philosophy and the Mirror of Nature* (Oxford: Basil Blackwell, 1990).

Smart, Carol, *Feminism and the Power of Law* (London: Routledge, 1989).

Smart, Patricia, *Feminist Jurisprudence* (Oxford: Clarendon Press, 1993).

Tallack, Douglas (ed.), *Critical Theory: A Reader* (Hemel Hempstead: Harvester Wheatsheaf, 1995).

Unger, Roberto, *False Necessity: Anti-necessitarian Social Theory in the Service of Radical Democracy* (Cambridge: Cambridge University Press, 1987).

Unger, Roberto, *Knowledge and Politics* (New York: Free Press, 1975).

Unger, Roberto, *Law in Modern Society: Toward a Criticism of Social Theory* (London: Collier-Macmillan, 1977).

Wacks, Raymond (ed.), *Hong Kong, China and 1997: Essays in Legal Theory* (Hong Kong: Hong Kong University Press, 1993).

Ward, Ian, *An Introduction to Critical Legal Theory* (London: Cavendish, 1998).

11 FUNDAMENTAL LEGAL CONCEPTS

Almost all courses in jurisprudence devote some (albeit diminishing) time to an analysis of certain key legal concepts. This often includes terms such as 'right', 'duty', 'ownership', 'possession', 'person', 'fault' and so on. Of course, you will have encountered many of these concepts in the substantive subjects to which they relate (thus, one would expect a course on the law of property to have examined and contrasted the concepts of 'ownership' and 'possession'; and in company law, you will have considered the concept of 'corporate personality'). But there they are normally treated merely as a means to explain certain specific rules and their operation in the context of that particular branch of the law. When they are encountered in jurisprudence they are viewed in a slightly different way: they represent the 'building blocks' of the law. It is therefore usual to consider the meaning of these concepts in a wider sense; attention is focused on their function in different branches of the law or even in different legal systems.

The difference between these two approaches is frequently captured by the distinction between 'general jurisprudence' (or 'legal theory') and 'particular jurisprudence' (or simply 'jurisprudence'). The former has been the subject we have been considering up till this point: the large questions about law and the legal system. The latter seeks to subject particular legal concepts (other than the concept of law itself!) to close scrutiny. Economists might call the former a macroscopic and the latter a microscopic approach.

DEFINITION IN THE LAW

Jurisprudence — and the law itself — is haunted by questions of definition. We can barely begin our analysis of the law and legal system without some shared understanding of what it is we are talking about. But the problem is easier to state than resolve. There is, however, a relatively simple means by which you can begin to clarify your thoughts on this important question: read Professor Hart's 'Definition and theory in jurisprudence' (1954) 70 LQR 37 (reprinted in his *Essays in Jurisprudence and Philosophy*). The fact that Hart devoted his inaugural lecture (after being elected to the Chair of Jurisprudence at Oxford in 1953) to this question gives you some indication of the importance he attached to the problem. In this essay, Hart (among other things) warns against the danger of 'theory on the back of definition'. By this he means that we should not confuse the act of attempting to *define* a legal concept with an account of what one might call its *ideological function*; to do so conflates logical and political criteria.

Broadly speaking, there are three main approaches to the problem of definition in general. The first argues that 'to mean is to denote' (G. Ryle, 'The theory of meaning' in Mace (ed.), *British Philosophy in Mid-Century*). In other words, all significant expressions are proper names — what they are the names of are what the expressions signify. But this raises immediate difficulties when it comes to, for instance, fictitious or non-existent things (Mickey Mouse or a unicorn). Surely, it cannot be correct (as Ryle puts it) 'that to every significant grammatical subject there must correspond an appropriate *denotatum* in the way in which Fido (the dog) answers to the name 'Fido''. A second approach therefore developed which rejects this 'denotationist' view; it is associated with the Cambridge philosopher, Wittgenstein, who said: 'Don't ask for the meaning, ask for the use'. The use of an expression is the *function* it is employed to do, as opposed to any thing or person or event which it is supposed to *denote*. Thus, to use one of Wittgenstein's own examples, a 'knight' has meaning only once we know the rules of chess; unless we know these rules, it is merely a piece of wood in the shape of a horse. The chief attraction of this approach is that it enables us to fix a meaning to certain legal concepts (see Hart's discussion of a 'corporation' in the above-mentioned essay and below) without the need to employ fictions to correspond with the meaning of certain concepts. A third approach, known as 'essentialism' argues that particular things have essences which serve to identify them as the particular things they are. Thus Austin and Kelsen sought to define law by reference to its fundamental nature (as commands of the sovereign or a normative system respectively).

You will, naturally, realise that in seeking 'definitions' of law or legal concepts, several difficulties lie in wait. Our political or ideological preferences will inevitably intrude, as will historical, social and moral considerations. Provided we are alive to these issues, we should not shy away from elucidating the ideas that infuse the legal system. Indeed, unless we do so, conceptual confusion may actually inhibit our attempt to improve the law. For example, I have tried to show how the concept of 'privacy' has suffered so much linguistic abuse by courts and lawyers that it may now be too late to redeem it from its state of incoherence (see R. Wacks, 'The poverty of 'privacy'' (1980) 96 LQR 73, *The Protection of Privacy*, ch. 1, and *Personal Information: Privacy and the Law*).

RIGHTS

By far the most important of the legal concepts that have attracted the attention of legal and moral philosophers is that of a 'right'. But to talk of rights immediately raises the distinction between what a right *is*, on the one hand, and what rights people actually *have* or should have, on the other. This is the distinction between *analytical* and *normative* jurisprudence respectively. It is hard to see how the two questions can be kept apart when it comes to seeking to understand the nature of rights (and attempts to do so may give rise to several difficult philosophical problems). Nevertheless it is a convenient separation which assists, I think, to clarify our thinking about rights. We should, however, recognise that the two are obviously closely related.

What is a Right?

It is not only lawyers who employ the term 'right' with more enthusiasm than precision. The concept invariably insinuates itself into discourses on ethics as well as in ordinary conversation. For the Scandinavian realists (see chapter 7) a 'right' was a mystical figment of one's imagination. You will find a concise, lucid statement of their position (and much else) in Professor White's admirable book *Rights*, pp. 2–4. Look, too, at the collection of essays edited by Carlos S. Nino, *Rights*.

This is a large subject and, for most students of jurisprudence, a fairly forbidding one. The ground has been well toiled by generations of legal and moral philosophers and the literature is enormous. You will benefit from a reading of the non-legal expositions of rights (which touch on anything from animal rights to rights of the dead and unborn), but most jurisprudence courses concentrate on the (sufficiently taxing!) subject of legal rights, and the starting-point of most expositions is the analysis by Wesley Hohfeld (whose name, I hope, you will recognise from the discussion in chapter 7 of American realism). You will, almost certainly, be expected to know how Hohfeld sought to elucidate the concept of a right, and the extent to which he succeeded. Most of the leading textbooks deal with his account, but (as always) it would be a good idea to read his own words in *Fundamental Legal Conceptions as Applied in Judicial Reasoning* (a useful extract from which you will find in *Lloyd's Introduction to Jurisprudence*, pp. 541–7).

Hohfeld sought to clarify the proposition 'X has a right to do R' which may, in his view, mean one of four things:

(a)   That Y (or anyone else) is under a duty to allow X to do R; this means, in effect, that X has a *claim* against Y. He calls this claim right simply a 'right'.

(b)   That X is free to do or refrain from doing something; Y owes *no duty* to X. He calls this a 'privilege' (though it is often described as a 'liberty').

(c)   That X has a power to do R; X is simply free to do an act which alters legal rights and duties or legal relations in general (e.g., sell his property) whether or not he has a claim right or privilege to do so. Hohfeld calls this a 'power'.

(d)   That X is not subject to Y's (or anyone's) power to change X's legal position. He calls this an 'immunity'.

Hohfeld conceived of these four 'rights' having both 'opposites' and 'correlatives' (i.e., the other side of the same coin) as shown in Table 10.1.

Table 10.1   Hohfeld's scheme of 'jural relations'

Opposites {	right	privilege	power	immunity
	no-right	duty	disability	liability
Correlatives {	right	privilege	power	immunity
	duty	no-right	liability	disability

Thus, to use Hohfeld's own example, if X has a *right* against Y that Y shall stay off X's land, the *correlative* (and equivalent) is that Y is under a *duty* to keep off the land. A *privilege* is the *opposite* of a *duty*, and the *correlative* of a *'no-right'*. Hence, whereas X has a *right* (or *claim*) that Y should stay off his land, X himself has the *privilege* of entering on the land, or, in other words, X does not have a duty to stay off.

It is important to note that, for Hohfeld, claim rights (i.e., rights in the normal sense) are strictly *correlative* to duties. To say that X has a claim right of some kind is to say that Y (or someone else) owes a certain duty to X. But to say that X has a certain liberty is *not* to say that anyone owes him a duty. Thus if X has a *privilege* (or liberty) to wear a hat, Y does not have a *duty* to X, but a *no-right* that X should not wear a hat. In other words, the *correlative* of a liberty is a no-right. Similarly the correlative of a power is a liability (i.e., being liable to have one's legal relations changed by another), the correlative of an immunity is a disability (i.e., the inability to change another's legal relations).

But is Hohfeld correct? Is it true that whenever I am under some duty someone else has a corresponding right? Or vice versa? In the first case, surely it is possible for me to have a duty without you (or anyone else) having a right that I should perform it. In the criminal law certain duties are imposed upon me, but no one has a correlative right to my performing these duties. This is because it is possible for there to be a duty to do something which is not a duty to *someone*; for instance, the duty imposed on a policeman to report offenders — he owes this duty to no one in particular, and, hence, it gives rise to no right in anyone. And even where someone owes a duty to *someone* to do something, the person to whom he owes such a duty does not necessarily have any corresponding right. Thus, I have certain duties toward my students, but this does not necessarily confer any rights upon them. Similarly we commonly accept that we owe certain duties to infants or animals; yet many argue that it does not follow from this that they have rights. You will have encountered several examples of the absence of correlativity of rights and duties in criminal law: the duty, say, to observe road signs contains no reference to any duty to others and therefore implies no rights vested in anyone.

On the other hand, it is, of course, common for me to have a right to do something, without you (or anyone else) having a corresponding duty. Lawyers, however, often assume that right and duty are correlatives. Hohfeld (*Fundamental Legal Conceptions*, p. 42) quotes Lord Lindley's dictum in *Quinn v Leatham* [1901] AC 495, 534, that the plaintiff had a right to earn his living as he pleased provided he did not infringe the law or the rights of others:

> This *liberty* is *a right* recognised by law; its *correlative* is the general *duty* of every one not to prevent the free exercise of this *liberty* except so far as his own liberty of action may justify him in so doing. (Emphasis added by Hohfeld.)

But this seems mistaken. And similar attacks have been made on Hohfeld's treating a power as a correlative of a liability, an immunity of a disability and so on.

Yet these criticisms may miss the point of Hohfeld's purpose. J. W. Harris (*Legal Philosophies*, pp. 81–3) offers a spirited defence of Hohfeld's position (which you should read closely). It is true that, in order to make sense of legal relations between persons, correlativity is part of the law's lowest common denominator — because every judicial issue involves two persons. In practice, therefore, *litigation* gives rise to opposing parties — even where, strictly speaking, the defendant does not owe a duty to the plaintiff. Thus my duty to pay tax on my income does not necessarily give rise to a right held by another; but the taxman will pursue me in the courts in order to recover tax owing. Hence, the court has to answer the question: does the defendant owe a duty *to the plaintiff*. Similarly, in those recent decisions in which the courts have had to consider whether private individuals have *locus standi* to enforce the duties imposed by the criminal law, or the duty of public authorities to provide various facilities such as health care and housing, the question is whether the defendant's conduct was in some way privileged — in relation to *the plaintiff* (remember, for instance, *Gouriet* v *Union of Post Office Workers* [1978] AC 435 and *Attorney-General (ex rel. Mc Whirter)* v *Independent Broadcasting Authority* [1973] QB 629). In other words, *someone* has to bring the action or, indeed, be sued. Correlatives seem a convenient way of describing the relationship between the plaintiff's action and the defendant's conduct. But, as Harris concedes, where a court holds (as it did, in, say, *Gouriet* v *Union of Post Office Workers* that in certain rare circumstances an injunction may be granted by a civil court to restrain a threatened breach of the criminal law) that a private person may bring an action only where he has a 'private right', this must mean that he has a 'private interest' — a non-Hohfeldian, non-relational conception of right. And, on the other hand, there will be cases where a general, uncorrelated 'duty' is the basis for recognising a certain relationship. So, in *Johnson* v *Phillips* [1976] 1 WLR 65, the duty of the police to promote the free flow of traffic was held to justify a constable, in an emergency, ordering a motorist to drive the wrong way down a one-way street. Here no correlative right arises. Perhaps the answer is that 'judicial reasoning [is] necessarily infused with moral and political ideas about private right and public duty, for which some non-Hohfeldian analysis is essential' (Harris, *Legal Philosophies*, p. 83).

All four of Hohfeld's rights (which, in modern accounts, are usually called claim rights, liberties, powers and immunities) are rights *against a specific person or persons*. As N. E. Simmonds (*Central Issues in Jurisprudence*, pp. 130–1) points out, students are often confused by the fact that, in Hohfeld's scheme, X's liberty does not entail any *duty* on Y's part not to interfere. Thus the fact that X has a liberty (as against Y) to wear a hat does *not* entail that Y is under a duty not to interfere with X's wearing a hat. Y would therefore be entitled to *prevent* X from wearing a hat (e.g., by buying up the supply of hats and refusing to sell X one).

You may discover other defects with the correlativity thesis; Professor MacCormick, for example, argues that duties are often imposed in order to *protect* rights rather than merely being correlative to such rights. And it is surely true that when we talk of imposing duties on people (such as the duty to wear seat-belts) we do not think of this duty as being owed to some person or persons. We do not, in other words, normally think that where there is a duty there is a right.

You should also consider the validity of the more general attack on Hohfeld: that he fails adequately to analyse the essential *nature* of rights and other legal concepts. J. W. Harris argues persuasively (in his *Law and Legal Science*, sect. 3) that we cannot understand the totality of any legal concept frozen in time in a 'momentary legal system'. We employ legal concepts in legal reasoning as part of what he calls the 'doctrine model of rationality'. In other words, all legal concepts exist in a historical context which requires reference to certain fundamental features of the legal system (e.g., our conception of property rights; see chapter 8). In addition, criticism is frequently made of Hohfeld's treatment of the concepts of 'duty' and 'power'. In particular, it is argued that he fails to distinguish the various *types* of duty and power: we use these terms in several ways which his analysis tends to neglect. For an interesting alternative analysis of legal rights, see J. Raz, 'Legal rights' (1984) 4 Oxford J Legal Stud 1. For a lucid exposition of rights as 'excess baggage' in the case for protecting animals, see R. G. Frey, *Interests and Rights*.

Theories of Rights

There are two principal theories of rights: the so-called 'will' (or 'choice') theory and the 'interest' theory. The former (advanced, most notably by Professor Hart; see *Essays on Bentham*, ch. 7) holds that when I have a right to do something, what is essentially protected is my *choice* whether or not to do it. It stresses the freedom and individual self-fulfilment that are regarded as essential values which the law ought to guarantee. The 'interest' theory, on the other hand (most effectively espoused by Professor MacCormick; see *Legal Right and Social Democracy*, ch. 8, and 'Rights in legislation', in Hacker and Raz (eds.), *Law, Morality and Society*), claims that the purpose of rights is to protect, not individual choice, but certain *interests* of the right-holder. It should be noted that the advocates of both theories (though not Professor MacCormick) normally accept the *correlativity* of rights and duties; indeed, this is (as we shall see) often central to their arguments.

In attacking the will theory, proponents of the interest theory raise two main arguments. First, they reject the view (at the heart of the will theory) that the essence of a right is the power to waive someone else's duty. Sometimes, they argue, the law *limits* my power of waiver without destroying my substantive right (e.g., I cannot consent to murder or contract out of certain rights). Secondly, there is a distinction between the substantive right and the right to *enforce* it. MacCormick gives the example of children: their rights are exercised by their parents or guardians; how can it be said, therefore, that the right-holder (i.e., the child) has any choice whether or not to waive such rights? It must, he argues, be concluded that children have no rights — which is absurd.

While the will theory, by arguing that the enforcement of Y's duty requires the exercise of will by X (or someone else), rests on the assumption of the correlativity of rights and duties, it is possible to postulate the interest theory (as MacCormick does) independently. Thus, it may be argued that conferring a right on someone (e.g., to housing) constitutes an acceptance that the interest represented by that right ought to be recognised and protected. There are two main versions of this theory. One asserts that X has a right whenever he is in a position to benefit from the performance of a duty. The other claims that X has a right whenever the protection of his interest is recognised as a reason for imposing duties — whether or not they are *actually* imposed. You should examine the virtues and deficiencies of both theories. A useful account may be found in Tom Campbell, *The Left and Rights*, chs 6 and 9. And see chapter 10 above.

Right-based Theories

Rights are 'in'. Human rights, animal rights, moral and political rights have assumed a central place in contemporary jurisprudence (to say nothing of moral and political philosophy). A modern trilogy (first introduced by Dworkin) of legal and moral theories which are *right-based, duty-based* and *goal-based* has emerged. A helpful reader is J. Waldron (ed.), *Theories of Rights*. Waldron (in his introduction) provides an example which illuminates this (sometimes elusive) distinction. We are opposed to torture. If our opposition is based on the suffering of the victim, our approach is *right*-based. If we believe that torture debases the torturer, our concern is *duty*-based. If we regard torture as unacceptable only when it affects the interests of those other than the parties involved, our approach is utilitarian *goal*-based.

Our principal concern is, of course, with right-based theories. We have already seen (in chapters 6 and 9) how rights, in modern legal theory, are taken very seriously. In particular, Professor Dworkin's 'rights thesis' argues for the primacy of rights over considerations of the general welfare. This view of 'rights as trumps' justifies their protection on a complex exclusion of 'external preferences'. I mentioned, in chapter 9, the distinction between 'personal' and 'external' preferences. The former refers to those things that I want for *myself*; the latter are the things I want for *others*. So, for example, I may want to be affluent, but not wish others to be. Dworkin argues that when we seek to improve the general welfare, external preferences should be excluded — because they undermine the 'basic right to equal concern and respect' which, in his theorem, is a fundamental political right — 'a postulate of political morality' (*TRS*, p. 272). Why do they have this effect? Because any imposition of external preferences is equivalent to a judgment that those on whom they are imposed are inferior, not to be treated as equals or 'with equal concern and respect'. I cannot here trace the elaborate argument which Dworkin deploys in support of this rejection of utilitarianism (or the counter-arguments which it has generated), but you will get a good idea of Dworkin's general conception of rights as trumps from chapters 7 and 12 of *TRS*. I also recommend the essays by Hart and Sartorius in M. Cohen (ed.), *Ronald Dworkin and Contemporary Jurisprudence*. Dworkin expresses his view so clearly in his reply to Sartorius (in *Ronald Dworkin and Contemporary Jurisprudence*, p. 281) that I think it is worth quoting the following passage at length:

Rights cannot be understood as things people have, come what may, no matter what general justification for political decisions is in play. We construct political theories as a package, and the rights that package assigns individuals must vary with what else is in the package. The idea of rights as trumps is a *formal* idea: it fixes the general function of rights within any particular theory that uses the idea at all. We can therefore think about the content of rights at two different levels of analysis. When we are engaged in constructing a general political theory, we must consider what package — what general justification for political decisions together with what rights — is most suitable.... But on other occasions we must take the general scheme of some political theory as fixed and consider what rights are necessary as trumps over the general background justification that theory proposes.

In other words (to use one of Dworkin's own examples) my strong preference for pistachio ice-cream is a reason for society producing pistachio, and it is a stronger reason than others that may be found for not producing it (such as your mild preference for vanilla). But it is pointless to speak of my *right* to have pistachio (or even my more general right to have my strong preferences satisfied) unless we mean that my preference provides a reason for producing pistachio even if the *collective* preferences of the community would be better served by producing vanilla. A political right, in Dworkin's account, arises only when the reasons for giving *me* what I want are stronger than some *collective* justification which normally provides a full political justification for a decision.

For Dworkin, therefore, no utilitarian view offers an adequate foundation for a theory that takes rights seriously, and only a restricted form of utilitarianism (which excludes external preferences) provides some support for the egalitarianism that is the main appeal of utilitarianism. Both Hart and Sartorius (and indeed other writers) accuse Dworkin of effectively adopting a utilitarian position, a charge which, as you will see, Dworkin skilfully refutes. Doubts do, however, remain. Dworkin concedes that 'to prevent a catastrophe or even to obtain a clear and major benefit' (*TRS*, p. 192) it may be necessary for individual rights to be overridden. Thus my right to free speech may have to give way when the public interest requires it (say during a state of emergency). But this suggests that there is an implicit recognition that even the most fundamental rights are not immune to the claims of utility — the public interest.

This, in turn, raises the question whether utilitarianism is itself inevitably hostile to individual rights? A utilitarian is committed to the proposition that all actions are to be judged according to the extent to which they advance or contribute to the general welfare. Does this mean that he is unable to accommodate rights into his felicific calculus? This is a controversy that cannot easily be resolved one way or the other. It has been argued that utilitarianism is compatible with individual rights because when an interest is shown, by reference to the general good, to be worthy of protection, a *right* to that interest may be recognised. But this means, first, that rights are at the mercy of the felicific calculus (a pretty fragile guarantee) and, secondly, that rights will always succumb to considerations of the general welfare. For a good, concise account of these difficulties, see Simmonds, *Central Issues in Jurisprudence,* pp. 143–5.

Another way out of the apparent impasse has been offered by Alan Gewirth in his remarkable books, *Reason and Morality,* and in *Human Rights.* Briefly, he argues that we cannot justify — in the interests of the general welfare — the denial of rights to others without accepting the importance of rights. At the very least, in order to persuade another that his rights should be denied, the latter should be accorded the right to freedom of thought — so that he can consider the argument against his right that is sought to be denied! You should be able to show the effects of this conflict on the protection of rights; your discussion will, of course, draw on the moral basis of act and rule utilitarianism, discussed in chapter 9.

HUMAN RIGHTS

The concept of human rights has been described as 'one of the greatest inventions of our civilisation [which] can be compared in its impact on human social life to the development of modern technological resources and their application to medicine, communication, and transportation' (C. Nino, *The Ethics of Human Rights,* p. 1). Similar praise abounds. The recognition in the eighteenth century of the apparently simple idea of human rights was plainly a significant intellectual moment in our history. The concept makes little sense unless it is understood as fundamental and inalienable, whether or not such rights are legally recognised and regardless of whether they emanate from a 'higher' natural law (see ch. 5).

The adoption by the United Nations, in the grim shadow of the Holocaust, of the Universal Declaration of Human Rights in 1948, and the International Covenants on Civil and Political Rights, and Economic, Social and Cultural rights in 1976, demonstrates, even to the most sceptical observer, a commitment by the international community to the universal conception and protection of human rights. This so-called International Bill of Rights, with its inevitably protean and slightly kaleidoscopic ideological character, reflects an extraordinary measure of cross-cultural consensus among nations.

The idea of human rights has passed through three generations. The first generation were the seventeenth and eighteenth-century, mostly negative civil and political rights. The second generation consist in the essentially positive economic, social and cultural rights. The third generation are primarily collective rights which are foreshadowed in art. 28 of the Universal Declaration which declares that 'everyone is entitled to a social and international order in which the rights set forth in this Declaration can be fully realised'. These 'solidarity' rights include the right to social and economic development and to participate in and benefit from the resources of the earth and space, scientific and technical information (which are especially important to the Third World), the right to a healthy environment, peace and humanitarian disaster relief.

Yet the idea both of rights (as we have seen) and of human rights continues to be attacked. Some see human rights as a Machiavellian plot by international capital to enslave the Third World. Others, of a more conservative persuasion, adopt Edmund Burke's reactionary view that spurns human rights on the ground that they inspire 'false ideas and vain expectations in men destined to travel in the obscure walk of laborious life'. Here I want to sketch some of the more important challenges. I have (following my paper, 'The end of human rights?' (1994) 24 HKLJ 372) identified the following seven. Snow White and the Seven Dwarfs? It is, I think, important to have a good understanding of these attacks, for they seem increasingly to insinuate themselves into jurisprudential debates about human rights in a post-communist world. I concentrate on the first for it constitutes a significant, though often misunderstood, assault on the very idea of individual rights.

Communitarianism

Community and communitarianism have assumed considerable importance, most conspicuously among legal and political theorists — and politicians — in the United States. The communitarian ideal is a bit of a Trojan Horse, containing a number of other associated ideas. Among communitarians, the individualism of theories of rights has generated widespread unease concerning the extent to which such theories neglect the interests of the community, civic virtue and social solidarity. The notions of rights (and justice) feature prominently in the theory of deontological liberalism which owes much to Kant. It is this political theory which communitarians so strongly invoke; the idea that:

> ... society, being composed of a plurality of persons, each with his own aims, interests, and conceptions of the good, is best arranged when it is governed by principles that do not *themselves* presuppose any particular conception of the good; what justifies these regulative principles above all is not that they maximise the social welfare or otherwise promote the good, but rather that they conform to the concept of *right*, a moral category given prior to the good and independent of it.
> (Michael Sandel, *Liberalism and the Limits of Justice*, p. 1.)

Or, to put it simply, the right is prior to the good. And this priority is, according to Kant, derived entirely from the concept of freedom in the relations between individuals; it has nothing to do with achieving happiness. Justice and right are antecedent to all other values which depend on want-satisfaction because justice and right stem from the idea of freedom which, in turn, is a prerequisite of all human ends. In Kant's words in his *Critique of Practical Reason*, 'the concept of good and evil must be defined after and by means of the [moral] law'.

I mention only one aspect of liberal, and particularly Kantian, epistemology: the concept of the human subject, for it goes to the heart of liberal theory and hence is central to the communitarian (and, as we saw in ch. 10, the postmodern) attack on human rights. It is an atomistic conception of the autonomous individual — which is found in 'those philosophical traditions which come to us from the seventeenth century and which started with the postulation of an extensionless subject, epistemologically a *tabula rasa* and politically a presuppositionless bearer of rights' (Charles Taylor, 'Atomism' in his *Philosophical Papers*, vol. 2, p. 210, quoted in Steven Lukes, *Moral Conflict and Politics*, p. 73). In other (simpler) words, as used by Sandel, for Kant, the subject of practial reason has an autonomous will which enables him to participate in an ideal, uncoditioned realm which is independent of our teleological, social and psychological inclinations.

This conception of the individual (which plainly has important consequences for liberal theories of rights and justice) is rejected by communitarians who conceive of persons, as Michael Sandel puts it, echoing the arguments of Hegel against Kant, as 'situated selves rather than unencumbered selves'. The communitarian response, articulated most effectively by Sandel, and Charles Taylor, is that individuals are partly defined by their communities. Moral obligation springs therefore from what Hegel called the '*Sittlichkeit*' of the society. The subject of deontological liberalism is thus a transcendental, detached, independent and autonomous agent. He or she 'stripped of all possible constitutive attachments, is less liberated than disempowered' (Sandel, p. 178). We cannot, in the view of communitarians, be understood as persons without reference to our social roles in the community: as citizens, members of a family, group or nation.

This is a powerful idea which has exerted considerable influence in moral, political and legal theory. And it appears to inflict serious damage on the concept of human rights. But is it possible to preserve a broadly Kantian moral system of universal rights without adopting Kant's transcendental idealism? Keep the moral baby and throw out the metaphysical bathwater? This is precisely what John Rawls seems to have attempted in his social contractarian theory of justice discussed in chapter 9. You will recall that 'people in the original position' determine principles of justice beneath a veil of ignorance which insulates them from their social condition.

In fact, according to Stephen Gardbaum, in his excellent essay, 'Law, politics, and the claims of community' (1992) 90 Mich L Rev 685, which I follow closely here, the communitarian claim seems to break down into three relatively discrete positions, and the adoption of one does not logically require the adoption of either or both of the others. First, the problem of 'agency' (which entails the arguments about individual and community which I have just mentioned). The atomistic thesis may be traced to Hobbesian social contract theory. In legal theory the communitarian move is central to both the critical legal studies project (discussed in chapter 10) and the recent Republican revival in the United States. It argues that the relationship between individual and community is constitutive, rather than merely contingent and instrumental. Legal Republicanism rejects the dominant instrumental conception of politics as an arena in which self-interest is advanced, and argues instead for the transformative potential of dialogue in public space (try to look at Frank Michelman's influential essay, 'Law's republic' (1988) 97 Yale LJ 1493). CLS adherents depict the law as constitutive of key social relationships: marriage, employment and so on. See J. M. Balkin, 'Ideology as constraint' (1991) 43 Stan L Rev 1133, and, if you have the stamina, R. W. Gordon, 'Critical legal histories' (1984) 36 Stan L Rev 57, 111.

But there is a second strand of the communitarian claim. It goes to the origin and form of normative structures generally and attempts, as Gardbaum puts it, to resolve the class tensions between universalism and particularism, foundationalism and contextualism, objectivism and relativism, rationalism and historicism. It contends that 'the particular moral and political context in which values are affirmed is always crucial to their validity' (Gardbaum (1992) 90 Mich L Rev 685, p. 694).

Two forms of this argument exist. The first (which I touched on in chapter 10) is postmodern in origin and generally regards appeals to universal values as redundant if not meaningless. Writers such as Jürgen Habermas and Richard Rorty belong here. A second argument (advanced, for example, by Michael Walzer) conceives of universal values as having 'no self-executing authority in the autonomous sphere of politics which has its own distinct criteria of validation based on the requirements of the political value of self-rule' (Gardbaum, p. 694).

In legal thory this form of community is most conspicuously, and successfully, articulated by Ronald Dworkin (see chapter 6) in which the community is the source or the author of law. Right answers are products not of universal legal truths or the personal predilections of judges, but of interpreting 'community morality' as expressed in legal doctrine. None the less if we are to take rights seriously they must, Dworkin argues, trump collective goals.

The third form of communitarianism explicitly attacks liberalism and (unlike the other two communitarian positions) postulates the substantive claim that the communitarian is a superior form of association. This position is taken by writers such as Sandel and Alisdair MacIntyre (*After Virtue: A Study in Moral Theory*).

Substantive communitarian ideas constitute a direct, postmodern challenge to liberalism and rights that is sceptical of the rationality of the individual human subject, and rejects Enlightenment foundationalist and universalistic modes of normative argument.

Relativism

Although cultural relativism has a fairly long pedigree in anthropology, it is only fairly recently that it has rejoined the assault on the human rights citadel. The doctrine maintains that 'there is an irreducible diversity among cultures because each culture is a unique whole with parts so intertwined that none of them can be understood or evaluated without reference to the other parts and so to the cultural whole, the so-called pattern of culture' (J. Ladd, 'Introduction' in J. Ladd (ed.), *Ethical Relativism*, p. 2). The thesis implies *ethical* relativism which claims that 'the moral rightness and wrongness of actions varies from society to society and that there are no absolute moral standards binding on all men at all times' (ibid., p. 1). Allowing the theory its most constructive interpretation, it appears to rest on the view that since moral beliefs depend on culture, language, economy and so on, and since such factors vary from society to society, morality is relative to each society.

Two principal arguments may be mobilised against the relativist. The first denies that morality depends on social factors at all; it may therefore be described as the absolutist position. The second denies the assertion that there has always been a diversity of cultures etc. and a diversity of moral beliefs. This is known as universalism. The absolutist position was held by Plato and claims that the validity of moral beliefs is logically independent of the social or cultural background of the person who accepts them; ethics is no less a scientific enterprise than mathematics. This so-called cognitivist position arises in two forms: *intuitionism* (which holds that ethical truths are known by a priori cognition, i.e., intuitions) and *naturalism* (which holds that ethical truths are known empirically). Discrimination is wrong in the same way as $1 + 1 = 2$.

Cognitivism in ethics has (as we saw in chapter 5) had something of a rough ride from philosophers. It is particularly vulnerable to the charge that it divorces moral thinking from the 'real world'; it compels us to think about morality in a vacuum. The universalist position is stigmatised as ethnocentric for its failure to apprehend cultural practices from the perspective of the culture in which a particular practice is transacted.

Utilitarianism

The utilitarian repudiation of the idea of individual rights, indeed the essential inconsistency between the two philosophies, continues to dominate political, moral and legal thinking about rights. This hostility to rights springs from the utilitarian concern to maximise general welfare (see chapter 9). Individual interests may therefore be sacrificed at the altar of utility: so, for example, free speech is to be protected only where it will maximise the general welfare of the community. Rights are stigmatised as individualist. They operate formally but do not necessarily assist those (the poor, oppressed, alienated) who most need them. They are merely 'excess baggage', superfluous in the condemnation of cruelty or exploitation. All we need, it is argued, is a fully developed theory of right and wrong. Moreover, as Professor Hart puts it, in uncharacteristically strong terms:

> Except for a few privileged and lucky persons, the ability to shape life for oneself and lead a meaningful life is something to be constructed by positive marshalling of social and economic resources. It is not something automatically guaranteed by a structure of negtive rights. Nothing is more likely to bring freedom into contempt and so endanger it than failure to support those who lack, through no fault of their own, the material and social conditions and opportunities which are needed if a man's freedom is to contribute to his welfare. ('Between utility and rights' in his *Essays on Bentham*, pp. 207–8.)

Utilitarianism's detractors considerably outnumber its supporters, and the attacks take numerous forms. As far as its approach to individual rights are concerned, it is criticised by both conservatives such as Robert Nozick (see chapter 9) for overriding what John Rawls calls 'the distinction between persons') and liberals like Ronald Dworkin (see chapter 6) for neglecting individuals' claims to equal concern and respect.

Socialism

The incompatability of individual rights and socialism has become something of a truism as we saw in chapter 9. There, I suggested that, put simply, the argument normally rests on both the irreconcilable conflict between the egotism of liberal theory and the communitarianism of socialism, and the denial that conditions of morality are inherent in human life. Against this position, Steven Lukes (*Marxism and Morality*, pp. 56–7) argues that there are four conditions which combine to make rights necessary: scarcity, egoism, conflicting conceptions of the good, and imperfect knowledge and understanding.

Positivism

Though they are not synonymous, the ideas of natural and human rights share certain common ground. The notion that certain rights are 'natural' is expressed most cogently in the social-contractarian political philosophies of Rousseau and Locke which inspired the French and American revolutions.

The lofty rhetoric of the Declaration of Independence of 1776 appealed to the natural rights of all Americans to 'life, liberty and the pursuit of happiness'. As the Declaration put it: 'We hold these truths to be self-evident, that all men are created equal, that they are endowed by their Creator with certain unalienable rights'. Similar sentiments were incorporated into the French 'Declaration of the Rights of Man and the Citizen' of 1789.

The moral scepticism that informs the writings especially of David Hume in the eighteenth century sought to deny the existence of objective values and, hence, natural rights which were founded on what G. E. Moore was much later to call the 'naturalistic fallacy': deriving an 'ought' from an 'is'. To Jeremy Bentham natural rights were 'bawling upon paper' (J. Bentham, *Anarchical Fallacies*, quoted in H. L. A. Hart, 'Between utility and rights' in his *Essays on Bentham*, p. 199). In his characteristically colourful prose, he describes rights-talk as 'the effusion of a hard heart operating on a cloudy mind. When a man is bent on having things his own way and gives no reason for it, he says: I have a right to have them so'. They are, moreover, a contradiction in terms: 'a son that never had a father', 'a species of cold heat, a sort of dry moisture, a kind of resplendent darkness', 'nonsense on stilts' (see J. Waldron (ed.), *Nonsense upon Stilts: Bentham, Burke and Marx on the Rights of Man*, p. 73). Much positivist and noncognitivist analysis therefore rejects rights-talk as meaningless or, at best, irrational 'emotional ejaculations'.

Critical Theory

As we have seen in chapter 10, a full-frontal assault on the concept of rights is an important feature of both the CLS movement and of postmodern accounts of society. An attack is also waged by radical feminists who generally argue that rights mask the real inequalities between the sexes, and may actually serve to preserve and maintain them.

The Future of Human Rights

The concept of human rights, though bruised and battered, still breathes. Stripped of the polemic that seems to characterise much of the debate, the matter ultimately and, I think, inescapably, boils down to the question of what it is to be a human being. (This is, of course, a profoundly *un*postmodern view.) I do not deny that the notion is culturally or historically contingent, but reflection on what John Finnis calls the 'basic forms of human flourishing' (see chapter 5) may reveal not only a considerable measure of common ground, but also that the competing perspectives are not nearly as irreconcilable as they may appear. Thus the tension between communitarian and individualistic conceptions of rights need not take the stark form it so readily assumes. In particular, the idea of human rights does not require a selfish, individual-centred rejection of community. The so-called International Bill of Rights, despite its imperfections and the claim that it does not enunciate justiciable rights, represents — even for the agnostic — a formidable, authoritative foundation for human rights norms. If human rights are an integral feature of both international law and custom, several of the challenges outlined above may be seriously undermined. So-called cultural imperialism, neo-colonialism and ethnocentricity are not to be lightly dismissed; international human rights must be mediated through local cultural circumstances.

You should ask whether it is not disingenuous to invoke the claim of relativism or contextualism to frustrate the legitimate and lawful expectations of individuals. Why is it almost always the oppressor, rather than the victim who cites local culture in support of an unjust practice? These questions are unlikely to go away in the next century. A proper grasp of the theories underpinning rights and human rights will help to clarify the arguments on all sides.

THE EXAMINATION

Most examination questions which are concerned with legal concepts confine themselves to a *specific concept* rather than a general analysis of the problem of definition itself. This immediately raises an obvious difficulty: if the concept selected happens to be 'rights', to what extent should you discuss the various theories of the nature of rights, or even right-based theories (in addition merely to focusing on Hohfeld's scheme and its limitations)? Much depends, of course, on the form in which the question is framed, but, as a general rule, you should always place your answer in the context of the general legal theory which is (often artificially) being sought. In other words, it would be unthinkable to omit from your answer to a question on the nature of rights, an account of Hohfeld's analysis. It should be abundantly clear from the question what the examiner is looking for (and, if it is not, err on the side of the most obvious construction). Thus a question which explicitly calls for a discussion of the nature of rights could legitimately be answered by restricting yourself to the 'analytical' aspects of the question, with only a cursory reference to the 'normative' theories of utilitarianism, Dworkin, Rawls and so on. However artificial this may strike you, you may rest assured that its artificiality has struck the examiner as well. But, in the space of 34 or

43 minutes, it would be impossible to cover this vast terrain. Having said this, however, I suggest that in *any* answer to a question on legal concepts (rights, duties, ownership, corporate personality etc.) you should discuss (as an introduction) the problems of 'definition' (see above). In *any* question on *rights*, you should discuss Hohfeld's correlativity thesis and its deficiencies, the interest and will theories of rights, and (in outline) right-based theories in legal and moral philosophy. Far too many students see a question on, say, 'ownership' and happily throw themselves into a description of what the concept 'means' (which is usually no more than a historical sketch of some of the developments in the growth of the modern idea of ownership). No attention is paid to the difficulties and, indeed, the perils, of definition itself. Nor do they attempt to analyse, explain or elucidate the concept.

If the question merely quotes a general observation which it invites you to discuss, you will have to plan your answer with care — always *telling* the examiner why you have interpreted the question in this way and how you propose to set about answering it. These questions often make unfair demands on you (and perhaps, for that reason, you may wish to choose another less demanding one) but that will not avail you! Take, for example, the following question from a recent LLB paper:

Rights are central to modern legal theory. But what are they?

The question succeeds in mixing a fine cocktail made up of equal parts of normative and analytical ingredients. It could, I suppose, be argued that, since the second sentence contains the directive words of the question, you would be justified in devoting the major part of your answer to the analytical matters it raises (see chapter 2). But why did the examiner refer to the centrality of rights in modern legal theory? He or she could simply have asked, 'What are rights?' This would have put the matter beyond doubt. It must be presumed that there is method in every examiner's (apparent) madness. I would therefore advise you to address some of your answer to the various theories of rights you have studied (Dworkin, Rawls etc.), but (having explained *why*) to devote the bulk of your answer to the analytical issues. This is, of course, a matter of individual judgment and, since you know what the emphasis of your course has been, of knowing the expectations of your teacher. Some courses, for example, would include (and therefore expect you to include) the attack on rights mounted by CLS and the postmodernists (see chapter 10).

One legal concept that seems to be particularly popular with examiners (apart from rights) is corporate personality — despite Professor Hart's observation that '... it is said by many that the juristic controversy over the nature of corporate personality is dead'! Though he goes on to add '... if so we have a corpse, and the opportunity to learn from its anatomy'! ('Definition and theory in jurisprudence', in *Essays in Jurisprudence and Philosophy*, p. 36). You should, at the very least, have read Hart's analysis of the concept in this important essay.

You will (as I suggested above) begin your answer by pointing to the problems of definition in general (referring to Ryle, Wittgenstein etc.) and in legal theory, in particular (referring to Hart etc.). Then, depending, of course, on how the question is couched, set out the various theories of corporate personality. There are five main theories (though many more have been proffered) to explain the concept of corporate personality.

(a) *The fiction theory*. It argues that since 'real' personality can attach only to human beings, the concept of corporate personality must be a fiction. It has a long and distinguished theory and is associated with the jurist Savigny and, in England, with Salmond. Corporate persons are therefore not 'persons' at all — except that the law accords them rights and duties. Thus the separation of a one-man company from its owner (as exemplified by the famous case of *Salomon* v *A. Salomon & Co. Ltd* [1897] AC 22) and the *ultra vires* rules are explicable by reference to the limited recognition by the law of the fiction of legal personality. In the latter instance, its powers to act are limited by the memorandum and articles of association. The theory does not explain *why* the law accords legal personality. Nor does it answer the question why, if a corporation has legal personality merely by virtue of a fiction, it may nevertheless be held liable in tort and criminal law for its acts.

(b) *The concession theory*. Closely related to the fiction theory, it argues that corporate bodies have no status as legal persons save in so far as it is conceded to them by the State. It is adopted by most of the adherents of the fiction theory: Savigny, Salmond and Dicey. To some extent, since it is only the law that can endow entities with legal personality, it is tautologous.

(c) *The symbolist theory*. Sometimes called the 'bracket' theory, it was held by Jhering to provide the best account of the concept of legal personality. It is based on the proposition that only human beings can have rights and interests; a corporation is therefore merely a legal device which facilitates our understanding of highly complex legal relations. When a company is formed by a group of individuals, it is unwieldy and inconvenient to refer to all of them. The law therefore places a bracket around them; it then gives this bracket a name. But, in order to understand the true position, the bracket must be removed. The theory therefore explains why it is sometimes necessary to 'pierce the veil' to establish what is actually taking place. But critics of the theory have pointed out that this occurs only in exceptional circumstances and hence the theory neglects the reality of the law which distinguishes between the rights and duties of the legal person, on the one hand, and of the actual individuals who constitute the legal person, on the other.

(d) *The purpose theory*. Its claim is (in common with Jhering) that only real human beings are persons. Nevertheless the law protects and promotes certain purposes and interests of individuals and, hence, the concept of legal personality is merely a device to attain these purposes.

(e) *The realist theory*. Also known as the organic theory, it is most closely associated with Gierke. It claims that the real existence of legal persons is the source of their legal personality. In other words, a corporation is a *real* person, it owes its legal personality not to the State (as per the concession theory), not to a fiction (as per the fiction theory) and not to its members (as per Jhering's bracket theory). It regards a corporation as having a mind, a will, and an independent power of action. Maitland is generally regarded as a realist; he put the matter as follows:

> It has often struck me that morally there is most personality where legally there is none. A man thinks of his club as a living being, honourable as well as honest, while the joint-stock company is only a sort of machine into which he puts money and out of which he draws dividends. (*Collected Papers*, vol. 3, p. 383.)

Hart says of Maitland:

> I do not understand why he is called a realist or thought to have accepted the doctrine of Gierke that he expounded, for though he was certain that fiction and collective-name theories 'denatured the facts', he left the matter with a final question to which he then saw no answer. (*Essays in Jurisprudence and Philosophy*, p. 37.)

That question involved an imaginary State which he called Nusquamia (Latin for never-never land). The State owes you money. The question Maitland asked was 'Who is it that really owes you money?' To reply 'Nusquamia' is no answer for it tells us nothing more than we already know. But, argues Hart, the statement that 'Nusquamia owes you £1,000' may be understood by reference to the laws of that territory and, in particular, the rules that impose a liability on persons to repay debts. In other words (Hart's), if we characterise adequately the distinctive manner in which expressions for corporate bodies are used in a legal system, there is no residual question of the form 'What is a corporation?' There only *seems* to be one if we insist on a form of definition or elucidation which (as in this instance) is inappropriate. The peculiarity of corporate bodies is not (as the other theories argue) their complexity or fictitious nature, but the distinctive characteristics of expressions which are used in the enunciation and application of rules. A typically Hartian explanation.

You would, in conclusion, be expected briefly to compare these competing theories and, perhaps (depending on the manner in which the question is framed) to refer to some of the practical difficulties (e.g., the *ultra vires* rule, the recognition of foreign corporations) that these theories may help to resolve.

FURTHER READING

Frey, R. G., *Interests and Rights: The Case Against Animals* (Oxford: Clarendon Press, 1980).

Gewirth, Alan, *Human Rights: Essays on Justification and Applications* (Chicago, Ill; London: University of Chicago Press, 1983).

Gewirth, Alan, *Reason and Morality* (Chicago, Ill; London: University of Chicago Press, 1978).

Hohfeld, Wesley Newcomb, *Fundamental Legal Conceptions as Applied in Judicial Reasoning*, ed. W. W. Cook (New Haven, Conn; London: Yale University Press, 1964).

Ladd, J. (ed.), *Ethical Relativism* (Belmont: Wadsworth, 1973).

Locke, John, *Two Treatises of Government*, ed. P. Laslett (Cambridge: Cambridge University Press, 1964).

Lukes, Stephen, *Moral Conflict and Politics* (Oxford: Clarendon Press, 1991).

MacCormick, Neil, *Legal Rights and Social Democracy: Essays in Legal and Political Philosophy* (Oxford: Clarendon Press, 1982).

MacIntyre, Alasdair, *After Virtue: A Study in Moral Theory* (London: Duckworth, 1982).

Maitland, F. W., *The Collected Papers of Frederic William Maitland*, ed. H. A. L. Fisher (Cambridge: Cambridge University Press, 1911).

Nino, Carlos S., *The Ethics of Human Rights* (Oxford: Clarendon Press, 1991).

Nino, Carlos S. (ed.), *Rights* (Aldershot: Dartmouth, 1992).

Raz, Joseph, *Ethics in the Public Domain: Essays in the Morality of Law and Politics* (Oxford: Clarendon Press, 1994).

Rorty, Richard, *Philosophy and the Mirror of Nature* (Oxford: Basil Blackwell, 1990).

Sandel, Michael, *Liberalism and the Limits of Justice* (Cambridge: Cambridge University Press, 1982).

Sumner, L. W., *The Moral Foundation of Rights* (Oxford: Clarendon Press, 1989).

Wacks, Raymond (ed.), *Human Rights in Hong Kong* (Hong Kong: Oxford University Press, 1992)

Wacks, Raymond, *Personal Information: Privacy and the Law* (Oxford: Clarendon Press, 1989).

Wacks, Raymond (ed.), *Privacy* (Aldershot: Dartmouth, 1993).

Wacks, Raymond, *Privacy and Press Freedom* (London: Blackstone Press, 1995).

Wacks, Raymond, *The Protection of Privacy* (London: Sweet & Maxwell, 1980).

Waldron, Jeremy (ed.), *Nonsense upon Stilts: Bentham, Burke and Marx on the Rights of Man* (London: Methuen, 1987).
Waldron, Jeremy (ed.), *Theories of Rights* (Oxford: Oxford University Press, 1984).
White, A. R., *Rights* (Oxford: Claredon Press, 1984).

INDEX

TITLES IN THE SERIES

SWOT Law of Torts
SWOT Law of Evidence
SWOT Company Law
SWOT Law of Contract
SWOT Family Law
SWOT Land Law
SWOT Criminal Law
SWOT English Legal System
SWOT Equity and Trusts
SWOT Commercial and Consumer Law
SWOT A Level Law
SWOT Constitutional and Administrative Law
SWOT Employment Law
SWOT Jurisprudence
SWOT Conveyancing
SWOT EC Law
SWOT Law of Succession
SWOT International Law